ROMANESQUE CHURCHES OF SPAIN

Peter Strafford is a distinguished journalist who worked on *The Times* for more than three decades, including in Paris and Brussels, and was, among other things, the *Times* correspondent in New York for five years and a leader-writer in London commenting on international affairs. His last position was editor of the *Times*'s special reports on foreign countries, many of which he visited himself. His acclaimed first book, *Romanesque Churches of France*, has recently been reprinted.

ROMANESQUE CHURCHES OF SPAIN

A Traveller's Guide
including the Earlier Churches of AD 600-1000

by

Peter Strafford

WITH PHOTOGRAPHS BY THE AUTHOR

dlm

First published in 2010
by Giles de la Mare Publishers Limited
53 Dartmouth Park Hill, London NW5 1JD

Typeset by Tom Knott
Maps by David Langworth
Printed in China
through Colorcraft Ltd, Hong Kong
All rights reserved

A CIP record of this book is available
from the British Library

ISBN 9781900357319 paperback original

for Jackie

the best of companions
and always perceptive

Acknowledgement

I should like to make an acknowledgement to the following authors and their publisher for the use of an extract that I have reproduced in my book:

Annie Shaver-Crandell and Paula Gerson, *The Pilgrim's Guide to Santiago de Compostela*, Harvey Miller Publishers, 1995, pages 31-2

Place Names

Spain is a country with several languages. Spanish, or Castilian, is the principal one, but Catalan, Basque and Galician are also spoken, as well as a few others that are less widely used. In regions with their own language, place-names are given in the local spelling in road-signs, maps and books: Girona and Lleida in Catalonia rather than Gerona and Lérida, for example, and A Coruña (Corunna) and Ourense in Galicia rather than La Coruña and Orense. So I have done the same.

Contents

Glossary

Abacus: strip running along the top edge of a column capital, sometimes carved

Ajimez: pair of horseshoe-shaped arches

Alfiz: rectangular stone frame that encloses an arch or pair of arches

Ambulatory: semicircular walkway round the outside of the choir and behind the altar

Apse: semicircular extension to a church; usually at the east end

Arcade: continuous line of arches

Arch:

    Blind arch: arch without windows

    Relieving arch: broad arch that encompasses two or more smaller ones

    Transverse arch: arch that supports the main vault, running across the nave

Archivolt: arch set immediately inside another, larger arch; often one of several such internal arches and sometimes carved

Bay: section of the nave consisting of the square or rectangular space formed by four columns or pillars, two on each side

Capital: decorative feature placed at the top of a column and often carved

Choir: part of the central body of the church that lies beyond the nave, or the transept crossing if there is one, and before the altar

Clerestory: uppermost level of the nave walls, usually containing windows

Cornice: overhanging edge of a sloping roof

Crypt: part of the church that is wholly or partly below ground level

Cupola: dome

Engaged column: half-column set into a flat or flattish surface

Gallery: raised section of the church running along the nave and divided from it by arches

Lantern tower: tower built over a transept crossing

Lombard bands: decorative feature consisting of rows of small blind arches divided by vertical pilasters

Mandorla: almond shape within which Christ is often seated in painting or sculpture

Mozarab: a Christian who lived in the Islamic part of Spain and often migrated to the north

Mudéjar: describes work by Muslims who continued to live in areas taken over by the Christians

Narthex: more or less enclosed space at the western end of some churches

Oculus: circular opening enclosing a window

Pendentive: concave triangle that provides support at each corner for a circular dome built over a square space

Pilaster: column with a square or rectangular cross-section

Squinch: small arched vault that provides support at each corner for a circular dome built over a square space

Transept: transverse part of many churches, built at a right angle to the nave, which it crosses

Transept crossing: space formed by the transept as it crosses the nave

Tribune: raised section in the nave or transept of a church

Triforium: section of nave wall above the main columns and usually marked by arcades

Tympanum: semicircular space above a doorway, often filled by sculpture

Vault:

> **Barrel vault**: round or pointed vault that runs the length of the nave, supporting the roof

> **Groin vault**: support system for the roof of a bay formed by the intersection of two barrel vaults

> **Rib vault**: support system for the roof of a bay formed by diagonal weight-bearing ribs

General Introduction

Spain was a turbulent place in the early Middle Ages, and one of the consequences is that the churches built in those centuries are remarkably diverse. As in other European countries, there are churches in Romanesque style, and some very fine ones. But they are not the only churches to be seen.

Much of Spain had been under Muslim rule since the early eighth century. The Romanesque churches date mainly from the eleventh, twelfth and early thirteenth centuries, when large parts of the country were still ruled by the Moors, but the Christian leaders in the north of the country had forced their way south, taking over new territory. The outstanding example is the cathedral in Santiago de Compostela, begun in the late eleventh century and completed at the beginning of the thirteenth.

There are others, large and small, across the north of the country. Cardona, in Catalonia, has one of the loveliest examples of the early Romanesque style, while Frómista, in Castile, has a well-structured church built some years later, complete with carved capitals. León has one of the best collections of Romanesque paintings to be seen anywhere, as well as outstanding capitals. Santo Domingo de Silos, also in Castile, has a superb cloister.

But if you visit the village of San Juan de Baños, in the heart of Castile, there is a well-preserved little church on the outskirts, complete with nave, side-aisles and horseshoe arches, that was consecrated a long time before, in the seventh century, when the Muslim occupation had still not taken place and Spain was ruled by the Visigoths. And it is not the only one from those days.

South-west of there, in San Cebrián de Mazote, is another church that has horseshoe arches, as well as capitals derived from the acanthus, Corinthian-style. This one is thought to date from the early tenth century, and it is one of several that were built in the course of that century by Mozarabs, the Christians who had lived under Muslim rule in the south of Spain and had migrated to the north, bringing their style of architecture with them.

Finally, there is an interesting group of churches around Oviedo, on the north

coast of Spain. This was the area that was never fully occupied by the Arab and Berber forces who invaded the Iberian peninsula in 711 and proceeded to take over most of it. The survivors created the tiny kingdom of Asturias, and there are some fine churches there, largely from the ninth century, that are built in a pre-Romanesque style.

So there is much to be seen, and very often in magnificent surroundings, for the traveller across northern Spain. Spain is a mountainous country, but it also has some vast open spaces in its central plateau – the *meseta*. While the larger churches

Navarre and
Basque Country

FRANCE

Vitoria-
Gasteiz

• Pamplona

Jaca

Vielha

Sant Pere
de Rodes

Estella

San Juan
de la Peña

Taüll

Sangüesa

Alquézar

La Seu
d'Urgell

Ripoll

San Millán
de la Cogolla

Loarre

Girona

Tudela

• Huesca

Aragon

Agramunt

Cardona

Soria

Ebro

Lleida

Catalonia

Terrassa

San Baudelio
de Berlanga

Barcelona

Tarragona

Spain

0 miles   60

0 kilometres   100

are in towns and cities, which are themselves often full of interest, several of the
smaller ones are in mountain villages or far out in the countryside, with splendid
views to be enjoyed.

Of the towns, Segovia is one of the most appealing. It is an ancient Roman city
that still has a magnificent aqueduct from those days, and also has a wealth of
Romanesque churches: more, perhaps, than any other city in Europe. Not far away
is Avila, which is surrounded by a mile and a half of impressive city walls, built in
the Romanesque period, and has some remarkable Romanesque churches as well.

Monastic church of Frómista (see page 220)

Out in the country is San Pantaleón de Losa, a small Romanesque chapel that stands high up on a sheer outcrop of rock in an area of rolling hills north-east of Burgos. South of Burgos, near the village of Quintanilla de las Viñas, is the surviving part of a church from the Visigothic period which also stands alone on a hill-side – and has some very fine carvings from that time.

When studying the story of medieval Spain, it is worth bearing in mind that from the days of the Roman Empire, of which it was an integral part, the country was linked to a culture that extended across the Mediterranean. Even after the collapse of the western Roman Empire, and the occupation of the Iberian peninsula by the Visigoths, the eastern empire and its capital, Constantinople, continued to have a cultural influence. This can be seen in the carvings at Quintanilla de las Viñas and in other churches of the Visigothic period.

The brilliant Islamic culture brought to Spain by the Arabs also had a Mediterranean dimension. So the Muslims of al-Andalus, as they called the Iberian peninsula, and the Christians who continued to live there often drew on the same centuries-old sources, not least in the elaborate patterns, often based on formalized plant motifs, that they carved on stone.

In addition, Spain had its own indigenous culture, which had given birth to one of the most striking features of its early medieval church architecture: the horse-

Cloister of Santo Domingo de Silos: Deposition from the Cross (see pages 258, 263)

Fragment of a Deposition from the Cross, preserved in the church of Vielha (see page 44)

shoe arch. This form of arch is often seen as essentially Islamic, but the fact is that it had been used in Spain well before the Muslims arrived there in the early eighth century.

Horseshoe arches had appeared as a decorative device on stone markers in Spain in the days of the Roman Empire. Then during the period of Visigothic rule they came to be used as part of the structure of churches – and a very prominent part – as can be seen at San Juan de Baños and elsewhere.

The Muslims adopted and developed the horseshoe arch after arriving in Spain; and the Mozarabs, who were heirs to the culture of the Visigothic period and at the same time open to influence from the Islamic style that was all round them, made full use of it, though it can be seen that, as in Islamic architecture, the upper, semicircular part of their arches was nearer to a complete circle than in those of Visigothic times. But in any case the arch's origins were much further back.

Around the year 1000 things changed. Since the eighth century the Muslim rulers in the south of Spain, who had their capital in Córdoba, had dominated the country politically and culturally. As late as the closing years of the tenth century and at the very beginning of the eleventh al-Mansur, the Muslim leader, had marched across the northern kingdoms, sacking cities from Barcelona to Santiago de Compostela.

But in the first years of the new millennium the caliphate which had ruled the

Nave of the collegiate church of Cardona (see page 44)

whole of Muslim Spain collapsed and was succeeded by a number of smaller, weaker states, known as *taifas*. At the same time Europe north of the Pyrenees, and France in particular, was emerging from the disarray of the so-called Dark Ages, and the disintegration of the Carolingian empire, with a new vigour.

The result was a shift in the balance of forces. The Christians were no longer overshadowed by a Muslim giant to the south; in fact they were increasingly able to bring pressure to bear on the *taifas*, exacting tribute from some of them and eventually taking them over altogether. And they developed new, closer contacts with the increasingly dynamic world beyond the Pyrenees.

One of the main features of this new orientation was the introduction of the Romanesque style in church architecture. Inspiration for this style came from northern Italy and France, and Romanesque almost entirely replaced the indigenous style of the Mozarabs, with its roots in the Visigothic period and its Islamic borrowings.

Some Islamic features were adopted, as indeed was also the case in France. The church of San Isidoro in León, for example, has a nave and transept built in Romanesque style in the twelfth century. But the high arches on either side of the transept crossing are cusped in Islamic style.

Even more remarkable is the delightful little Romanesque chapel in the village of Torres del Rio, south-west of Pamplona. This has an octagonal cupola with sophisticated vaulting which is clearly inspired by similar vaulting in Córdoba.

There was one feature, however, that never became part of the vocabulary of Romanesque, and that was the horseshoe arch.

This, then, was the background against which Romanesque arrived in Spain. It did not mark a radical departure since many of the earlier churches, Visigothic, Asturian and Mozarabic, also had a basic plan of nave and side-aisles, derived originally from the Roman basilica. But in Romanesque churches this plan was developed and refined, often very elaborately, as the style developed.

Naves were covered with barrel vaulting – something that had been done, but only on a small scale, in some Asturian churches, and a century later in Catalonia – and they were made more imposing. Cupolas were inserted over transept crossings. Care was lavished on the east end, and a cluster of three semicircular apses came to be a common feature of the outside of the larger churches, replacing the rectangular form.

Also visible on the outside were the towers, some erected over the transept crossing, some over other parts of the church or more or less free-standing. And an important feature was the cloisters that were built onto the body of the church, their column capitals decorated with carving.

Zamora cathedral: Bishop's Façade (see page 327)

One of the most attractive characteristics of Romanesque is the widespread use of sculpture, both formalistic and figurative. It serves, not just as decoration, but as an integral part of a church's design; and there is much of it to be seen in Spain. There is lively and original carving, not merely on column capitals, but on a great number of doorways and, very often, a whole façade. Ripoll, in Catalonia, has a magnificent façade, and there are doorways that are covered, and surrounded, by carving in Santiago de Compostela, Sangüesa and many other places.

Romanesque style was first introduced in Catalonia late in the tenth or early in the eleventh century. This was a region that had developed separately from the rest of Spain because the Muslim occupiers had been driven out of much of it by Charlemagne and his Carolingian dynasty in the late eighth and early ninth century. So it had had less than a century of Muslim occupation. It had links to France and Italy, and by the tenth century it had become prosperous.

The style of the first Catalan churches is known as the First Southern Romanesque. It had been developed in Lombardy and spread from there to southern France and Burgundy; then further west to Catalonia. So Catalonia has a great number of these early Romanesque churches, which have barrel vaults built in stone and a decorative device on their walls known as 'Lombard bands', consisting of rows of small blind arches divided by vertical pilasters.

It also has churches built in later forms of Romanesque as the style evolved, and some lovely cloisters attached to them. So for those who enjoy the style, Catalonia is full of riches. A late example is the monastery of Poblet, south-east of Lleida, whose church was built by the Cistercians towards the end of the twelfth century and shows that the transition to Gothic was already under way.

The other route by which Romanesque reached Spain, and a very significant one, was further west, over the Pyrenean passes. As the Christian kingdoms became more self-confident they increased their contacts with the rulers, and the religious institutions, to the north; and since they needed people to settle in the towns and, often, the vast open spaces taken from the Moors over the years, there was a flow of immigrants, ideas and techniques. Romanesque churches were built in Aragon, Navarre, León, Castile and not least Galicia in the far west.

One of the first to promote these contacts was Sancho el Mayor (the Great) (970-1035), the king of Navarre who had also taken over Castile and León and was the most powerful of the Christian rulers of his time. Sancho developed close relations with the great Burgundian abbey of Cluny, inviting its monks into his dominions, and over the years Cluny acquired great influence in Spain, above all on monastic life there.

One of the main areas of Cluniac influence, and the channel by which people

St James with Christ, Portada de las Platerías, cathedral of Santiago de Compostela (see page 378)

and ideas reached Spain from elsewhere in Europe, was the pilgrimage to Santiago de Compostela. Santiago's fame derived from the announcement, made in about 813, that the tomb of the Apostle James the Greater, brother of St John, had been discovered there. Pilgrimage to it became one of the features of life in the Middle Ages, encouraged by Cluny and by local rulers.

The passage of large numbers of pilgrims called for both hospices and churches. So many of the Romanesque churches are on or near the Camino de Santiago, which the pilgrims followed across northern Spain to the remote Galician shrine. There are outstanding churches in, for instance, Jaca, Frómista, Sahagún and León. But there are many others to be seen across the whole of northern Spain.

Historical Background

The Iberian peninsula was invaded and occupied in ancient times by a number of foreign peoples, most notably the Romans, the Visigoths and the Arabs. Each left their mark, but the Arabs, or at least their descendants, remained the longest; and they came to be known as Moors.

So one of the principal themes of Spanish history in the Middle Ages is the *reconquista*, the long and complex process by which over the centuries the Christian rulers in the north recovered land from the Muslims who occupied most of the centre and south.

Before that, however, there were the Visigoths. This warlike Teutonic people had migrated over the years from their homeland somewhere near the Baltic. They tangled frequently with the Romans, threatened Constantinople in the fourth century, and in 410 sacked Rome itself, before settling in agreement with the Romans in what is now south-western France early in the fifth century. In due course they set up their capital in Toulouse.

By then the Roman Empire was in a weakened state, and the Visigoths had already made forays into Spain, where they defeated various Teutonic and other peoples that had settled there earlier. By the middle of the fifth century they controlled most of the Iberian peninsula, as well as much of southern France. They were, however, defeated at Vouillé, near Poitiers, by the Franks in 507, and withdrew to their possessions south of the Pyrenees, retaining a small strip of southern France. In time they established a new capital in Toledo.

The state that the Visigoths created there lasted for another two centuries. It was always fragile, because of internal dissension, and lacking in economic dynamism, but it eventually included the whole Iberian peninsula after they had defeated the

Suevi, another Germanic people who had taken over Galicia, in 585, and finally driven out the Byzantines, who had occupied a part of southern Spain in 554, in 624. There was much cultural activity, including the building of churches.

The Visigoths adopted many features of the Roman way of life, including the Latin language, and they maintained contacts with the eastern Roman Empire and its capital, Constantinople. They were always a minority of the population, and they eventually merged with the Hispano-Romans.

One significant development was the official abandonment in 589 of Arianism, the heretical Christian belief that the Visigoths had adopted years before. Basically this held that as the Son of God Christ was younger than God the Father and so did not have the same nature, just one that was like God's.

Under the leadership of King Reccared the Visigoths officially adopted Catholicism, and from then on the Catholic Church came to be a powerful force. Its most prominent figure was St Isidore, a learned man who was bishop of Seville in the seventh century for nearly forty years. He was the author of several erudite works, among them *Etymologiae*, a twenty-volume summary of human knowledge at that time.

One of the legacies of the Visigoths was the notion that Spain, or the Iberian peninsula as a whole, was a kingdom in its own right, rather than a mere province of an empire as it had been in Roman times. This notion was subsequently taken up by the Christian rulers in the small area in the far north of Spain that the Arabs never fully occupied, where they proclaimed themselves the rightful descendants of the Visigoths when they launched their campaigns of *reconquista*.

Visigothic rule came to an end in 711, very largely as a result of the internal divisions. A new king, Roderic, had been elected the previous year, and his opponents invited the Arabs, who were close at hand having already overrun most of North Africa, to help them to overthrow him. They apparently believed that the Arabs would do this and return to their territories across the strait.

In the event the Arabs carried out a reconnaissance in 710 and landed in force the following year. They were led by Tarik – whose feat has been commemorated ever since in the name of Gibraltar, which derives from Gebel-Tarik, or 'rock of Tarik' – and proceeded to defeat Roderic on the banks of the Guadalete, near Jerez de la Frontera. They then went on, instead of returning to North Africa, to occupy most of the Iberian peninsula.

The new regime was not without its internal difficulties, and there was some fighting, much of it caused by the fact that while the leaders were generally Arab, most of the troops were Berber. But the situation was transformed by the arrival in Spain in 755 of Abd al-Rahman, the sole survivor of the Umayyad dynasty of

Damascus, the former rulers of the Arab empire who had been overthrown, and almost all massacred, in 750 by the Abbasids.

Abd al-Rahman defeated the Abbasid-backed emir and proclaimed himself emir as Abd al-Rahman I. He and his descendants then proceeded over the next two and a half centuries to create a glittering civilisation centred on Córdoba, the capital, which not only revived the Iberian economy by developing agriculture, industry and trade, but was culturally and intellectually active, outshining any other centre in western Europe. It reached its peak in the tenth century under Abd al-Rahman III (912-61), the greatest of Córdoba's rulers.

The Abbasids in Baghdad came in time to accept the virtual autonomy of al-Andalus, as the Iberian peninsula was known in Arabic, and there were many contacts between the two centres. But in 928 Abd al-Rahman III declared formal independence by announcing that he himself was the rightful caliph, or head of the whole Muslim world, and from then on the Cordoban regime was known as a caliphate.

Christians and Jews were officially tolerated in al-Andalus, as enjoined by the Koran, and allowed to continue their communal life provided they paid a tax. There was often an element of hostility in day-to-day contacts, but some members of both communities were still living in areas that had been ruled by Muslims for centuries when they were taken over by the Christians.

After an initial period of harmony, however, relations between the Mozarabs, the Christians who, as already recounted, continued to live under Muslim rule, and the Islamic authorities became more strained. They deteriorated sharply in the ninth century, when a number of 'martyrs' were executed for publicly expressing their opposition to Islam.

The background to this was that over the years many of those living in the Muslim-ruled part of Spain had converted to Islam, partly because it made life easier for them, but also because of the attractions offered by a culture that was at its peak. Those who resisted these attractions were all the more inclined to be radical in their opposition, many of them drawing a parallel with the early days of Christianity, when its believers were persecuted by the Romans.

The outcome was that many of them decided to speak out; and many Mozarabs, particularly some monastic communities, decided to emigrate to the north, where they were welcomed by the rulers of the expanding Christian kingdoms there. Numbers of them were settled in the early tenth century, for instance, in what became the kingdom of León, often in the lands just north of the river Duero that had been taken from the Muslims and needed to be resettled.

There the Mozarabic monks built themselves new monasteries, with churches

San Pedro de la Nave, Visigothic period: Daniel in the lions' den (see page 314)

San Pedro de la Nave: Sacrifice of Isaac (see page 314)

at the centre of them. Their style derived originally from that of the Visigothic period, but incorporated various structural and decorative features that they had adopted from Islamic work in the south: a modified horseshoe arch, for instance (see page 6), distinctive corbels, and the *ajimez* and *alfiz*, one a pair of arches, the other a rectangular stonework frame that enclosed an arch or arches.

The fact was that many Christians had regrouped in the north after the Arab occupation, numbers of them in the remote areas in and beyond the Cantabrian mountains where neither the Romans nor the Visigoths had made much headway. Nor were the Arabs any more successful. They had appointed a governor in Gijón, and in 718 they sent a small force into the mountains of Asturias. But it was defeated at Covadonga by a combination of local people and refugees from the Visigothic regime led by a certain Pelayo, and from then on the Christians controlled that part of Spain, initially very small.

Pelayo was later said to have been a dignitary at the Visigothic court, to have been sent as a hostage to Córdoba by the local Arab leader, to have escaped and to have rallied the local people on his return. But this is not certain.

What is certain is that though Covadonga was a small affair, it became a symbolic event that was subsequently taken as the marking of the beginning of the *reconquista* – and specifically the rebirth of the Visigothic regime. Pelayo had been elected king of Asturias, and under him and his successors this remote little kingdom, which eventually had Oviedo as its capital, proceeded to go from strength to strength.

The first Asturian capital was Cangas de Onís, followed by Pravia. Alfonso II, who ruled from 791 to 842, moved it to Oviedo, which he had to rebuild after Moorish raids in 794 and 795. He set out to recreate something of the grandeur of Toledo, the former Visigothic capital, and it is interesting that he was in close contact with Charlemagne at the end of the eighth century. He discussed making a formal pact of alliance with him, but the idea was rejected, it seems, by the Asturian nobles.

In the course of the eighth and ninth centuries the Asturians expanded into areas that the Arabs had neither the will nor the resources to defend properly – west into Galicia, and south and south-east into the empty plains of the central plateau, the *meseta*. They had resettled the *campos góticos*, the 'Gothic lands', as the north bank of the river Duero was known, by the beginning of the tenth century.

It was a significant step, therefore, when Ordoño II moved the capital south, beyond the protective wall of the Cantabrians, from Oviedo to León in 914. From then on it was the kingdom, not of Asturias, but of León.

Asturias was not the only area, however, in which Christians were organizing themselves against the Muslim occupiers. Further to the east, and also protected by the Cantabrian mountains, were the Basques, who were equally intolerant of any foreign incursion, and they were instrumental in creating what became, by the late ninth or early tenth century, the kingdom of Navarre. This had its capital in Pamplona and for a time came to control Aragon and other areas further west in the Pyrenean foothills.

Then there was Catalonia, where the Carolingians were active. Charlemagne had crossed the Pyrenees in 778, apparently as an ally of the Abbasids against the rebel emir, Abd al-Rahman. But he failed to win over Arab-held Saragossa (Zaragoza), and proceeded to sack Pamplona. The attack on his rearguard at the Roncesvalles pass as he withdrew across the Pyrenees was the theme of the famous twelfth-century *Chanson de Roland* – though in it the attackers were presented as Muslims, for obviously political reasons, when in fact they had been Basques.

Charlemagne returned to Spain in 785, however, when he took Girona from the Arabs; and his son Louis took Barcelona in 801. So the greater part of Catalonia had Muslim rule for less than a century, as I wrote earlier, and this differentiated it from much of the rest of Spain. For a time it was part of the Carolingian empire, known as the *marca hispanica*. But it became virtually independent, and in 987 it shook off any subordination to the Frankish kings by refusing to accept the accession of Hugh Capet.

The Catalans were not able to expand far to the west because the powerful Moorish *taifa* of Saragossa stood in their way. So they looked eastwards, across the Mediterranean, where they developed extensive trading links, and by the early eleventh century they had become prosperous. In time they embarked on expansion to the south.

On their side the Arabs appear to have treated Covadonga as a matter of little consequence, and to have decided that it was not worth their while to make a further attempt to stamp out opposition in remote Asturias. They also decided not to occupy or to take steps to make a serious defence of the empty expanses in the northern part of the *meseta*. So this became a no man's land, and though the Arabs made often devastating raids into these areas, the Christian expansion into them continued.

The Christian powers were, however, still puny when compared with the might of the Islamic regime in the south. There had been the sacking of Oviedo in 794 and 795, and in the tenth century Abd al-Rahman III made expeditions against León and Navarre, in both of which he caused great damage – though he was heavily defeated at Simancas in 939. Even more telling were those twenty or so years at the end of that century and the beginning of the eleventh when al-Mansur, the Cordoban dictator, marched across the Christian territories sacking and burning.

But this situation did not last, as already observed. Al-Mansur died in 1002, and soon after that the Cordoban regime was engulfed in internal fighting that led to the formal dissolution of the caliphate in 1031. That was the end of unified rule in al-Andalus. The caliphate was succeeded by the *taifas*, which were often seriously at odds with each other; and though they continued to be culturally active and influential, in political and military terms they were far less able to resist the pressures from the increasingly strong Christian states to the north.

The result was a complex situation in which there was fighting between Christians and Moors, but also much interaction at all levels. The *reconquista* was a centuries-long process, and there were numerous occasions on which alliances were struck, or dynastic marriages arranged, between rulers on different sides of the religious divide.

By 1000 the rulers of the various Christian states had already made gradual but significant advances, and with the collapse of the caliphate in Córdoba this process continued. The kingdom of León was able to reinforce its authority over areas to its south and east, not least through the activities of the counts of Castile, whose capital, Burgos, had been founded in 882.

Castile, named after its many castles, became one of the most dynamic parts of the kingdom and, though it remained subordinate for a time to León, it came to overshadow its former rulers.

Meanwhile the kingdom of Navarre had extended its rule over Aragon and other Pyrenean valleys in the early tenth century; while further east the counts of Barcelona had brought the other Catalan counties under their control – including several north of the Pyrenees in what is now France – and so created a unified Catalonia, though they never claimed the title of king. Between the two was Saragossa, which continued to stand in the way of the Christians' advance.

The reign of Sancho el Mayor, the Great, who was king of Navarre from 1004 to 1035, was an important stage in the development of the various Christian kingdoms. Sancho was an activist and powerful monarch, as I have written, and by the end of his life he had come to rule, not just Navarre, which included Aragon, but León and Castile as well.

On his death these remained separate entities. They were divided up between his sons, and after some fighting two new kingdoms eventually emerged, each ruled by one of them. Ferdinand was crowned Ferdinand I, king of Castile, and proceeded to take over León and Galicia. Ramiro, an illegitimate son, became Ramiro I, king of Aragon, and he too extended his realm, taking over the counties to the east.

Ninth-century church of Santa María de Naranco, outside Oviedo (see page 342)

Ferdinand, in particular, proved another activist ruler who seized new territories to the south. He was followed in this by his son, Alfonso VI, who was king of León from 1065 and of both Castile and León from 1072 to 1109. He achieved the resounding feat of capturing Toledo, the former Visigothic capital, in 1085.

Alfonso was helped in this task by some knights from France, and it was this that led to the creation of the separate kingdom of Portugal. One of the knights, Count Henry of Burgundy, married one of his daughters, Teresa, and as a dowry Teresa received lands south of the river Minho. Their son, Afonso Henriques, inherited them, and in 1139 he proclaimed himself the first king of Portugal. He too went on to capture territory, including Lisbon, from the Moors. Alfonso VII, king of León and Castile, accepted this independence in 1143.

But though the Christians had their successes, they also had setbacks. There was a substantial setback in 1086 when, in response to the capture of Toledo, there was a new invasion by Moors from North Africa. These were the Almoravids, a fanatical Berber tribe who crossed into Spain and inflicted several defeats on Alfonso VI's army. They recovered much Muslim-ruled territory, though not Toledo, and incorporated several of the *taifas* into their North African empire. This put an end, for a time, to the Christians' expansion.

Not for long, however. In 1096 Pedro I, king of Aragon, captured the Moorish stronghold of Huesca; and in 1118 there was a significant Christian victory when, with the help of more French knights, the great fortress of Saragossa fell to his successor, Alfonso I of Aragon, known as el Batallador, the Fighter of Battles. Alfonso carried out raids into Moorish territory further south, and showed that Aragon, too, was a force to be reckoned with.

Meanwhile the Catalans had captured the port of Tarragona in 1091, and in 1137 there was another far-reaching development when Ramon Berenguer IV, count of Barcelona, was engaged to marry Petronila, heiress to the throne of Aragon. The marriage did not take place for some years, but from then on Catalonia and Aragon formed part of the same kingdom, with Ramon Berenguer as regent. It was known as Aragon, though the Catalans tended to be the dominant partner. In 1149 they captured Lleida, another Moorish stronghold.

The kings of Castile and León were determined to show, however, that they, the heirs to the Visigoths, were the true rulers of Spain. So in 1135 Alfonso VII had proclaimed himself emperor, and he was formally acknowledged as such by the king of Navarre, the count of Barcelona, and various lesser rulers. In 1144 he too marched south and succeeded in capturing Córdoba itself, as well as sacking Seville and Granada.

But then came another shock. In 1146 a second, even more fanatical Berber group, the Almohads, landed in Spain, and they not only recovered Córdoba but, like the Almoravids before them, took over most of Muslim Spain and made it a mere part of a North African empire. In 1195 they defeated the army of Alfonso VIII, king of Castile, at Alarcos, showing that the Christians were not going to have everything their own way.

Both the Almoravids and the Almohads were intolerant towards the Christians who remained in their respective territories after they had taken over. They demolished churches, and this explains why, though it is known that there were numerous churches and monasteries in existence in al-Andalus in the ninth century, and possibly later, there is barely a trace of them, apart from a few ruins in the hills near Málaga and others near Toledo, to be seen today.

One factor that contributed to the Christian defeat was the divisions between the various states which, from the earliest days of the *reconquista*, had generally been determined to retain their independence – and were quite prepared to fight each other. At Alarcos, for example, Alfonso VIII had been promised the help of León, but it did not arrive.

Some years later, however, in 1212, he fought another battle with the Almohads at Las Navas de Tolosa, and this time Castile was not alone. By then Alfonso had received the support of the Pope, who had declared a crusade, and with the help of some other Christians – but not León – he won a resounding victory.

This was a turning point in the *reconquista*, and the beginning of the end for al-Andalus. In the course of the thirteenth century the various Christian armies were able to take over most of the cities that had for centuries been under Muslim rule: Badajoz, Córdoba, Murcia, Seville, Valencia. By 1300 only Granada remained, and it survived until taken by Ferdinand and Isabella in 1492.

Castile and León had become one kingdom once again in 1230, and this time they remained together.

Monasteries

In Spain, as elsewhere in western Europe, monastic communities were established in late Roman times, some as early as the fourth century. Monastic life continued under the Visigoths, and in some places even after the greater part of the Iberian peninsula was occupied by the Arabs in the eighth century, though over the years the monks found life in the Muslim-ruled south increasingly difficult, as recorded, and often migrated to the Christian north.

Once an area had been recovered by the Christians, the situation changed, and the monasteries and convents, some long-established, some new, took on great importance, both economically and politically. The foundation of a monastery gave a boost to the process of resettlement, and the monks or nuns, while leading an austere life themselves, often became wealthy landowners collectively as a result of the donations they received.

They also, of course, built churches, and many of the surviving Romanesque churches were originally built by or for monasteries or convents. Others, like the lovely church in Cardona (see page 44), belonged to colleges of canons regular.

The canons formed communities that were monastic, but less rigorous than the fully-fledged monasteries. They were often attached to a church or cathedral, and tended to follow the Rule of St Augustine, a modified version of principles set out by St Augustine of Hippo in the late fourth and early fifth century.

In addition to their religious activities, and the part they played in the local economy, the various monastic communities also had a broader, cultural role. The abbey of Ripoll in Catalonia (page 74), for instance, originally founded in the late ninth century, accumulated an outstanding collection of manuscripts, secular as

Monastery of Sant Pere de Rodes (see page 91)

well as devotional. So did Santo Domingo de Silos in Castile (page 258) and many others.

Ripoll was one of the leading monasteries, and very influential. Another prominent one was Sant Pere de Rodes (page 91), which is also in Catalonia and, like Ripoll, was founded in the ninth century after the region had been taken from the Arabs by the Carolingians.

Further west were San Juan de la Peña in Aragon (page 141), which was founded in the tenth century and became for a time a burial place for the Aragonese kings; and Leyre (page 174), which had a similar position in Navarre. Leyre is known to have been in existence in the middle of the ninth century and may well have been even older.

One early foundation was San Millán de la Cogolla (page 241), which can be dated to the sixth century, when Spain was still ruled by the Visigoths. San Miguel de Escalada (page 309) and San Cebrián de Mazote (page 231) are examples of monasteries founded in the early tenth century by monks who came from the Muslim-ruled part of Spain, as I wrote earlier. They brought their Mozarabic architectural style, and much else, with them.

One of the main issues which confronted the monasteries in those days – and the Spanish Church in general – was differences in the pattern of monastic life and

Mozarabic monastery of San Miguel de Escalada (see page 309)

in church ritual. Most of the Spanish monasteries, and particularly the older ones, had practices that had been passed down through the centuries, often since the days of the Visigoths, and they were unlike those in use elsewhere in western Europe.

As early as the ninth century Charlemagne had set out to create a single pattern when he was promoting monastic life throughout his empire. He stipulated that the Benedictine Rule, which was first set out in the sixth century by St Benedict of Nursia and specified how life should be conducted in a monastery, should be the universal standard. He was only partially successful, and the process was taken further by his son, Louis the Pious. But only a small strip of northern Spain, south of the Pyrenees, was ever part of the Carolingian empire.

There was, however, an important development in 910, when the abbey of Cluny was founded in Burgundy by William the Pious, duke of Aquitaine. The Benedictine Rule was observed there from the beginning, and Cluny became one of the most influential institutions of the day, often called in to advise other monasteries on the observance of the Rule. It eventually became the centre of a vast, but loosely linked empire of some 1,450 monastic institutions, spread all round western Europe.

The Rule set out a number of principles, such as who could be admitted to a monastery or convent, the pattern of life for the monks and nuns, the overriding importance of humility and obedience, the rule of the abbot or abbess, and the procedure for electing a new one.

Sancho el Mayor, who was king of Navarre from 1004 to 1035 and also ruled León, Castile and Aragon, made a point of cultivating Cluny, as we have seen, and that was the beginning of a process by which Cluny acquired extensive influence in Spain. With Sancho's encouragement monks from the Burgundian abbey advised on the introduction of the Benedictine Rule in San Juan de la Peña, and later in the century the monastery was put completely in the hands of Cluny – as over the years were many others.

There was a significant growth in Cluny's presence in Spain during the reign of Alfonso VI, who was king of León from 1065 and of both León and Castile from 1072 to 1109, as already recorded. Alfonso had particularly close links to Cluny. One of his wives was the niece of St Hugh, the long-serving abbot, and he made a substantial contribution to the building of Cluny III, the abbey's great Roman-esque church, after his capture of Toledo in 1085. He presented Cluny with several monasteries.

When Cluny took over a monastery, it usually insisted on its being re-classed as a priory. But the Cluniac community was very loosely structured, and very often Cluny did not itself actually take control, but simply encouraged the monks to accept Cluniac principles, including the Benedictine Rule.

This was the case of the great abbey of Sahagún (page 302), little of which remains today. It was required by Alfonso to adopt Cluny's ways, as well as a Cluniac monk as abbot, but it remained independent. It became one of the most influential monasteries in Spain, and was itself responsible for the growth in Cluny-style observance in León and Castile.

It was during Alfonso's reign that another important step was taken, also at the behest of Cluny, which affected church ritual. The liturgy that had been in use, with modifications, since the days of the Visigoths, and was still used by the Mozarabic communities, was replaced in the parts of Spain where Alfonso's writ ran by the Roman liturgy used elsewhere in western Europe.

Catalonia was different, then as now. We saw that its northern parts were occupied by the Arabs for less than a century, and it was for a time part of the Carolingian empire. The Catalans had replaced the Mozarabic liturgy by the Roman one by the middle of the ninth century, and as links with the Carolingians weakened, they moved into a closer relationship with the papacy in Rome.

Monastic reform, as well as the extensive building of churches, was carried out there in the early eleventh century by Oliba, who was not only abbot of Ripoll and

St-Michel-de-Cuxa – now in France, but then part of greater Catalonia – but bishop of Vic. His influence extended beyond Catalonia: he was, for instance, an adviser to Sancho el Mayor.

Cluny's influence was limited in Catalonia, therefore. But it did take over some Catalan monasteries in the late eleventh century: Sant Pere de Cassérres (page 89), for instance, and Sant Ponç de Corbera (page 47).

There were other French monasteries that had a presence in Spain: Saint-Victoire-de-Marseille, which controlled Ripoll for about a century from 1070, and Saint-Ruf-d'Avignon. But the most active were the Cistercians, who had been established at the end of the eleventh century in reaction to Cluny, which they criticized for being too lax and self-indulgent, particularly in its application of the Benedictine Rule.

The Cistercians set up monasteries and convents in many parts of western Europe. They began to move into Spain in the first half of the twelfth century with the encouragement of the various rulers, Alfonso VII and Alfonso VIII in Castile and León and Ramón Berenguer IV, count of Barcelona, in Aragon and Catalonia. The first group arrived at Moreruela, north of Zamora, in 1131, backed by Alfonso VII; their church is now a spectacular ruin.

It was some time before they began to build their churches, and by then Romanesque style was already beginning to be replaced by Gothic. The Cistercians were influential in bringing about the spread of the latter. But some of their earliest churches were initially Romanesque, with later, Gothic additions. That is true of three monastic institutions in the hilly area north of Tarragona, all set up in the second half of the twelfth century: the monasteries of Poblet and Santes Creus and the convent of Vallbona de les Monges (page 65).

The Cistercians took over Leyre (page 174) at the beginning of the fourteenth century after a long battle with the monks who had been in charge until then.

Pilgrimages

Pilgrims first began making their way to Santiago de Compostela, in remote Galicia, in the ninth century, and they have been doing so, on foot or on horseback, ever since. In the early days they crossed the Pyrenees at the western end and then followed a route that took them past Vitoria, in the Basque Country, and along the north coast through Oviedo.

Later, when the threat from the Moors in the south had receded, they were able to take a more southerly route; and it was along this route, known as the Camino

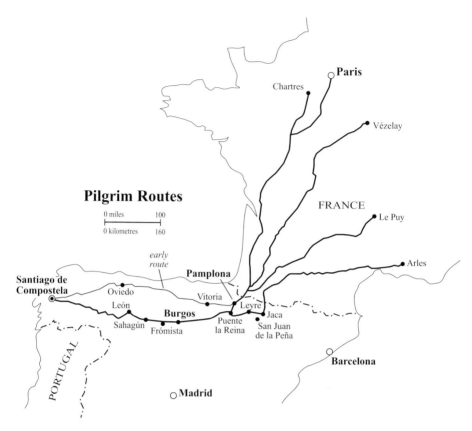

Pilgrim Routes

0 miles   100

0 kilometres   160

de Santiago or Camino Francés because it was largely used by French people, that some fine Romanesque churches were built in the eleventh and twelfth centuries.

They include the cathedral in Jaca (page 130), just south of the Pyrenees, the churches in Frómista (page 220), Sahagún (page 302) and León (page 295), and many others that are either on or near the pilgrim route.

The pilgrims had their own reasons for making this extremely arduous journey. Some wanted to carry out an act of penance; many more were keen to venerate the saintly relics that they found in the churches along the route – and especially in Compostela itself. But for the rulers of the Christian kingdoms there were political and economic motivations, as well as religious ones, for encouraging this inflow of travellers, and the other immigrants who were drawn in with them.

This was of course the time of the *reconquista*, or reconquest, when territory that had quite recently been recovered from the Moors needed to be resettled; and though the greatest danger was removed with the dissolution of the caliphate in

Córdoba in the early eleventh century, there were still hostilities with the various Moorish *taifas* that succeeded it. So from the earliest days the pilgrimage was seen in the context of the struggle between the Christians in the north of Spain and the Muslims in the south.

It all began with the announcement, made in about 813 as already noted, that the bones of St James, the Apostle and brother of St John, had been discovered in a field near Iria Flavia, a settlement on the west coast of Galicia that dated back to Roman times. According to a later account Theodomir, the local bishop, and Pelagius, a hermit, had been led by a star to the site, where they found a tomb containing three sarcophagi.

The two men had no doubt that the sarcophagi contained the remains of St James and two companions, St Athanasius and St Theodore. The belief was that St James had been charged by Christ himself with converting the people of the Iberian peninsula, and that he had actually spent a brief if unsuccessful time there before returning to Palestine.

There he was condemned to death by Herod Agrippa I and beheaded in AD 42 or 44. St Athanasius and St Theodore then put his remains into a boat, and they and the coffin were carried by wind, tide and divine guidance across the Mediterranean, through the straits of Gibraltar and north to the coast of Galicia, where they came ashore near the modern town of Padrón after a seven-day journey.

The two men buried St James there, and in due course were themselves buried with him, only to be discovered almost eight centuries later.

The discovery was a momentous one, because St James was the only Apostle to have been buried in western Europe outside Rome – where the tomb of St Peter was. It is perhaps significant that it was made almost exactly a century after the Arab-led forces, all of them Muslim, had invaded and occupied the greater part of the Iberian peninsula. In any case it was made much of by Alfonso II, who was king of Asturias at the time and as such ruled Galicia.

The site became known as Compostela, which is often said to be a corruption of *campus stellae*, or 'field of the star', because of the way the tomb had been found, though this is disputed; an alternative explanation is that it derives from a Latin word for a cemetery.

Alfonso needed support from elsewhere in western Europe, and it was not long before it came. Compostela quickly became a local pilgrimage centre, and soon a Benedictine monastery was established there. Within fifty years the festival of St James, on 25th July then as now, was listed as far away as Metz in the martyrology of the cathedral. The pilgrimage to Compostela became one of the most important in the Christian world, almost on a par with the one to Rome.

Funerary chapel of Eunate (see page 172)

In 844 Alfonso's successor, Ramiro I, received support from St James himself when a knight in shining armour mounted on a charger and bearing a white standard with a red cross upon it appeared at the battle of Clavijo and helped him to defeat the Moors. The knight was recognized as St James, and from that moment the Apostle was converted into 'Santiago Matamoros', the Slayer of Moors.

He became the champion of the Christians in the centuries-long war against the infidel, and is seen in that martial role, cutting down the enemies of the Church, in sculptures in the cathedral in Compostela and elsewhere.

The practice of pilgrimage was encouraged, not just by the Christian rulers, but also by the monastic institutions and in particular by the great Burgundian abbey of Cluny. In the eleventh century Cluny became an important presence in Spain, as already described. It took over control of many of the monasteries and persuaded others to adopt the Cluniac rule; and it too promoted the pilgrimage.

A big role in all of this was played by Sancho el Mayor, who was king of Navarre from 1004 to 1035 and also ruled León, Castile and Aragon, as I have already stated. He developed good relations with Cluny, encouraging its interest in Spain, and its principles began to be introduced south of the Pyrenees during his reign.

Sancho was also responsible for fixing the pilgrim route to Compostela. Until his time the route was not well defined, and there were variations, some of them used by only a small number of pilgrims, which could be dangerous for them. After crossing the Pyrenees and arriving in Pamplona, the capital of Navarre, many of them then headed west from there along an old Roman road.

Sancho laid out a route that went south-west from Pamplona to Logroño and then on to Burgos in Castile. From there it passed through Frómista, Sahagún and León. This became the definitive route, though there were minor variations, and towns such as Puente la Reina and Estella (see page 162) were founded along it to provide for the needs of the pilgrims.

Sancho did much to make the route more attractive, and this process continued over the succeeding years. Roads were repaired or re-directed. Bridges were built. Monasteries were founded along the route, and hospices and inns built to accommodate the pilgrims. There were even new towns that sprang up, for which artisans of all sorts were needed.

Some of the stopping places were not actually on the route, but were not far from it, so that the pilgrims were able to reach them without too much extra effort. That was true of San Juan de la Peña (see page 141), for instance, in the hills west of Jaca, and Sangüesa (see page 180), in Navarre.

Those travelling from Britain or Ireland did not necessarily make the long walk across northern Spain. Ships sailed from the south coast of Cornwall, for instance, to A Coruña (Corunna) on the Galician coast, from where it was only about fifty miles overland to Compostela. But others sailed to Soulac, near Bordeaux, where they joined the westernmost of the main routes across France.

By the twelfth century there were four such routes, all well-established. Three of them merged just north of the Pyrenees, which the pilgrims then crossed by the Roncesvalles pass; the fourth used the Somport pass, which was further east. The western route took the pilgrims through Pamplona, and the eastern through Jaca, in Aragon. They joined at Puente la Reina, from where the single route laid out by Sancho led to Compostela.

There is still an elegant bridge at Puente la Reina that was built in the eleventh century by a queen of Navarre – though it is not known which.

It was not easy going, since the roads were often bad, and there were rivers, forests and mountains to be crossed; and it was often dangerous, with desolate stretches on which the pilgrims could be attacked by bandits or wolves. So the pilgrims took as little as possible with them. The traditional pilgrim's equipment consisted of a broad-brimmed hat, a long cloak, a small pouch or scrip for some food and personal belongings, a gourd or something similar to carry water, and sandals. He or she would also have a long stick tipped with an iron ferrule to serve both as a walking stick and as a weapon in case of attack.

Bridge of Puente la Reina (see page 29)

Pilgrims were entitled to wear the cockleshell which was the symbol of the pilgrimage, but only after they had reached Compostela.

The contrast between the rigours of the road and the magnificence of much of the architecture that they encountered must have been extreme. This was particularly true at a time when most people were illiterate and hardly saw images of any sort, so that the impact of the buildings, with their paintings and sculpture, must have been far greater than they would be today.

They were able to take advantage of the benefits that, for many, made such a journey possible. There was a general requirement that pilgrims should be offered hospitality, and that applied particularly to monasteries and other religious institutions, which had hospices for them. But in spite of that the pilgrims had to pay for much of their board and lodging along the way. In addition, there were also, of course, the many temptations that might be met in the towns; and they could be fleeced or worse by toll-keepers, ferry-owners or innkeepers.

The pilgrim routes, and the hazards that the pilgrims encountered along the way, were described in a remarkable document, *The Pilgrim's Guide to Santiago de Compostela*, which was written in Latin and is thought to have been compiled in the 1130s. This early guidebook was one section of a collection of manuscripts known variously as the *Codex Calistinus* and the *Book of St James*, all of them to do with the cult of St James.

It gave practical information, often colourful but not always trustworthy, on the nature of the regions through which the pilgrims would travel, the people who inhabited them, and the important shrines along the route. There was more on the French shrines than those in Spain – there are just brief references to Santo Domingo de la Calzada, Sahagún and León – but the guide included a detailed description of the cathedral in Santiago de Compostela as it was at that time.

There are some lively passages. On crossing rivers, for instance: 'At a place called Lorca, in the eastern part, runs a river called the Salty Brook. Be careful not to let it touch your lips or allow your horse to drink there, for this river is deadly. On its bank, while we were going to Santiago, we met two men of Navarre sitting sharpening their knives; they are in the habit of skinning the mounts of pilgrims that drink that water and die.

'When questioned by us, these liars said that it was safe to drink. We therefore watered our horses, and immediately two of them died, which these people skinned on the spot.'

It is not known who the author was, but it is clear that he was French. It seems that he followed the route that began at St-Denis, outside Paris, since he gives full descriptions of the shrines along that route and omits several important ones on the other routes; he seems to have relied on written sources for those routes. It also appears that given his references to horses, and the time he allowed for covering the various distances, he himself travelled on horseback.

His account is engagingly subjective, and he does not hesitate to be extremely critical, and even offensive, about some of the people to be encountered. He is very complimentary about the people of Poitou – which suggests that that was where he himself came from – but rude about the Basques and the Navarrese.

On the Navarrese: 'This is a barbarous race unlike all other races in customs and character, full of malice, swarthy in colour, evil of face, depraved, perverse, perfidious, empty of faith and corrupt, libidinous, drunken…', and so on. He adds that they practise 'unchaste fornication with animals'.

The author likes Castile, on the other hand: 'This country is full of riches, gold and silver, blessed with fodder and very strong horses, well-provided with bread, wine, fish, milk and honey.' But he adds: 'However, it is devoid of wood and full of wicked and vicious people.'

He also likes Galicia, and even has a special word of praise for its people, though his praise is qualified. 'This is wooded and has rivers and is well-provided with meadows and excellent orchards, with equally good fruits and very clear springs; there are few cities, towns or cornfields. It is short of wheaten bread and wine, bountiful in rye bread and cider, well-stocked with cattle and horses, milk and honey, ocean fish both gigantic and small, and wealthy in gold, silver, fabrics, and furs of forest animals and other riches, as well as Saracen treasures.'

He adds: 'The Galicians, in truth, more than all the other uncultivated Spanish peoples, are those who most resemble our French race by their manners. But they are alleged to be irascible and very litigious.'

Before Romanesque

There are four churches from the Visigothic period that are especially interesting:

Baños de Cerrato (page 217)
Quintanilla de las Viñas (page 223)
San Pedro de la Nave (page 313)
Santa Comba de Bande (page 365)

The churches and chapels that date back to the kingdom of Asturias are all in and around Oviedo. They are all in the Asturias section (pages 337-52), and include:

Cámara Santa, Oviedo
Santullano, Oviedo
Santa María de Naranco
San Miguel de Lillo
San Salvador de Priesca
San Salvador de Valdediós
Santa Cristina de Lena

The churches built by Mozarabs include:

San Baudelio de Berlanga (page 228)
San Cebrián de Mazote (page 231)
San Juan de la Peña (in part) (page 141)
San Miguel de Celanova (page 361)
San Miguel de Escalada (page 309)
San Millán de la Cogolla (in part) (page 241)
Santa María de Lebeña (page 201)
Santa María de Wamba (in part) (page 253)
Santiago de Peñalba (page 321)

Catalonia

Catalonia is a region of great variety, and its many Romanesque churches can be found in some very different places: the foothills of the Pyrenees, large cities such as Barcelona and Tarragona that border the Mediterranean, smaller cities and towns, and remote sites far out in the countryside. As I have already mentioned, these churches range from some of the earliest to be built in Romanesque style in Spain to others from a later period that foreshadow the arrival of Gothic.

There is also much to be seen in the museums. Both the Museu Nacional d'Art de Catalunya (MNAC) in Barcelona and the Museu Episcopal in Vic have collections of paintings and works of sculpture that have been taken from Catalan churches.

The region began to take shape in the ninth century, after the Arabs had been driven out of the northern parts by the Carolingians. It was then made up of a number of more or less independent counties on both sides of the Pyrenees, but they were brought together and resettled by a man known as Guifré el Pelós, or Wilfred the Hairy, who was initially count of Urgell and became count of Barcelona.

As such he and his successors were the effective rulers of, first, Old Catalonia, comprising the northern parts of the region, and later, areas further south as they were taken from the Moors.

Catalonia was hard hit by the devastating raids carried out in the late tenth century by al-Mansur, the Cordoban leader, when Barcelona and other centres were sacked. It recovered in the course of the following century, after the collapse of the caliphate in Córdoba, and as it became more prosperous, there was extensive rebuilding and building of churches.

One of the driving forces in this was Oliba, a member of an aristocratic family – his father was Oliba Cabreta, count of Besalú – who was not only abbot of Ripoll and St-Michel-de-Cuxa, now in France, but bishop of Vic, as we saw earlier. He himself was responsible for giving a new, Romanesque form to the abbey church in Ripoll and the cathedral of Vic, and he was influential over a wide area,

Bossòst
Salardù
Vielha
Erill la Vall
Boí
Barruera
Taüll
Durro
260
Gerri
de la Sal
ANDORRA
FRANCE
La Seu
d'Urgell
260
Sant Pere
de Rodes
260
Sant Joan
de les Abadesses
Frontanyà
Ripoll
Besalú
Figueres
AP7
17
Sant Pere
de Cassérres
Girona
Ponts
Cardona
Vic
L'Estany
Agramunt
25
Sant Benet
de Bages
Lleida
Santa Cecilia
de Montserrat
C16
AP7
A2
Terrassa
Vallbona de
les Monges
La Tossa
de Montbui
Sant Cugat
del Vallès
Barcelona
Poblet
AP2
Corbera
Catalonia
Santes
Creus
0 miles   30
AP7
0 kilometres   50
Tarragona

Bell-tower of Vic cathedral

in Catalonia and beyond. Cardona, to the west of Vic, and Sant Pere de Cassérres, to the north-east, are among the churches built at that time.

The cathedral of Vic was later largely reconstructed in Gothic style, but the splendid Romanesque bell-tower, dating from the eleventh century, and the crypt survive.

These churches were the work of Lombard stonemasons who brought their own distinctive style with them from northern Italy, and modified it to accommodate the round barrel vaults, built in stone, that already existed in Catalonia. The churches have a stylish form, but no carved decoration.

There was also, however, another tradition in the architecture of Catalonia, which did include carved decoration. It can be seen in the capitals of the early monastic church of Sant Pere de Rodes, north-east of Girona, and it later produced the great porch at the west end of the church in Ripoll, as well as beautifully worked cloisters in Girona, Sant Cugat del Vallès, Sant Benet de Bages and L'Estany.

There are of course some earlier churches in Catalonia that are wholly or partly pre-Romanesque. There is a group of three in Terrassa, a few miles north-west of Barcelona, and a little church on a hillside at La Tossa de Montbui, west of there, that has Lombard features added onto an older structure.

Santa Cecilia, which stands on the slopes of Montserrat, the centuries-old pilgrimage centre, is an early example of pure Romanesque style. So are two other churches in remote settings: Sant Ponç de Corbera, which is far out in the countryside west of Barcelona, and Sant Jaume de Frontanyà, in a small village in the foothills of the Pyrenees.

Catalan builders became much attached to Romanesque, and they continued to use the style for many years. In the course of the twelfth century churches were built in such different places as the hillside outside Ponts, north-east of Lleida, the town of Agramunt, a few miles to the south of there, the fortified town of Besalú, north-west of Girona, and Gerri de la Sal, the site of a monastery far to the north on the bank of the river Noguera Pallaresa.

Romanesque was, naturally enough, used for cathedrals too. La Seu d'Urgell was built over a long period, beginning in the first quarter of the twelfth century. Tarragona and Lleida were both begun much later, Tarragona in 1171 and Lleida in 1203, but both were initially late Romanesque in style, with Gothic additions. Lleida has some fine late Romanesque capitals.

In Barcelona the cathedral is Gothic, and so is Santa María del Mar, another of its principal churches. But there is a small late Romanesque church there, Sant Pau del Camp, which dates from the early thirteenth century and has interesting Moorish-type features in its cloister.

Some of the latest Romanesque churches in Catalonia are those built for the three Cistercian communities, in Poblet, Santes Creus and Vallbona de les Monges, all to the north of Tarragona. Like the cathedrals in Tarragona and Lleida, they were initially Romanesque, but have much that is Gothic.

There is a particularly appealing corner of Catalonia in the mountainous country in its far north-west. There the Vall de Boí has a group of churches dating from the twelfth century which are structurally quite simple, but include several with tall bell-towers. Above all, they have some excellent Romanesque paintings or, rather, good copies, the originals having been removed for their protection and now on show in the MNAC in Barcelona.

As well as the paintings, there is also some attractive Romanesque sculpture to be seen in Catalonia. Erill la Vall, one of the churches in the Vall de Boí, has a good copy of a group of seven figures, carved in wood, that make up a Deposition from the Cross: the originals are split between the museums in Barcelona and Vic.

There are small original works, also carved in wood, in the churches of Vielha and Salardú in the Vall d'Aran, another mountain valley in the north-west.

The outstanding work of sculpture, for itself and for its setting, is another group of seven figures, also making up a Deposition from the Cross, which is still in place in Sant Joan de les Abadesses, a few miles north-east of Ripoll, and is worth a trip on its own.

Barcelona: Sant Pau del Camp

Tucked away in one of the shabbier side-streets of Barcelona, but only a short walk from the Ramblas, is the little Romanesque church of **Sant Pau del Camp**. It is surrounded by palms and other trees, so that its form is not immediately obvious, but it has a handsome west front with carved figures on it and three good-sized apses, complete with Lombard bands, at its east end.

Above all, it has a small cloister which not only has a varied collection of capitals, but a feature that is very rare, and perhaps unique. The arches are cusped in Moorish style, some with five lobes, some with three, so that the effect is decidedly exotic.

The origins of Sant Pau are unknown. Both the church and the cloister have been dated to the beginning of the thirteenth century, when they were part of a priory subordinate to the abbey of Sant Cugat del Vallès (see page 83). But a monastery is known to have existed there, outside the walls of Barcelona, long

Cloister of Sant Pau del Camp, Barcelona

before that; at least since the late eleventh century, when it was already owned by
Sant Cugat. So it is assumed that there was an earlier church on the site.

Like many others, the monastery underwent changes over the centuries.
Monastic life came to an end in the nineteenth century, and the church was turned
over to parish work. The cloister and related buildings were handed over to the
War Ministry, which set up a barracks in them, and the cloister was in danger of
being demolished, but was saved by being declared a national monument in 1879.

Since then much has been restored and, apart from the worn state of the cloister capitals, there is little indication of this disturbed past. The west front makes an
impressive introduction with its decorative doorway, a circular window and on
either side lines of blind arches resting on tiny heads and other carvings. Above it
is a small turret, apparently defensive, and behind that a tall octagonal tower that
encloses the cupola inside and has a pair of baroque arches built onto it.

The doorway has a tympanum on which Christ is seated in the middle and is
being reverently approached by St Peter and St Paul, one on each side, to whom
he is holding out his hands. It is surrounded by an archivolt filled with tiny carved
shapes, many of them circular. But the most striking aspect is the representations
of the four evangelists, especially St Matthew and St John.

Up above and standing out from the smooth surface of the stone are, on one

Capitals in cloister of Sant Pau del Camp, Barcelona

side, a winged man holding out a gospel for St Matthew and on the other an eagle, also holding a gospel, for St John. Between them, slightly higher, is the Hand of God set in a circular frame. The quartet of evangelists is completed by a lion's head for St Mark and a calf's for St Luke, placed one on either side at the base of the archivolt.

There are other interesting, and intriguing, features of the doorway. It has a column on either side of the door, and each of them is topped by a capital that dates from the Visigothic period and must have come from some earlier building; one has Corinthian-style acanthus, the other a more formal design, also made up of leaves. The stone above them and the lintel between have a cross, stars and other patterns carved in low relief.

Inside, it is the height and spaciousness of the church that make an immediate impression. Sant Pau has only a single, short nave, which is barrel-vaulted and quite plain. But it is wide and so is the transept crossing into which it leads. This is formed by four tall arches and has the octagonal cupola, supported by squinches, rising high above it.

The three apses are also large, but they too are plain, with only small windows set into them.

The cloister is another world, with its array of cusped arches and no less than forty-eight carved capitals, set on paired columns. Most of the capitals are made up of Corinthian-style acanthus leaves, but there are some more formal designs and a number of naive, but vigorous creatures, real and mythological: lions, eagles, griffins and sirens among them.

One capital shows a warrior fighting a monster that has a bird's wings but the body of a reptile and two scaly tails that end in dragon heads. Next to it is one that has another warrior who is fighting a losing battle with a lion.

There are just two historiated capitals. One has a tree with a serpent twisted round its trunk and Adam and Eve on either side. Another has the theme of a woman being punished for lust: she is raising her hands in horror while two large toads suck at her breasts.

Besalú

The little town of Besalú, on the banks of the river Fluvià north-west of Girona, once played a much more important role on the Catalan scene, as the heart of a county that was independent from 877 to 1114. Today the castle of its counts has gone, but the town is most picturesque, with narrow streets and pleasant squares, some fine old houses, and three churches that date back to the Romanesque period.

Its outstanding feature is a long and handsome bridge across the river, with seven arches and a fortified tower, which can also be seen as Romanesque, as it has been there since the eleventh or twelfth century. It has often been restored since then, not least after losing two of its arches during the Spanish Civil War, but it is well preserved and makes an impressive entrance to the town, with the houses and towers reflected in the water under its arches.

Of the three churches, it is worth walking through the town to **Sant Vicenç**, which has an attractive east end and a setting among cypresses. **Santa Maria** also has a stylish east end that has recently been restored and is in a prominent position, but it is largely a ruin, with only the east end and the transept left, so that you cannot visit the interior.

Sant Pere, a former monastic church which dominates one of the squares, is the most rewarding. It dates from the mid-twelfth century – though it has a seventeenth-century bell-tower – and it has some good capitals. Its west front is largely plain, but it has an arched window complete with columns and carved capitals high up in the centre; and on either side is a splendidly savage lion, each of them trampling some benighted human figures, presumably sinners.

Capital in Sant Pere, Besalú

Inside, the nave is quite plain, with a barrel vault and solid rectangular pillars that divide it from the two side-aisles. But the eye is drawn to the east end, where there is a semicircular colonnade that rings the sanctuary, linking it to an ambulatory, and this has pairs of columns topped by vigorously carved capitals.

There are some Biblical scenes: the journey of the Magi, the Flight into Egypt, the Massacre of the Innocents. There are also Corinthian-style acanthi, and some lively capitals on which a human face appears between two monsters that are pulling in opposite directions.

Not far from Sant Pere is a decorated

Nave of Sant Pere, Besalú

Lion on west front of Sant Pere, Besalú

doorway which forms the entrance to what was once the Sant Julià hospital. It has an arch and several receding archivolts, as well as some columns and capitals, and it is thought that it may once have been part of the west front of Sant Pere, forming the entrance to the church.

There too the capitals are worth looking at. One is Corinthian, but there are also monsters maltreating humans, including one with two bodies that is apparently devouring a human head.

Bossòst and the Vall d'Aran

Bossòst is a pleasant little town a few miles south of the French frontier which is surrounded by mountains and has the Garona (Garonne) flowing through it. It also has a small Romanesque church dating from the late twelfth and early thirteenth centuries that has two carved doorways and a fine bell-tower.

The carving is rustic but moving, especially on the doorway on the north side, which has a tympanum showing Christ in Majesty. He sits bolt upright, his right hand raised in blessing, his left holding a scroll, with tiny faces representing the sun and moon on either side; and he is flanked by the 'four beasts of the

Tympanum on north door of church of Bossòst

Apocalypse' that represent the evangelists, the bull or calf for St Luke, the eagle for St John, the lion for St Mark and the winged man for St Matthew.

The tympanum is surrounded by a chequerboard pattern, and there is the chi-rho symbol in the middle of the lintel. Another chequerboard pattern runs over the top of the doorway, which has round archivolts. There is more carving, including a pair of monsters, on the capitals of the four columns.

The doorway on the south side is later, probably from the early thirteenth century, since it has a slightly pointed arch. It is also simpler. It has a chi-rho symbol in the centre of its tympanum and a frieze of formalized tendrils across the lintel. There are no columns, but it too has a chequerboard pattern running over the top.

The bell-tower stands well against the backdrop of the mountainside. It has three tiers of open arches, the two lower ones topped by Lombard bands, some of them damaged, and a pointed spire. There are more Lombard bands on two of the three apses – the northerly one has been remade in modern style on the outside.

Inside, the church has a slightly pointed barrel vault over the nave and half-barrel vaulting over the two side-aisles, which are divided from the nave by pointed arches resting on columns. The three apses also have pointed barrel vaulting.

Bossòst is in the lower reaches of the Vall d'Aran, which is cut off physically by

Crucifixion in church of Salardú

mountains from the rest of Catalonia – it once came under the rule of the counts of Comminges, on the far side of the Pyrenees – and still has a Romance language of its own, Aranes. It is a beautiful valley, and several of its villages have churches that are at least partly Romanesque.

Two of them have exceptional pieces of sculpture from that period. In **Vielha** the church has a life-size wooden bust of Christ, once part of a Deposition from the Cross, as is shown by a hand, presumably that of Joseph of Arimathea, that can still be seen on Christ's ribs. It is a powerful work that was originally in the church of Mijaran, now in ruins. (See page 6.)

In **Salardú** there is a Crucifixion that is much smaller, but is also in wood and may well have been carved by the same sculptor. It is intact and, like the Christ in Vielha, a work of great power.

Cardona

The collegiate church of **Sant Vicenç** in Cardona, in remote hilly country west of Vic, is one of the masterpieces of early Romanesque architecture in Catalonia; and it is remarkable not only for that. It also has a superb setting, perched as it is on a tall outcrop of rock and surrounded by the walls of the castle with which it once shared the site.

The castle itself has gone, and the buildings that replaced it now serve as a *parador*, or hotel. But the church is still there, and it is an unforgettable sight as you make your way up the winding road to the top of the rock, with the three apses of its east end, a short transept and a lantern tower over the crossing.

The church was consecrated in 1040, when it must have been complete or nearly so, and is one of the outstanding examples of the style introduced at that time by masons from Lombardy. Like other churches in that style it has no carved decoration. It relies for its effect on immaculate stonework, soaring lines and the interplay of round arches.

The rock on which it stands has a long history. It was strategically placed near some important routes and had valuable salt mines immediately below. A garrison was established there in 798 by Louis the Pious, the son of Charlemagne, as he prepared to attack Barcelona, which he took from the Arabs in 801. The next years were turbulent, and Cardona was later abandoned, but resettlement was begun in 879 by Guifré el Pelós, who was count of Urgell and also of Barcelona, as already recorded, and is generally regarded as the founder of a unified Catalonia.

East end of collegiate church of Cardona

Like much of northern Spain, Cardona suffered a century later during the campaigns of al-Mansur, the Cordoban dictator, who sacked Barcelona in 985. But resettlement began again in 986, when the rock and the town below came under the control of the viscounts of Ausona, who already ruled Vic.

The threat from the Islamic south faded soon after that, and the town became prosperous, partly because of the salt-mines, and partly because it was on a route for trade with the south. The viscounts took the name of Cardona, and came to play an important role in the politics of Catalonia.

There had been an earlier church on the rock, but in the early eleventh century Count Bremond began the building of a new one, having first taken the advice of Oliba, the influential bishop of Vic who was also abbot of Ripoll (see page 75) and St Michel de Cuxa, now in France, as I have written. At the same time he established a college of canons to take charge. The church was completed after Bremond's death by his brother and successor, Eriball, who was both viscount and bishop of Urgell and carried out the consecration himself.

The canons were considerable landowners, and they remained there for several centuries. But the site offered great attractions to the military. They gradually moved into various buildings, and in 1794 the church itself was handed over to them to become a barracks and store-room. This caused considerable damage, including the crumbling of the lantern tower over the transept crossing. The military left in the twentieth century, however, and the church has been extensively restored.

It was originally built in a relatively short time, and as a result is homogeneous in style. The main decoration is on the outside, where Lombard bands form a simple, but stylish pattern on the three apses, the two façades of the transept, and the walls of the nave. The main apse is tall and imposing. It has an ornamental ring of blind, arched windows under the cornice, but apart from that only a single central window at its upper level and three tiny ones, which light the crypt, far below.

The west front is largely plain, but has round arches which lead into a well-proportioned porch that has five bays covered by groin vaulting, and beyond that into the nave itself.

This makes a wonderful impression, demonstrating the beauty achieved by the masons of the First Southern Romanesque. High overhead is a round barrel vault supported by transverse arches. On either side are three tall round arches that divide the nave from the side-aisles, which have an arrangement of three groin vaults in each bay. The side-aisles are lower than the nave, and so round-topped windows set into the wall above the arches provide light. (See page 7.)

Beyond the nave is a short transept, also covered by barrel vaulting, and over the crossing a cupola supported on squinches. At the far end are a short choir bay that is raised above the level of the nave to accommodate the crypt below and a simple but elegant apse. It has the single window in the centre and on either side three tall, shallow niches with round tops.

Down below is the crypt, which is another appealing feature of the church. It has the same outline as the choir bay and apse. There is a short nave and side-aisles, with each of the bays framed by round arches and covered by groin vaulting. The columns that support the arches have the simplest of capitals and are thought to have come from the earlier church on the site.

As I have already written, there is no carved sculpture in this early Romanesque church. But like others built in Catalonia at the same time, it has a distinctive beauty that derives from the expert handling of the stone, and the way in which height, depth and rounded forms are combined in an inspiring whole.

Corbera

The church of **Sant Ponç de Corbera** is in wooded country a short distance west of Barcelona, on the far side of the river Llobregat. It is quite hard to find, and is not often open. But it is well worth making the effort, because in addition to being in a beautiful setting it is a good example of the First Southern Romanesque, with the simplicity and the pure lines of that style.

The church stands on a slight rise above a handful of rural buildings, with a row of hills in the background. As you walk up to it you see the west front, which is tall and imposing but plain. It has two pairs of round-topped windows in it, the upper ones set together with a column between them, but otherwise has only Lombard bands as decoration.

There are more Lombard bands along the outer wall of the nave, and there too they add a touch of elegance to a surface that is plain apart from a pair of small windows.

The east end is more elaborate, and unusually so. There are three apses, the central one larger than the two at the sides. Behind them is a short stretch of sloping roof that covers the choir bay, and beyond that more sloping roofs over the two arms of the transept. In the centre a rectangular tower over the crossing encloses the cupola that is inside the church, and at the top is a delicate belfry with two tiers of open windows.

No one knows exactly when Sant Ponç was built, or by whom. But the assumption is that it dates from the first half or the middle of the eleventh century. It is

Priory church of Corbera

known that there was a priory there, and that like several other Catalan monasteries it was taken over by the great Burgundian abbey of Cluny towards the end of
the eleventh century.

The inside of the church is well preserved, with the form and the proportions
that give the style its appeal. There is no carved decoration, just impeccable stonework and round arches everywhere. The single nave is covered by a barrel vault
that is supported by transverse arches. Beyond it is a short transept, which also has
barrel vaulting over its two arms and has the three apses leading off it.

In the centre the choir bay leads to the apse proper, which has three small, deep-
set windows, three niches below them and, most remarkably, some surviving paintings on the wall between the windows. There are entwined plants, birds and a
four-footed animal, and they too are dated to the eleventh century.

Rising above the transept crossing is another of the church's distinctive features,
the cupola. This is an ingenious and attractive construction. It is supported by
arches of different heights – low ones between the crossing and the two arms of
the transept, taller ones linking it to the nave to the east and the sanctuary to the
west – and at the top has four squinches that transform the square into a circle.

There as elsewhere the stone has been lovingly worked and that, together with the interplay of the various arches, creates a most satisfying effect. It would of course have been different in the eleventh century, when the walls would have been covered by paintings like those in the main apse. But the plain walls have their own appeal, and that is enhanced by the light that comes in through the windows. They are all small, but well distributed around different parts of the church.

L'Estany

The church of **L'Estany**, a village a few miles west of Vic, has a small and delightful cloister with a wide range of capitals. They include a sequence of scenes from the Old and the New Testament, formal arrangements of plants, birds and animals, and one or two capitals that are almost racy: a girl combing her hair, for instance, while beside her a couple embrace.

The church itself has been much restored. It originally belonged to a college of canons founded in 1080, and was consecrated in 1133. But it was badly damaged by an earthquake in 1428, which caused the collapse of the bell-tower, the vaulting of the nave and much else. A certain amount of rebuilding was carried out over

East end of collegiate church of L'Estany

Capital in cloister of L'Estany: the Magi before Herod

the succeeding century. The brick barrel vaulting over the nave was installed later, in 1670, and the two side-apses were only added on in the second half of the twentieth century.

The restoration has been well done, however, in keeping with Romanesque style, and the cloister, which was also rebuilt and rearranged, with the addition of an upper level, still has its original capitals. They cover a long period. The earliest, which are in the north wing and include the Biblical scenes, date from the second half of the twelfth century. The latest are those in the south wing, where there are a number of formal patterns, as well as some human and animal figures, which were completed in the late thirteenth or early fourteenth century.

The Biblical scenes have a moving simplicity. They begin with the story of Adam and Eve. One capital shows Eve emerging from Adam's ribs; then her taking the apple from the serpent coiled round the Tree of Knowledge while Adam, already complete with fig-leaf, looks on; and finally Adam ploughing with two oxen, while Eve holds up a spindle, after their expulsion from the Garden of Eden.

Next are scenes from the life of Christ, which begin with the Annunciation and give a full account of the various events – though they are not always in chronological order. First come the Nativity, the Adoration of the Magi and the Flight into Egypt. Then there are the Baptism of Christ, his Temptation and the Marriage in Cana. The story ends with the Kiss of Judas and the Crucifixion, followed by the Weighing of Souls, in which the archangel Michael holds the scales and two devils try to pull down one side.

They are an appealing collection. Among the most striking are the appearance of the three Magi before Herod, the Massacre of the Innocents, in which a distraught mother holds her head in her hands as two children have their throats cut, and a long procession of Apostles, their bodies closely packed together and tapering down towards their feet, who are accompanying Christ during his Entry into Jerusalem.

The capital in which the girl is combing her hair is in the east wing of the cloister, and that has several lively subjects. There is a musician who is playing a string instrument while a woman wearing an elaborate head-dress dances with castanets in her hands; and there is a scene of an engagement, in which the man holds out a scroll towards his fiancée. Another capital has an ox that is playing a string instrument.

There is also a scene of country life – two peasants holding a sheaf of corn – and there are some fine carvings of birds, animals and monsters confronting each other in heraldic poses. Perhaps surprisingly, there are even two religious subjects: an Annunciation and a Christ in Majesty surrounded by the lion, calf, eagle and winged man that represent the four evangelists.

There are good capitals in the other two wings too, and it is possible to spend a long and happy time looking at them all. In the south wing is an abbot who is flanked by two acolytes as he gives a blessing and sprinkles holy water; and elsewhere two peasants are holding up a dead hare. In the western there is a hunter with a falcon on his wrist and two dogs that are chasing a hare; and on the same capital a peasant slaughtering a pig.

Not least, there is an array of formal patterns throughout the cloister, and of posturing birds, animals and monsters.

Capital in cloister of L'Estany: Palm Sunday

Frontanyà

The village of Frontanyà, hidden away in mountainous country north-west of Vic, has only a handful of houses. But it also has a large and handsome church that was built in Lombard style in the later half of the eleventh century and that towers over the tiled roofs.

Up above the village is a high outcrop of rock, so that the setting as a whole, with wooded hills all round, is a magnificent one.

The church, which is dedicated to **Sant Jaume**, or St James, has largely retained its unity of style. So there is no carved decoration, and its appeal, like that of other churches of its period and style, derives from the pure lines of its stonework, its rounded forms and its combination of height and depth.

The west front has two later additions: a belfry at the top and a circular window in the centre. But it still has its bare elegance, with an arched doorway flanked on either side by Lombard bands, and more Lombard bands overhead, carved at an angle and rising to a peak in the centre. A distinctive touch is the tiny cross-shaped window just under that peak.

The east end is more elaborate. There are three tall apses, each with a single round-topped window: the central one has Lombard bands, while the two side ones have just a ring of blind arches under the cornice. But the dominant feature is the twelve-sided tower over the transept crossing, which is encircled by the arches of tiny blind windows.

Protruding from the tower are four small triangular structures that cover the squinches inside. The two with sides facing east have Lombard bands and flank a window. Together with the arms of the transept on either side, the apses below and the tower above, they make an unforgettable ensemble, with the rock rising up behind.

Frontanyà is in an area that was taken from the Arabs by the Carolingian Franks late in the eighth century and early in the ninth. The first

Nave of collegiate church of Frontanyà

Collegiate church of Frontanyà, from east

attempts at resettlement came to nothing, but a new programme was set in motion towards the end of the ninth century, and in 905 a church was consecrated on the summit of the rock above Frontanyà, where it was easy to defend.

In the course of the eleventh century conditions became calmer, and the present church was constructed at the foot of the rock, where it served a college of canons. As elsewhere, it received donations from local aristocrats.

The plan of the church is a straightforward one, with a single nave of two bays covered by a round barrel vault. There is a short transept that is also barrel-vaulted and has an octagonal cupola, supported by the squinches, over the crossing. Beyond that are the three apses, each framed by a round arch.

The central apse has a feature that is characteristic of the Lombard style: five tall, shallow niches, each with a round arch at the top; and a narrow window in the central one.

There are only small windows anywhere in the church, which means that the light is limited. But it is enough for the enjoyment of a building of great beauty.

Gerri de la Sal

The monastic church of **Gerri de la Sal** is a simple, harmonious structure that dates from the middle of the twelfth century and has great charm. It is also set in picturesque surroundings. It stands alone, surrounded by trees, on one bank of the Noguera Pallaresa river, and there is a fine view of it from the village on the other bank.

Mountains rise steeply on both sides, and the river makes its way through a gap between them. You cross from one bank to the other by a high and ancient bridge from which you see fishermen wading in the water below.

The most prominent feature of the church is the tall belfry which rises above a porch at the west end and has three tiers of open arches which, interestingly, are cusped in Moorish style. Behind it are two ranges of blind arches that run along the outside of the nave, one on each side high up under the eaves, and a third range that runs above the south side-aisle.

There are three apses at the east end, all ringed by Lombard bands, and beyond them a sacristy that was attached to it some time later.

Gerri has been the site of a church for a long time. It is known that there was a monastery there, and a newly built church, in 807, and it is possible that the

Monastic church of Gerri de la Sal, from north-east

monastery was founded long before that, in Visigothic times, though there is no firm evidence for that. What is certain is that the existing church was built for the monastery and was consecrated in 1149 by the archbishop of Tarragona; also that it was quite an occasion because the bishops of Urgell, Barcelona, Vic, Girona, Lleida and Saragossa were all there too.

Additions have been made to it since then – the belfry, the porch and the ranges of blind arches – but the body of the church has remained as it was. It has a relatively tall, well-proportioned nave with a round barrel vault that rests on transverse arches and two side-aisles with half-barrel vaulting.

There is no transept, and so the nave leads straight to a choir bay above the sanctuary and beyond that the central apse. This has a stylish arrangement of tall, shallow niches topped by round arches, with windows in three of them. There is a smaller apse on either side.

In the nave the transverse arches supporting the vault rest on pilasters that run up from the floor and have engaged columns set onto them. There are capitals at the top of the columns – birds, animals, monsters and the occasional human, simply carved – and more on the engaged columns that support the round arches that divide the nave from the side-aisles.

The porch at the west end of the church has three sections, each covered by groin vaulting and divided from each other by round arches. The central section encloses the doorway into the church, which has round archivolts and on each side an engaged column topped by a capital. There are also capitals elsewhere in the porch. Some of them are quite worn, but one apparently shows Daniel between two lions,

Girona

The cathedral of Girona, which towers above the old town, with the river Onyar down below, is largely Gothic, and an impressive example of the style. But there were other cathedrals on the site before this one was built, and two features of an earlier, Romanesque complex survive: a bell-tower and, above all, one of the outstanding cloisters of the twelfth century.

The cloister is unusual in having, not just some fine column capitals, but carved friezes on which a number of stories, mainly from the Old Testament, are graphically told; and the bell-tower soars above its south side.

Parts of the medieval city walls also survive, and run close by the cathedral. Down below are gardens and, surrounded by an array of cypresses, two

Romanesque churches that were built outside the walls, also in the twelfth century: the tiny Sant Nicolau and the much larger Sant Pere de Galligants, which was once part of a Benedictine abbey and has a small cloister with an excellent collection of capitals.

Girona is an ancient city, and it is a pleasure to walk around these older parts. But there is also another, compelling reason to visit it. The **cathedral** has a museum that has an extensive collection of manuscripts, paintings, metalwork and much else. It includes a unique object: a superb piece of embroidery known as the Tapestry of the Creation that was woven in the eleventh or twelfth century.

It is damaged at the edges, but is largely intact, and is a complex and dramatic work, full of fascinating detail. In the centre is Christ, a boyish but commanding figure who is sitting inside a circle with his right arm raised in a masterful gesture. Around him, in segments set inside a larger circle, are vivid little scenes representing the events of the Creation. They include the separation of light and darkness and the division of the waters.

In one segment Eve is shown emerging from Adam's rib, and in another Adam is confronting a line of animals, including a unicorn. One enchanting scene has an array of exotic birds and beneath them various ungainly creatures swimming around in the sea.

Further out, and set in the corners of a square, are four naked young men who represent the winds and are blowing long horns while sitting on what look like inflated goatskins. On the outer edge, where it survives, are more little scenes. Samson and Abel are both there, and there is a range of other figures. One represents one of the rivers of Paradise (another of the rivers was in the part that is lost), others the year as a whole, the seasons and several of the months.

Then there is the cloister. This is built along the north side of the cathedral, and has a slightly irregular shape, with some sides longer than the others, because it had to be fitted in between the cathedral and the town walls. But it is a place of great charm, shaded by cedars and with a well in the middle, and it has identical round arches, beautifully shaped, on all four sides.

Up above is the bell-tower, an impressive structure that has no less than seven tiers, each topped by a line of Lombard bands. The two lower tiers are plain apart from the Lombard bands, the next one has blind arches, and the top four all have pairs of open arches.

Most of the cloister's arches rest on pairs of columns, set a few feet apart. But there are also some substantial pillars, both at the four corners of the cloister and at various points on the sides. They appear to have been set there for structural reasons, being more robust than the columns, but they have been integrated into

Cloister of Girona cathedral

the overall design, with engaged columns at each corner. Most critically, they also provide the space for the friezes.

Many of the stories on the friezes are told step by step. Adam and Eve are given dramatic treatment, including a scene in which they are standing on either side of the Tree of Knowledge; the serpent is curled around the tree as it reaches out towards Eve, and Adam is eating the forbidden fruit. So are several other stories, among them those of Cain and Abel and Abraham and Isaac.

On one of the friezes Noah and his son are shown working as carpenters to build the Ark. Then later you see Noah, followed by a young man and a woman, presumably his son and his wife, approaching the completed Ark, which already has animals and birds looking out of the windows.

Not all the scenes come from the Old Testament, however. A frieze on one of the pillars shows Christ's descent into Hell, where he knocks down the gates with his cross and reaches out to Adam to free him. Another frieze on the same pillar presents a gruesome picture of Hell in which the busts of three people emerge from a huge cauldron that has flames blazing underneath while on either side horned devils are hauling in further victims.

And a much more positive note is struck by friezes which have a contemporary theme. They appear to illustrate the process of building the cloister, or perhaps the

Frieze in cloister of Girona cathedral: Noah, his wife and son boarding the Ark

cathedral itself. In one, there are labourers who are hauling in water in a huge cistern; in another, craftsmen who are crouching over their work while a bishop is arriving at one side, presumably to see what they are doing.

These narrative friezes are mostly on the south side of the cloister, which was the first to be built. In addition to telling a story they have another attractive feature. At each end of the frieze is a purely decorative design: birds with necks entwined in one place, pairs of angels in another.

There is of course more to be seen in this cloister. There are friezes that do not tell a story but have some exquisite formal designs, often with birds, animals or tendrils all caught up in complex patterns. There is also a large number of column capitals, whose decoration ranges from Corinthian-style acanthus leaves to subjects taken from both the Old and New Testament.

These too are vigorously carved. They are in no particular order, and the narrative subjects include the Massacre of the Innocents, Moses carrying the tablets of the law and Christ's entry into Jerusalem. Then there are Christ's washing of the disciples' feet, the death of the Virgin Mary, and the parable of the rich man and Lazarus.

There are also purely decorative capitals, often made up of pairs of birds or animals, and by way of contrast, a number of action scenes. Warriors are shown fighting each other, for instance, or struggling with animals, and one capital has a boar hunt. It is altogether a rich collection.

Sant Nicolau and **Sant Pere de Galligants** are not far away, and close to each other. Sant Nicolau has a well-shaped exterior, with an east end made up of three apses and a lantern tower that are all decorated with Lombard bands. Across the road is the west façade of Sant Pere, which is largely plain, but has a carved doorway in the centre and, unusually, a rose window up above.

More impressive is Sant Pere's bell-tower, a tall hexagonal structure that has two tiers of paired arches at the top, all topped by Lombard bands, and dominates the church's east end. It is built above the north arm of the transept, with two apses attached to it, and together with the large central apse and two smaller apses attached to the south arm of the transept they make up a well-balanced composition.

The interior of Sant Pere has the harmony and the sense of height and space that are the mark of Romanesque. A high barrel vault supported by transverse arches covers the nave, and it leads to a lower arch that frames the apse and the semicircular ring of arches below it. There is a short transept, which has a total of four small apses leading off it, three on its east side and one at the end of the north arm.

Bell-tower of Sant Pere de Galligants, Girona

The tall arches that divide the nave from the two side-aisles are not decorated, but above them the transverse arches that support the barrel vault rest on capitals. They are quite elaborate, with a pack of snarling lions on one and on another a human figure who is raising what look like weights with both hands. A third has a man standing between two centaurs.

There are more capitals, and some very accomplished ones, in Sant Pere's little cloister. This is a delightful place, with a hydrangea and other plants in the centre, and capitals that range from versions of the Corinthian-style acanthus to stories from the New Testament. They include the Visitation, the Nativity, the Adoration of the Magi and the Flight into Egypt.

It is thought that the cloister dates from the second half of the twelfth century, and that its capitals were carved slightly earlier than those of the cathedral cloister, which they resemble. They too are a fine collection, and as well as the New Testament scenes it is possible to see sirens with double tails, harpies and battles against lions. There is a dance scene and even a bishop officiating at an altar.

Lleida

Lleida was once a Moorish fortress, captured by Catalan forces in 1149, and the modern town is still dominated by fortifications that surround the hill on which the citadel stood. Within the fortifications are the remains of the castle occupied by the Christians after their victory and, above all, the cathedral that they built there over the site of the mosque.

This is now known as the **Seu Vella**, or old cathedral, since there is another, newer cathedral in the lower part of the city. But the Seu Vella continues to tower above the rooftops and the river Segre, so that it can be seen from miles away; and it is remarkable for illustrating the transition from Romanesque to Gothic, as well as having some exceptional late Romanesque carving.

Its most prominent feature is the very tall, slim Gothic bell-tower that was erected in the fourteenth and fifteenth centuries. At its foot is a cloister that also dates largely from the fourteenth century and is in a particularly ornate Gothic style. But the body of the cathedral is mainly late Romanesque. It has features that anticipate Gothic, as well as some fully Gothic additions, and it has a wealth of carved capitals both inside the church and on the outside of various doorways.

It is thought that many of the craftsmen who were responsible for the carving were Moors who had stayed on in Lleida after the city had been taken over by the Christians. They formed part of what has been called the Lleida school, which was influential in surrounding areas, including Agramunt (see page 71).

Building of the cathedral only began in 1203, as already noted. By then the much smaller church that had been put up soon after the conquest was found to be too small – it stood on the north side of what later became the cloister. The new cathedral was consecrated in 1278. Other features continued to be added after that, but at the beginning of the eighteenth century the whole hilltop area was turned over to the military for their use and the cathedral became a barracks. Restoration began in the middle of the twentieth century, when the military left, and has necessarily been extensive.

The cathedral's plan is a traditional Romanesque one, with a nave, two side-

Lleida: old cathedral

aisles, a transept and, at the time it was built, five apses leading off the transept.
The east end is not quite what it once was because one of the four side-apses,
which was at the end of the north arm of the transept, is no longer there, and the
two on the south arm have both been remodelled in Gothic style.

But if you walk round the outside you see that the central apse is still there in
its original form, with three round-topped windows, and it has a smaller Romanesque apse beside it. Behind it is the transept, which is also Romanesque and has
more round-topped windows, and above that the Gothic lantern tower.

At the west end is the cloister. This is an unusual position for it, but it seems that
it was the only place with the necessary space, given the lie of the land on Lleida's
hilltop. It means that you enter the cathedral through a Romanesque doorway of
the thirteenth century, and a decorative one that has a combination of geometrical
patterns and intricate plant designs, in the east wall of the Gothic cloister.

Once you are inside, the nave is majestic, with the marked sense of upward
movement that is typical of the transition from Romanesque to Gothic. The three
bays are each covered by rib vaulting, with pointed transverse arches between the
vaults. There are more pointed arches on either side of the nave, dividing it from
the side-aisles, and rib vaulting in the side-aisles and both arms of the transept.

There are rose windows at each end of the transept. But the only round arches

Capitals in old cathedral, Lleida

are over the smaller windows that are high up in the nave, the side-aisles, the transept and the choir bay.

A cupola that is supported on squinches and is wholly Gothic rises from the four pointed arches of the transept crossing. Beyond it, the central apse makes an appealing focal point. It is framed by the pointed arches of the choir bay, which is also rib-vaulted, and has its three windows in the semicircle of wall below.

The many capitals can be seen throughout the cathedral, and they add a distinctive touch, with subjects that range from Biblical scenes to purely ornamental patterns. Some are placed at the top of the engaged columns that run all the way up the sides of the nave, providing support for the arches of the vault, others on the shorter columns that support the arches of the nave; and there are more in the side-aisles and in the transept.

Generally speaking, the Old Testament scenes are in the transept and the apses, while those from the New Testament are in the nave and the side-aisles. Alongside them is an extraordinary collection of purely fanciful subjects: winged monsters confronting each other, a centaur armed with a bow and arrow, a warrior swinging a club at a monster with wings and a crown, another fighting with sword and buckler, as well as designs consisting of no more than ingeniously entwined plants and tendrils.

Capitals in old cathedral, Lleida

There are more carvings on the doorways that are another of the glories of the cathedral. A formal doorway at the north end of the transept is plain, but the western entrance to the nave is decorated, as has already been seen; and there is fine workmanship on two doorways on the south side of the cathedral, one at the south end of the transept, the other forming the entrance to the side-aisle.

These are all Romanesque, with round arches and archivolts, but there is yet another doorway on the far, western side of the cloister which, like the cloister as a whole, is purely Gothic and has a sharply pointed arch.

The doorway at the south end of the transept is the oldest of the three that have carving, dating from 1215. It is known as La Anunciata because it once had two statues representing the scene of the Annunciation. They have gone, but the niches in which they stood still have cusped arches that may, it is thought, have come from the mosque that once stood on the site.

Along the top is a cornice that has a row of corbels, as well as an inscription giving the words spoken by the Archangel Gabriel to the Virgin Mary and in the centre the chi-rho symbol. Below them, the archivolts and the column capitals that frame the doorway have carvings of an extraordinary richness, with animals and birds caught in a maze of picturesque tendrils.

There is a similar richness in the other doorway on the south side of the cathedral, a little way to the west. This too is late Romanesque and dates from the second half of the thirteenth century, but it stands inside a porch that was added in the fourteenth century and is framed by a broad Gothic arch.

Here too is a line of corbels under the cornice, as well as geometrical patterns similar to those on the western doorway on the archivolts. Together with them are the exquisite carvings of animals and birds caught in tendrils that were the speciality of the Lleida school.

Montserrat: Santa Cecilia

The mountain of Montserrat, north-west of Barcelona, is one of the most dramatic natural features in Catalonia, a jagged ridge that is visible from miles around. The ancient monastery which had stood on its heights since the ninth century was sacked by French troops in 1812, and the present church is a nineteenth-century replacement. But it still attracts large numbers of pilgrims, not least for its twelfth-century wooden statue, the Black Madonna.

Even if not for that, Montserrat is well worth visiting, not just for its magnificent views, but for a small early Romanesque church, **Santa Cecilia**, which is on the

Santa Cecilia, on slopes of Montserrat

lower slopes of the mountain. With its three apses and a simple belfry, you see it set against the mountain peaks soaring behind it; and there are also views of the plain far below.

It is a plain but well-built church that was erected in the eleventh century in the First Southern Romanesque style. Its apses have small, deep-set windows with round tops, and are decorated on the outside with Lombard bands.

Inside, it has a nave that is covered by a barrel vault. At its east end, just before the three apses, there is an arch on each side that links the nave to the side-aisles, creating the effect of a transept. The side-aisles are shorter than the nave.

Poblet, Santes Creus and Vallbona de les Monges

The Cistercians came to play an active role in Catalonia, and the three monastic communities that they established in the area north of Tarragona – the monasteries of Poblet and Santes Creus and the convent of Vallbona de les Monges – are outstanding examples of their architecture. The building of all three began only in the second half of the twelfth century, and continued for some time after that, so that much is Gothic or later, as I have already written. But they all also have parts that are Romanesque.

All their naves were originally Romanesque in conception, and each of them has its own appeal. There are also Romanesque features in the three cloisters, alongside the more prominent Gothic.

The Cistercians were brought in and supported by the kings of Aragon (which after 1137 included Catalonia), partly because of the attraction of their religious practices, but also because of their agricultural skills. By the middle of the twelfth century southern or 'New' Catalonia had been taken from the Moors – Tortosa in 1148, Lleida in 1149 – and it consisted of large stretches of land that needed to be resettled and redeveloped.

So in 1150 Ramón Berenguer IV, count of Barcelona and also the effective regent of Aragon, invited Cistercian monks from Fontfroide, in what is now France, to found the monastery of Poblet. Santes Creus was founded at about the same time by monks from La Grande-Selve, near-Toulouse, though they only moved to the present site in 1169 after abandoning an earlier one that had proved unsatisfactory.

Vallbona also had its origins in the 1150s, as a community of both monks and nuns. It became a Cistercian convent in 1176 after the monks had moved elsewhere and a group of Cistercian nuns had come from Tulebras in Navarre.

Cloister of monastery church of Poblet

Over the years all three institutions became substantial landowners as a result of support, and donations, from the Aragonese royal family and other nobles. They have royal tombs, and all three continue to boast the title of 'royal' in their official names.

Poblet, which is still an active monastery, is the largest and, with its array of buildings, many of them surmounted by towers, and the walls and turrets that surround it, it makes a powerful, almost exotic, impression when you arrive at its gate.

When you enter the church, however, you are in the late twelfth century, with a slightly pointed barrel vault soaring high above you and on either side a line of six pointed arches that divide the nave from the side-aisle. Engaged columns rest on brackets a few feet from the ground and run up each side of the nave to support the transverse arches. There are round-topped windows above each of the bays.

A short transept, also barrel-vaulted in both arms, extends on either side of the nave, and beyond it is an unusually complex east end. The principal apse is segmented, with a sixteenth-century reredos beneath it. Behind it is an ambulatory with rib vaulting over its bays and five smaller apses.

Since this is a Cistercian building, there are only the simplest of capitals on the columns that support the arches of the nave. But the purity of line and impeccable stonework are characteristic.

The other Romanesque features at Poblet are in the cloister which, like the church, was begun in the twelfth century. The south side dates from that time – unlike the other sides, which are Gothic – and it has pairs of round arches that are each set within a pointed relieving arch, as well as capitals with simple plant motifs. There are more round arches and plant motifs in the hexagonal lavatorium in the centre of the cloister, a delightful structure that is also twelfth-century.

The church of **Santes Creus** also has a tall nave that dates from the late twelfth century, though it was only completed in the early thirteenth. It is narrower, heavier and even more austere than that of Poblet, and so considered to be closer to the original principles of the Cistercians. Plain round arches divide the nave from the side-aisles, massive square pillars are placed between them, and there are no capitals at all. But it is uplifting in its own way.

This church too was originally intended to have a barrel vault, but the plans were changed in the course of construction and it was given rib vaulting instead. The east end has a square-ended sanctuary in the centre and two chapels on the east side of each arm of the transept, also square-ended.

The cloister of Santes Creus is largely Gothic, and has some surprisingly explicit carvings, not just of plants, but also of Biblical stories, monsters and assorted humans, among them a rich man with his bag of gold and a stonemason holding

Capital in cloister of Santes Creus

Nave of monastery church of Santes Creus

a hammer and chisel. But as at Poblet, the lavatorium in the centre is Romanesque in style, and it is another appealing hexagonal building, with round arches and plant motifs.

Like Poblet, the convent of **Vallbona de les Monges** has an active religious community. It dominates the little town that surrounds it, and there is an attractive view to be had of it from the outskirts, its two Gothic lantern towers rising above the rooftops.

Unlike the other two, it has a formal doorway in Romanesque style of the thirteenth century that stands at one side of a small square and provides an entrance to the north arm of the transept. The tympanum has a carving of the Virgin and Child with an angel on either side.

In its interior, the church has a square-ended sanctuary in the centre of the east end, and a square-ended chapel leading off each arm of the transept. This is similar to the arrangement in Santes Creus, and it can be regarded as late Romanesque, but the greater part of the church, which has rib vaulting over the nave and transept, and a cupola over the crossing, is Gothic.

There is something of both styles in the cloister, which is interesting for having been built over a very long period. The south side was the first to be built, in the late twelfth century, and it is very simple Romanesque; it has round arches and

Tympanum of doorway of convent church of Vallbona de les Monges

Doorway of convent church of Vallbona de les Monges

most of its capitals are not decorated at all. The east side came next, in the thirteenth century, and the style was still Romanesque. There are round arches in sets of three, with a round window and a relieving arch above them, and the capitals have plant motifs.

Attitudes had changed by the time the north side came to be built in the fourteenth century, and this has tall pointed arches in an elaborate Gothic style. But there was a change of heart in the fifteenth century when plans were made for the final, western side of the cloister. It appears to have been felt that the north side was too flamboyant, and it was decided to revert to the simpler manner of earlier days, with small round arches and quite simple capitals.

Ponts and Agramunt

Romanesque churches can be found all over Catalonia, as we have seen, some in cities and towns, others in remote country settings. There is one of each in the area of hills and valleys north-east of Lleida: Sant Pere, which stands alone on a hillside outside Ponts, and Santa Maria, in the centre of the town of Agramunt, not far away.

Sant Pere de Ponts is in a superb position, as you see when you make your way up to it from below. It rises on the far side of a dip in the land, surrounded by small pine-trees and with a view of hills in the distance behind it. It has a tall, octagonal lantern tower ringed by two tiers of double arches, and down below it an east end made up of three apses, each decorated by a semicircle of round arches, all of them open.

The church belonged to a college of canons, and was built at the beginning of the twelfth century, probably on the site of an earlier structure. By the twentieth century it was in ruins, but it has been thoroughly restored. In addition to its visual appeal, it is interesting for its use of Lombard bands, particularly on the three apses, where they provide a framework for the arches. The arches are blind, but are set deep into the stone and appear like windows.

Tiny blind arches also decorate the outside walls of the nave, and there are more of them above each of the double arches that decorate the lantern tower.

Like many other churches in remote corners of Spain, Sant Pere is not normally open, so that arrangements have to be made to see the interior. It has a single nave covered by a round barrel vault resting on transverse arches, leading to a high octagonal cupola below the lantern tower. Two of the apses open out from the space below that, one on either side. The central apse has three tiny apses set into it.

Collegiate church of Sant Pere de Ponts

Santa Maria in Agramunt is also a work of the twelfth century, but it is many years later and rather different. It has a nave and two side-aisles that are all covered by pointed barrel vaulting and that lead to three apses at the east end. There are a few capitals on engaged columns that run up the sides of the nave as far as the transverse arches that support the vault.

The church's main interest, however, is the very elaborate, and exquisitely worked, west doorway that was added on later and is thought to be the work of stonemasons from Lleida (see page 60). It has a succession of archivolts that recede far inwards and that are all decorated, some with simple patterns, others with little figures or formal designs; and they rest on two lines of columns that are topped with some intricately carved capitals.

In the centre, over the innermost arch, is a little group that was set there, according to an inscription, in 1283 – a late date for a Romanesque work. It has a Virgin and Child, each of them crowned and flanked by two small angels, in the middle. On one side is the Annunciation, and on the other the Adoration of the three Magi, the first of whom is kneeling and has taken off his crown.

There is so much detail on this doorway that it is worth spending time looking at the various parts. The innermost archivolt has six virgins, three on each side,

West doorway of church of Agramunt

Carving on west doorway of Agramunt: Adoration of the Magi and Annunciation

Capitals on west doorway of Agramunt

who are or were each holding a book and a flask of perfume. Surrounding them on the next archivolt is a more complex design in which tiny kneeling figures are surrounded by tendrils. Around that are eighteen female figures, some standing and some sitting, who are all carrying books, except for one who is holding a child. One of the outer archivolts has more little standing figures.

One of the most striking features is the immaculately carved capitals on top of the columns, and the little strip that extends from them on either side towards the central door. The little strip has monsters that are fighting each other. The capitals have more monsters, as well as other animals and humans, all of them caught up in various fanciful arrangements of plants and their tendrils.

Ripoll

Ripoll, a town set among the wooded foothills of the Pyrenees, near the junction of the rivers Ter and Freser, once had one of the most important abbeys in Catalonia. Its church is largely a nineteenth-century reconstruction, carried out after it had fallen into ruin, but it still has a twelfth-century porch at its western end that is one of the great achievements of Romanesque art, as well as a cloister that is partly Romanesque.

The porch has the form of a Roman triumphal arch, with a deep doorway in the centre framed by a succession of archivolts, all covered with little carved figures and scenes. Above it and on both sides are more carvings, illustrating an extraordinary array of subjects: from Christ in Majesty at the top, flanked by angels, to episodes from the Old Testament, the stories of St Peter and St Paul, and depictions of the work carried out by country people in the fields each month of the year.

The abbey was originally founded in the late ninth century by Guifré el Pelós, the count of Barcelona and creator of a unified Catalonia (whose remains are preserved in a modern tomb in the north transept of the church). The church was rebuilt more than once, and in its final form, inspired by Oliba, abbot of Ripoll and one of the most influential men of his time (see page 24), was consecrated in 1032.

Oliba was also abbot of St-Michel-de-Cuxa, now in France, and bishop of Vic, as already stated. Under his guidance the church was given a nave that was flanked by two side-aisles on each side and a long transept that had one central apse leading off it and no less than three smaller ones on each side. At the western end it had two tall bell-towers similar to those Oliba had built at St-Michel-de-Cuxa. This is the basic form of the church as it has been reconstructed.

West porch of abbey church of Ripoll

Thanks in large part to Oliba, Ripoll became a leading centre, not just for religious observance, but for letters and learning in general. It came to own an extensive library of manuscripts, including the works of both Christian and classical writers. It was during the time of Ramón de Berga, abbot from 1172 to 1206, that in all likelihood the western porch was built. He is known to have been responsible for the north wing of the cloister.

Serious damage was done to the church by the earthquake of 1428, and repairs were carried out, largely in Gothic style. More damage was done by a fire that broke out in the course of disturbances in 1835, and paintings and photographs from the nineteenth century show the ruinous state that it was in after that. Moves to rebuild it began in 1885, and it was consecrated once again in 1893.

The idea was to recreate Oliba's Romanesque church. At the western end one of his two bell-towers, the southern, was still largely intact; it was restored and battlements were built onto it at the top. The other had been badly damaged by the 1428 earthquake and has been given a conical top. The body of the church was rebuilt and, in spite of good intentions, very obviously lacks authenticity.

The porch, however, has survived, under a protective portico erected in the thirteenth century. Sadly, much of the carving is in poor condition, since the stone is diseased and has been worn away by centuries of exposure. But the figures on the inside of the arch, which were more protected, are better preserved. They include the stories of St Peter and St Paul and those of Jonah, Daniel, and Cain and Abel, as well as the signs of the Zodiac and the labours of the months. And the overall effect is still one of great vitality.

The Christ in Majesty is a powerful and serene figure who is surrounded, not only by angels, but by symbolic representations of the four evangelists: the eagle of St John, the winged man of St Matthew, and at a lower level, the lion of St Mark and the bull or calf of St Luke. On either side are the twenty-four Elders of the Apocalypse, who are

Detail of Ripoll porch: Cain's offering and his burial of Abel

Detail of Ripoll porch: beheading of St Paul

each carrying a stringed instrument and a cup of perfume and are shown, not seated as they often were, but standing in a line and almost dancing.

Below them is a line of saints, and below that there are two rows of scenes from the Old Testament – as well as a decorative stork in the triangular space on either side of the arch. On the left are scenes from the life of Solomon: among them the dream in which he asked for wisdom, his judgment in the case of the disputed child, and his anointment as king. Below that are the Ark of the Covenant being conveyed to Jerusalem, Jerusalem afflicted by plague, and the prophet Gad telling David to make a sacrifice to Jehovah.

On the right of the arch Moses is shown drawing water from the rock, which the Israelites are clamouring for. Further to the right the Israelites are being guided by an angel and the column of fire; and then there are the miraculous appearances of quails and manna. Below are action scenes from the battle of Rephidim, when Joshua led the Israelites against the Amalekhites: Moses is being supported by Aaron and another companion, and horsemen with lances are charging each other.

Lower still are a row of arches, five on either side of the doorway, which each contain a full-length figure. On the left is David surrounded by musicians. On the right Christ is shown delivering the Law to Moses, Aaron, and two other people, one dressed as a bishop, the other as a nobleman.

The two most prominent figures on the porch are St Peter and St Paul, who are represented by life-size statues standing on either side of the arch, with an archivolt above them. Unfortunately, their two heads are both missing, but above each of them in the archivolt is a sequence of little scenes from his life – St Peter curing a cripple, for example, and St Paul being baptized – ending with their respective martyrdoms.

Further into the arch, another archivolt tells the stories of Jonah, on the left, and Daniel, on the right; and the innermost one recounts the events that led to Cain's murder of Abel.

The labours of the months are on the upright columns on either side of the door – January to June on the right, July to December on the left. They are vivid little scenes that include cheese-making, harvesting wheat and grapes and slaughtering a pig.

There is much else to be seen on this porch, which has innumerable decorative details, not least the carving on the various columns. There are even little scenes, for instance, on the two outer sides of the porch which are linked to the events on the front: on the right, the crossing of the Red Sea and a battle between two horse-

Capitals in cloister of Ripoll

men; on the left, Elijah being taken up to Heaven in a chariot of fire and a group of musicians.

There is less to be seen in the cloister. But it is a harmonious place with a fountain in the middle and two levels of identical round arches, each resting on pairs of columns. From it there is a fine view of the taller bell-tower, with its Lombard bands and tiers of open windows.

Only the lower level of the north wing is Romanesque. The other wings on that level and the whole upper level were added in later centuries, beginning in the late fourteenth century, when Gothic had taken over. But the later builders preserved the form of that first wing, with its round arches, and only the style of the column capitals is noticeably different.

The capitals of the north wing have a full repertoire of Romanesque subjects. Several of them have plant designs, often derived from Corinthian-style acanthus. There are also animals, eagles and monsters, sirens with double tails, angels with outstretched wings, and little human figures caught up in tendrils. In one capital little men look out from the corners, apparently emerging from waves. In another a bearded man, perhaps Daniel, has each of his arms caught in a lion's jaws.

There is a badly worn relief carving of Ramón de Berga in the north-east corner of the cloister.

Sant Benet de Bages

The former monastery of **Sant Benet de Bages** has a lovely setting in the countryside near the village of Navarcles, between Manresa and Vic. Its church is late Romanesque, from the end of the twelfth and the beginning of the thirteenth century, and it has a small cloister that was added on soon afterwards.

The cloister has considerable charm, with a few trees and shrubs creating a dappled effect in the centre, and round arches that rest on relatively short, stocky columns on each side. The column capitals are an interesting collection, though many of them are rather obviously restored. They include a number of purely decorative designs, often very elaborate, with leaves and tendrils intertwined, but also human figures, animals, birds and monsters.

The history of Sant Benet goes back to the tenth century, when the first church was built. Turbulent times followed, not least when al-Mansur, the Moorish leader from Córdoba, ravaged Catalonia at the end of that century; and there was another raid by Moors in about 1114-15, when the monastery was sacked. It was only at the end of the twelfth century that work could begin on the new church.

Since then there have been modifications and a number of additions, many of them in Baroque style, but the plan of the Romanesque building has been retained.

Monastery of Sant Benet de Bages

It has a single nave with a slightly pointed barrel vault, a short transept with two apsidal chapels leading off it, and a central apse. Below that is a simple crypt.

On the outside you see only one of the apses, the large central one, since the two smaller ones are incorporated in the wall of the transept. It has no decorative carving, but the east end as a whole is impressive. Above the apse is a pretty bell-tower with two tiers of open arches, single at the lower level and paired in the upper. At the far end of the church is a tall, plain tower that survives from the earlier building.

The west door is well worth stopping at because it has several good capitals: two lions mauling a small person, other lions with shaggy manes and bushy tails, pairs of birds sitting on leafage and an involved scene in which lions and birds are caught in tendrils.

In the cloister there are two capitals that must have come from the earlier, tenth-century church. They are both on the east side, which was the first one to be built, and form a pair. One, which is badly worn, has formalized acanthus leaves and is Islamic in style. The other, which is very different from all the others in the cloister, has carving in low relief on all four faces: Christ in Majesty, the Annunciation, a man standing with his arms raised and a leafy plant.

The standing man is often described as someone praying. But there is a small

Capital on doorway of Sant Benet de Bages

Capitals in cloister of Sant Benet de Bages

figure at his side and a bird perched on one of his hands, which has suggested a
more ingenious interpretation: that the man is St Benedict and that this describes
a miracle in which the small figure tried to give him poisoned food and the bird
intervened to save him by removing the food.

There are other capitals on the cloister's east side that may well have come from
an earlier building, even if they do not date from the tenth century. They would
have been brought in when the cloister was being built. But the capitals on the
other three sides were in all likelihood newly carved at that time.

There is an tantalizing mystery about who was responsible. A capital inside the
cloister, on the angle between the western and southern sides, has an inscription in
Latin which says that it was the work of 'Bernad'. It has generally been assumed
that this referred either to the master mason or, more probably, to the abbot of the
day – and there was an abbot at about that time called Bernat Sanespleda.

But there is another possibility. One of the capitals carries the coat of arms of
the Rocafort family, aristocrats who had links with Sant Benet, and it seems that
several of them were called Bernat.

The figured capitals are well worth a careful look. Three of them have the Virgin
Mary sitting and holding the infant Jesus, with Joseph in the background on two
of them; and there are angels with outstretched wings on one. Apart from them

none are overtly Biblical, but they range from pairs of birds sipping from a tall vase to horsemen with shields.

One intriguing capital has two men facing each other and blowing hunting horns while a bird of prey sits on the ground between them with its catch between its claws. Behind them is a subject that also appears on two other capitals: a man who is sitting and has between his legs a plant that grows up out of the ground and spreads out on either side of him.

Elsewhere is a scene in which two lambs are facing each other and above them is a monster with two bodies and a single head; and another capital has an eagle with outstretched wings that has its prey, probably a rabbit, in its talons.

Sant Cugat del Vallès

The monastery of **Sant Cugat del Vallès**, in the town of that name just outside Barcelona, has one of several notable cloisters built in Catalonia in late Romanesque style, as I have already mentioned. It dates from the early thirteenth century, and has an irresistible mix of Biblical, ornamental and other subjects, all beautifully carved, on its capitals.

There are even four capitals showing monks engaged in various activities: ringing a church bell, carrying a sacred book, sitting and writing. Interestingly, one of them is sitting on a stool and handing a bowl to a sculptor who is also sitting and is at work carving a capital. Alongside is an inscription that is carved in the stone and gives the sculptor's name: Arnau Cadell. So this must be a rare self-portrait by a Romanesque artist, and an illustration of the hospitality offered him by the monks.

Altogether there are no less than one hundred and forty-four columns, most of them standing in pairs with round arches between them. They include a fine collection of largely decorative capitals – Corinthian-style acanthus leaves, elaborate patterns of entangled plants and fruit – and also formal groupings of various birds, lions and monsters. Not least, there are numerous scenes from both the Old and the New Testament, ranging from the story of Adam and Eve to the Resurrection.

The story of the monastery begins far back in the past because according to legend Cugat was a Christian missionary from North Africa, properly known as Cucufas, who was martyred in about 304 in a Roman fort outside Barcelona. It was the time of Diocletian's persecutions. Cugat's remains were placed in a cemetery, where they were venerated, and this became the site of a succession of buildings, most of which did not survive the disturbed centuries that followed.

Cloister of church of Sant Cugat del Vallès

The monastery was reduced to ruins in 717 when the Arabs, who had invaded the Iberian peninsula in 711, marched into Catalonia; and again in 985, when al-Mansur, the Cordoban leader, sacked Barcelona and the surrounding towns. Finally, there were Moorish attacks, and perhaps more destruction, in the first half of the twelfth century.

You would not guess this violent past when you see the monastery and its church today. They stand on the edge of a broad and pleasant square in the centre of the town, and could not be more peaceful. The church's west front is fourteenth-century Gothic, as is the lantern tower over the transept crossing. But the main body of the tall bell-tower is Romanesque – though smaller turrets were put on top of it in later years – and so are the three apses at the east end.

The church was built over a period of time, beginning in the twelfth century and continuing into the thirteenth, after calmer conditions had returned to Catalonia. Its basic form is Romanesque, with a nave, two side-aisles, a short tran-sept and the three apses. The style evolved over the years, however, and there are Gothic features, not least the rib vaulting over the nave which replaced the barrel vault originally planned.

The cloister was built in the early thirteenth century, at about the same time as the cloisters of Sant Pere de Galligants and the cathedral in Girona (see page 55) – and it is known from documents that Arnau Cadell was present at that time, and presumably playing a leading role. It now has two levels because an upper floor was added on in the sixteenth century. But the upper level is much simpler, con-sisting of four ranges of slender columns and round arches, and it does not detract from the effect of the Romanesque display below.

So this cloister too is a peaceful and fascinating place, with a cypress in one corner and a fountain in the centre; and it has an interesting feature. Excavations have revealed the foundations of earlier buildings under the ground in the middle, and in particular those of a church of the Visigothic period, complete with a horse-shoe-shaped apse.

You need time to look properly at all the capitals. Most of the Biblical scenes are on the south side of the cloister, and it is evident that they are on the inside columns, presumably so that they could be more easily seen by the monks, while the more ornamental capitals are on the outside, facing into the open space at the centre of the cloister.

There are only a few Old Testament stories, but they are vividly presented. Adam and Eve are shown receiving instructions from Jehovah, committing their sin and then cowering before him afterwards. Noah appears hard at work building the Ark, then peering out of it as it floats on the waters and the dove, perched on the roof, indicates that the flood has subsided, and finally in a drunken stupor. Abraham receives and entertains the three angels who visit him.

The New Testament scenes are not in chronological order, but they are worth searching out. A capital on the east side of the cloister has both the Nativity and the Adoration of the Magi. Another shows the Presentation in the Temple. A third shows a much later event, Jesus washing the feet of the Apostles.

There are several more scenes, and some that are full of action, on the south side. One capital combines the horror of the Massacre of the Innocents – Herod giving his orders, the soldiers seizing the children from their

Capital in cloister of Sant Cugat del Vallès

mothers – with the Flight into Egypt. Another shows Christ's entry into Jerusalem, accompanied by people waving palms. Then there is the Resurrection, illustrated by the Three Marys going to buy unguents from two seated vendors.

But there is much more to be seen in this cloister, not just the formalized acanthus leaves and the exquisitely entwined patterns, or the pairs of birds and monsters standing and confronting each other, but scenes of men fighting lions, men fighting each other, shepherds fighting off wolves, hunters going after wild boars. There is a capital showing musicians and dancers, with the dancers doing handstands at the corners; and another in which an armoured figure representing a virtue is spearing a small crouching figure that represents a vice.

Some of the most striking, and mysterious, figures are four bearded men who are sitting, each on one face of a capital on the east side. Each holds a pair of what look like studded plant stems that rise from between his legs, cross over in front of him and disappear into strangely shaped objects at the corners.

Sant Joan de les Abadesses

The church of **Sant Joan de les Abadesses**, a pleasant little town on the river Ter, a few miles north-west of Ripoll, has an unusually elaborate east end consisting of

Sant Joan de les Abadesses: Deposition from the Cross

an ambulatory and five apses. It also has a magnificent group of statues inside, as already noted, that are in the central apse and make up a Descent from the Cross.

The Descent from the Cross is a subject often found in Catalan churches, in Erill-la-Vall, for instance (see page 109). This one is late Romanesque, dating from about 1250 when style was evolving towards Gothic, and is a powerful work that is exceptional in being preserved nearly intact in the church for which it was intended.

Only the figure of the good thief, on a cross on the left of the group, is a modern copy, the original having been burnt in 1936 in disturbances at the outbreak of the Spanish Civil War. The central figures are Nicodemus and Joseph of Arimathea, who are carefully taking down the body of the dead Christ, and the Virgin Mary and St John, who are standing on either side and are both visibly grieving.

The group is known as the 'Santíssim Misteri', or most holy mystery, because of the discovery in 1426 of a consecrated host in a cavity behind a tiny door in Christ's forehead. It had apparently been there since the statues were put in place in 1251. It was put back and was much venerated over the years, but it too was destroyed in 1936.

The present church was the third to be built on the site. The first was consecrated in 887, at a time when Guifré el Pelós, the count of Barcelona, was resettling the area, which had been taken from the Arabs not so long before. He founded a convent there and installed his daughter Emma as the abbess. She proved to be a dynamic figure who was responsible for the construction of a number of new churches in the area.

The nuns were removed by order of the papacy in the eleventh century, and a college of canons took their place. The present church, consecrated in 1150, was the second that they built.

Its style, and specifically its east end, was influenced by features often found north of the Pyrenees in what is now France and very rarely in Spain. This is particularly true of the ambulatory, which has three apses radiating out from it and was originally separated from the sanctuary by a semicircle of columns. West of it is a long transept that has two more apses leading off it on its eastern side.

There is only a single, barrel-vaulted nave, which is short and undecorated, possibly because funds ran out. It has no side-aisles, and there is no doorway on the west front.

Sadly, the east end was badly damaged by the powerful earthquake that hit Sant Joan de les Abadesses and other churches in the region in 1428 – causing more than forty deaths in Sant Joan alone.
The vault of the ambulatory fell in and was replaced by the barrel vault resting on four robust pillars that is there now and is somewhat incongruous.

It is, however, possible to see the outer rim of the ambulatory. It still has the three apses radiating out, and also windows set into the wall between them; and they are all quite ornate. The central apse is framed by two tall columns topped by capitals, and has three round arches supported by slender columns, also topped by capitals, on the semicircular wall below. Two of the arches are blind; the central one has a narrow window.

There are more round arches and capitals in the two apses that lead off the transept.

Sant Joan de les Abadesses: capital on east end

There are a great number of capitals in Sant Joan, both inside the church and on the outside, and they are a varied and vigorous collection. The subjects range from stylized versions of the Corinthian acanthus to contorted monsters and Biblical scenes: the bathing of the infant Jesus, for example. They include a centaur, Samson grappling with a lion, a pair of lions confronting each other and even the fable of the fox and the stork.

Much of the outside is plain, with a few small windows. The west front has only a frieze of blind arches under the cornice, and the same is true of the façades of the two arms of the transept. But at the east end the central apse has two tiers of round arches, most of them blind, and is flanked by the two windows of the ambulatory, both with arches. There too there are some fine capitals: pairs of men who share a single bearded face and more animals and monsters.

Sant Pere de Cassérres

Like several others in Catalonia, the small monastic church of **Sant Pere de Cassérres**, a few miles north-east of Vic, has a remote and beautiful setting. It stands high up on a wooded promontory, with the river Ter forming a loop round it down below and distant views of hills in all directions. It is also an attractive example of early Romanesque style, dating as it does from the first half of the eleventh century.

It has a short nave that has only two bays but is quite wide, with a round barrel vault supported by transverse arches overhead, and that gives its interior a spaciousness that is exceptional in such a small church. Round arches divide the nave from the two side-aisles, which also have barrel vaulting. There is no transept. A short choir bay continues the vaulting of the nave, and beyond that is an apse, which has three round-topped windows.

There is no carved decoration, and the walls are bare. But the sense of space and the interplay of round arches give the church its appeal. A door in the south side-aisle leads to the interior of the bell-tower, which is built onto the outer wall of the aisle and has a cupola in the form of an irregular octagon resting on squinches.

The known history of the promontory goes back to 798, when the troops of Louis the Pious, the son of Charlemagne, occupied a castle there during their campaign against the Arabs. It was only resettled in 879, however, when conditions were calmer, and a first church was built on the site.

By the early eleventh century that church was quite dilapidated, and in 1006 Ermetruit, viscountess of Ausona, decided to found a monastery there and to

Monastery church of Sant Pere de Cassérres

build a new church as part of it. In due course her daughter-in-law, Enguncia, took over from her, and the present church was consecrated in 1050. Enguncia was the mother of the viscounts Bremond and Eriball, who between them built the great church at Cardona (see page 44).

In about 1080 the monastery was taken over by Cluny, the influential Burgundian abbey, and, as was Cluny's way, became a priory. It flourished for a time with the support of local aristocrats and ecclesiastics, but went into decline in the fourteenth century.

The church was badly damaged, like a number of others in the surrounding area, by an earthquake in 1428. This led to the demolition of the north side-aisle, and several other parts of the monastery, including the cloister, had to be rebuilt. Further restoration was carried out in the late twentieth century, not least of the cloister, which has a number of simple capitals, and of several monastic buildings that surround it.

Sant Pere stands alone, and you have to approach it on foot. There are splendid views along the way of the Ter and the rocks that line it, and you see the church rising high above them on its outcrop. The bell-tower has pairs of round-topped windows. To one side of it is the plain west front, to the other an east end that has three apses and is more decorative than the rest of the church.

The central apse has a ring of blind windows, framed by Lombard bands, under the cornice, and there are more Lombard bands on the two smaller apses and on the outer walls of the choir bay.

Sant Pere de Rodes

Many of Spain's early churches are in spectacular settings, but none is more spectacular than that of the monastic church of **Sant Pere de Rodes**. The church and other monastery buildings stand alone on a steeply sloping hillside high above the Mediterranean north-east of Figueres, some twenty miles south of the French frontier. (See page 22.)

In its day Sant Pere was one of the most prominent monasteries in Catalonia, and its church is a beautiful product of the early eleventh century, with features that are unique. But it went into decline after the twelfth century, and though there was new building over the years it was in ruins by the nineteenth century. Even today, after much restoration, many parts of the monastery are still that way.

The church itself is largely intact, and there are two surviving towers, visible from far away as you walk the last stretch of the road that crosses the hillside, with the sea and the little harbour town of Port de la Selva far below and the ruins of a castle on the cliff above. One is relatively plain and known as the Tower of Homage; the other a more ornate bell-tower in a characteristically Romanesque style of the twelfth century, with four levels of open windows, the two higher ones topped by Lombard bands.

It is the interior of Sant Pere, however, and the nave in particular, that is exceptional. The nave has bare stone walls and no pews, but it is tall, spacious and well-proportioned, with a round barrel vault supported by transverse arches. Beyond it are a short transept and three apses at the east end. Round arches divide the nave from the two side-aisles and, remarkably, they are structured and decorated in a way that is reminiscent of Roman style of the classical period.

At the foot of the arches are solid stone plinths, and resting on them columns on two levels, one above the other, all of them topped by some intricately carved capitals. Some of the columns at the lower level support the arches. Others provide a base for the columns at the higher level which, in turn, support the transverse arches of the vault.

This arrangement is not just a very handsome one; it is also unique for eleventh-century Catalonia. It is quite unlike the style of other churches being built at about the same time, such as Cardona (see page 44), which have lovely lines but no carved decoration. And it raises an interesting question, much debated by specialists: should Sant Pere be categorized as Romanesque or pre-Romanesque?

It is known that the church was consecrated in 1022, and it is assumed that though it may well not have been complete by then – perhaps only the east end and the outer walls had been built – it would have been finished in the next few years. There was certainly later building, at least until the end of the twelfth century, but the basic structure of the church is a product of the first half of the eleventh.

One interesting point is that the arch that frames the entrance to the choir is slightly horseshoe-shaped, a feature that is associated with the Mozarabs. Another early feature is the ambulatory, which circles the sanctuary but does not have radiating chapels built onto it.

Then there are the capitals, many of them variations on the theme of the Corinthian acanthus, others an exquisite mix of entwined plants and tendrils. It is suggested that the craftsmen who carved them drew on ancient decorative traditions while also reflecting influences from the Islamic world to the south and the Carolingian to the north.

Whatever the verdict, Sant Pere is an extraordinary monument which was created over several centuries and reflects the history of Catalonia. According to legend, the hillside on which the monastery was built had once been the site of a temple of Venus. What is certain is that a monastic community was established there during the ninth century, after northern Catalonia had been taken from the Arabs by the Carolingians.

These monks may well have been refugees from the Arab-ruled south. In 926 they came under the control of a local aristocrat, Count Tassi, and it was under his guidance, and that of his heirs, that the monastery emerged as a power in the land. Tassi carried out some rebuilding – and he became a member of the monastic community himself – but his work was replaced when construction of the existing church began in the first years of the eleventh century.

It was not an easy job because of the slope of the land. One of the earliest parts of the new church was the crypt, a simple arched structure that was set under the sanctuary and was important for the relics that it held – and also served to shore up the apse. Above it is the ambulatory, which leads directly off the two side-aisles and was originally on one level but was given an upper level later, perhaps in the early twelfth century.

The transept, like the nave, is barrel-vaulted, and has two apses, also added at a later stage, attached to it.

One intriguing fact is that a cloister was erected on the south side of the church

Nave of Sant Pere de Rodes

in the first half of the eleventh century, but was demolished in the late twelfth century because it was felt to be not large enough for an increasingly important monastery. It was replaced by a bigger one in a different position further to the west, and traces of it were only discovered during excavations in 1989. It is possible to see what has been found of this earlier cloister. The later one is largely intact, but only because it has been extensively restored.

At the far end of the church a narthex, or galilee, was built onto the west front towards the end of the eleventh century, and it remains in place, though it has suffered from wear and tear over the years. The intention was to provide a more impressive entrance, and also a place for the burial of the ruling family. To embellish it further, the doorway into the nave was decorated in the second half of the twelfth century by the sculptor known as the Master of Cabestany.

Who this sculptor was is a mystery, but his work is found in a number of places in France, Italy and Spain, recognized by its distinctive style: expressive faces, for instance, in which the eyes are emphasized by two holes drilled one on either side of the eyeball. He is linked to Cabestany, a small town near Perpignan in France, because one of his best-known works, a tympanum illustrating the glorification of the Virgin Mary, is in a church there.

The Sant Pere doorway was one of his major projects but, sadly, it was stripped of most of its sculpture in the nineteenth century, and there are only tiny fragments left. However, two works from the doorway can now be seen in the Museu Frederic Marès in Barcelona, and there are copies of them in the narthex of Sant Pere. One is a most powerful creation, the Appearance of Christ to the Apostles, in which Christ is standing and gesturing to two Apostles who are in a boat; the other the Lamb of God, set in an oval frame.

La Seu d'Urgell

The cathedral of **La Seu d'Urgell**, an ancient city in the foothills of the Pyrenees, has the look of a fortress when you walk up to it from the north; and that is what, in effect, it had to be at one time. But behind the high wall and the towers its interior is a good example of twelfth-century Romanesque, tall and spacious, and there is a big cloister on the south side that was built soon afterwards and has columns and capitals on three of its sides.

Above all the cathedral is notable for certain features that show the influence of contemporary Italian style. This is true in particular of the sizable, and decorative, apse that you see when you walk round the outside to the east end.

East end of cathedral of La Seu d'Urgell

At its top it is ringed by a semicircular gallery complete with round arches, capitals and other carvings that is similar to those found in a number of Italian churches – Modena, Bergamo – and that sets it apart from most other churches in Catalonia.

The history of Urgell and its bishopric goes far back in time. It has a strategic position in a valley flanked by high and spectacular mountains, and the Romans founded the city of Orgellia on a nearby hilltop in the second century BC after defeating the local tribes. This later became an early centre of Christianity, and it is known that there was a bishop of Urgell, St Just, by the first half of the sixth century, if not before.

Because of its remote position, the see survived the Arab occupation of the early eighth century. Bishops continued to succeed each other – though one of them, Nambad, was burned at the stake by the invaders in 731. The town was taken from the Arabs by Charlemagne's troops in 788, but was sacked in 793 by an Arab force that was diverted to the area after failing to seize Narbonne.

Some time after that the population moved from its hilltop, now known as Castellciutat, to the present site of Urgell, a short distance away, and erected the first of the three cathedrals that succeeded each other there. Fighting with the Arabs continued, but over the years the towns to the south were taken from them, and the bishop of Urgell came to be the head of an extensive diocese with the political power that went with it.

Fighting was often with rival Christian rulers over territory as much as with the Arabs. But deals were made, and one far-reaching outcome was a treaty signed in 1278 by which the bishop of Urgell and the count of Foix, in what is now France, agreed to share jurisdiction over Andorra, which is made up of mountain valleys north of Urgell.

This arrangement is still in force today. The bishop of Urgell continues to be a co-ruler of Andorra, while the rights of the count of Foix passed first to the king of France and then to the president of the French Republic, who still has them.

In spite of the prestige of its bishop, construction of the cathedral was a slow business, and it was never completely finished. This shows in the two massive, but truncated towers that rise from the arms of the transept, in the smaller turrets that stand at each end of the west front, and in the lantern tower over the transept crossing, none of which has an appropriate top.

It seems to have been a question of money. It is known that building of the cathedral, to replace an older structure that had become decrepit, began in 1116. But by 1175 only the walls had been erected, and a seven-year contract was signed with a Lombard mason, Ramon, and four other Lombards for the vaulting, the lantern tower and bell-towers.

Ramon and his workmen were responsible for much of what can be seen today, but the cathedral remained incomplete. One factor was tension between the bishop and a neighbouring warlord, the viscount of Castellbó. The viscount's men sacked the city in 1195, and work never resumed in a big way after that. The cathedral itself was adapted for defence.

In spite of that, there is much in it to be seen and enjoyed. The apse at the east end is a splendid creation, with carved capitals on the columns that make up the gallery, some of them free-standing in pairs, some set on the sides of rectangular pillars; and there are little faces, several of them grimacing, just above.

Below the gallery the apse has three windows, all elaborately decorated with archivolts. Up above is a rose window, and above that the lantern tower over the transept crossing, now topped by a small belfry.

There are two smaller apses on either side which can be seen inside the church but are not visible outside, since they are enclosed within the thick wall of the transept. But there is a gallery built into the wall high up on the east-facing side of each arm of the transept, and three arched windows from each of those galleries can be seen flanking the main apse.

At either end are the two huge towers. Both are largely plain, and have been restored, but are decorated with Lombard bands. The northern one came nearer to completion, and has faces carved at the base of the little blind arches.

There is another point of great interest if you go further along the east end of the cathedral, beyond the southern tower. This is the little church of Sant Miquel, formerly known as Sant Pere, which is attached to the south part of the cathedral buildings – and can be visited from the cloister. It is much older than the cathedral, dating from the first half of the eleventh century, and its east end, made up of three apses, a transept and a simple bell-tower, is a delightful survival from that time.

By comparison with the east end, the north side of the cathedral is quite forbidding, though there is a small doorway that has columns, capitals and several round archivolts, as well as a short stretch of Lombard bands in the wall above it. Apart from that, the wall is largely plain, with towers at each end. This was useful for defence, but there is another explanation for it.

It seems that there was a miscalculation when the body of the church was being constructed. The nave was made very tall, and there was too great a difference in height between it and the two side-aisles, which were much less high, with the result that their vaulting did not provide the support that was needed for the vault of the nave. There was a danger of collapse.

The solution, which was presumably devised and put in place by Ramon and his fellow Lombards, was to erect an extra stretch of wall above the northern side-aisle, where the danger must have been greatest, and link it to the upper part of the wall of the nave with flying buttresses. Together with the extra wall, these provide the necessary support.

If the north side of the cathedral is largely plain, however, the west front, by contrast, is ornate, and includes some fine carved detail. It has the two turrets, which are built onto unadorned stretches of wall at each end. But between them there are three arched doorways, all with receding archivolts, and above them two rows of windows. The upper row, made up of one arched and two circular windows, is enclosed within an arrangement of blind arches, and the cornice above is richly patterned, with a dog-tooth design running down each side.

At the top is a little turret that has two tiers of open arches, one above the other.

The central doorway has a pair of columns on each side, all four topped by lively capitals. More arresting are the carvings on the wall that surrounds it. High up on either side is a lion that is apparently devouring a human figure sprawled beneath it and has another stretched out on its back. Two similar lions can be seen at ground level, though they are largely worn away, and there are two lion heads at the level of the capitals.

West front of cathedral of La Seu d'Urgell

Up above is a frieze that has a range of tiny figures, human and animal, all full of movement. They include sirens with double tails, more lions, a person holding a staff and grimacing, a dragon, a hunter and much else.

The interior of the cathedral has the sense of height and space that are characteristic of Romanesque style. The nave is tall, with a barrel vault that is supported by transverse arches, round but slightly flattened, which rest on pilasters that run all the way up from the floor. Similar pilasters support the round arches that divide the nave from the two side-aisles, so that the pillars on either side of the nave are cross-shaped.

The effect is quite massive, but it is lightened by some decorative features. There are engaged columns in the angles between the pilasters, with carved capitals on top of them; and there is a line of corbel-like faces running along the walls of the nave immediately under the barrel vault. A feature that stands out is the little balls that have been carved on the corners of all the pilasters.

The sanctuary, which opens out beyond the transept crossing, forms the focal point of the nave, and has a most appealing design, made up of an array of round forms. There is a tall choir bay and, leading from it, an unusually complex arrangement in which a small apse is set into the larger one.

The smaller apse has a window in the centre, set within several archivolts, and tall blind arches and capitals on either side. Above it in the semicircle of the larger apse is another window, also set within archivolts, and on either side three very tall narrow arches that run up from ground level, two of them blind and the central one having a window set into the top.

The transept is also tall, with round barrel vaulting over each arm and a rectangular lantern tower that rests on squinches over the crossing. The west-facing side of the two arms is plain, but the east-facing side of each of them is particularly appealing. Each side has its two apses and, up above them, the gallery, which has a row of three arched double windows, complete with pairs of columns, all of them set into the wall.

The cloister is another pleasure. Across its broad open space there is a fine view of the south side of the cathedral, with the little two-tiered turret at the west end; and the capitals on the three sides that survive from the Romanesque period are, if a bit coarse because they were carved from granite, full of vitality.

The east side was originally in the same style as the others, but was demolished in 1603 and replaced by the rather plain structure that you see today. The other three were due to suffer the same fate in a plan that was adopted in 1781 but, fortunately, not put into effect.

The cloister is thought to have been built soon after the cathedral and by the

Cathedral of La Seu d'Urgell: capital in cloister

same masons. The capitals, which rest on single columns, have a range of animals and humans, vigorously and often grotesquely presented. One of the most engaging has a bearded man, seated and playing a stringed instrument, at each of its four corners.

Tarragona

Tarragona was the most important city in Spain in Roman times, when it was known as Tarraco and was the capital of a province; and there are a number of evocative remains from that period: walls, an aqueduct, an amphitheatre and, on the outskirts, the villa of Centcelles, which has early Christian mosaics of the fourth century. The city continued to be important in the Middle Ages, as is shown by the **cathedral** that dominates the old part.

This was many years in the building, from 1174 to 1331, when it was consecrated, and so much of it is Gothic. But the initial plan was Romanesque – a nave and two side-aisles, a transept and five apses – and there is late Romanesque carving to be seen both inside the church and in the cloister.

On the outside the central apse is tall and largely plain, but it has a ring of quite ornate blind arches, complete with corbels, under the cornice. The other two apses on the south side, which are much smaller, have also survived from the Romanesque period, but those on the north side, between the church and the cloister, have been replaced by later structures.

In the interior, the nave is tall and wide, and though it is basically late Romanesque, it illustrates the way in which that style evolved into Gothic. It, the side-aisles and the transept are all covered by rib vaulting, and pointed arches divide the nave from the side-aisles. A cupola over the crossing also rests on pointed arches, and has rib vaults. On the other hand there are a few carved capitals that can be seen high up on either side of the nave and that give a Romanesque touch.

The main apse is largely Romanesque, though it is partly hidden behind a fifteenth-century reredos, and so are the two smaller apses leading off the south arm of the transept. One attractive feature is the capitals on the columns that frame the entrance to the choir – warriors fighting, a centaur with a bow and arrow, ravening lions – and there are more on the columns that mark the two bays.

The doorway that leads from the church to the cloister is pure Romanesque, and has more good carvings on the cloister side. On the tympanum is Christ in Majesty, seated in a mandorla with a book on his knee and surrounded by the symbolic

Tarragona cathedral: cloister

figures of the evangelists: the lion of
St Mark, the bull or calf of St Luke, the
eagle of St John and the winged man of
St Matthew.

Down below, the capital on the central column has touching scenes of
the Nativity and the Adoration of the
Magi; and there are more carved capitals on the columns on either side.

The cloister was built between 1194
and 1214, and is large and handsome,
with a distinctive arrangement of arches
on all four sides; and it has the main
apse and other parts of the cathedral
towering over it all. It has sets of three
round arches that are raised slightly
above ground level and are each enclosed within a relieving arch; and there
is a pair of small round windows, filled

Tarragona cathedral: capital in cloister

with a carved pattern, in the space immediately above them.

Between the relieving arches a pilaster runs up the wall with an engaged column
set onto it; and between the pilasters is a horizontal line of tiny blind arches that
are cusped in Islamic style and have little faces, several of them grimacing, at their
base.

There are carved capitals at the top of the engaged columns, and more on some,
but not all, of the columns that surround the cloister. They include Biblical scenes
from both the Old and the New Testament – the angel waking the three Magi is
a charming example – but also simple plant designs like those favoured by the
Cistercians.

And there are a few scenes from ancient fables. Across one of the abaci is the
Procession of Rats, in which a cat that is pretending to be dead is being carried
along on a bier for burial by rats, but is secretly waiting for the right moment to
jump up and carry out a mass killing.

Taüll and the Vall de Boí

The two churches of Taüll, high up on the mountainside above the Vall de Boí,
the Boí valley, are stylish constructions that have a perfect natural setting. Sant

Climent, in particular, which is on the outskirts of the village, is an unforgettable sight, with its tall bell-tower and three apses standing out against the surrounding mountains.

Santa Maria, which is in the centre of the village, also has three apses and a similar, but shorter bell-tower, and this too can be seen from far away, rising above a mass of closely packed slate roofs with the mountains in the background.

Both were built in the early twelfth century, and are the outstanding members of the group of small Romanesque churches that are dotted around the mountain slopes of the Vall de Boí. They include one in Boí itself, and others in Erill la Vall, Barruera and Durro.

The two churches in **Taüll** are remarkable, not just for their handsome bell-towers, which were modelled on contemporary Italian designs, but, as already described, for the superb wall-paintings that once covered their interiors and have survived in part. Most of them were removed between 1919 and 1923, and they can be seen as the masterpieces they are in the Museu Nacional d'Art de Catalunya (MNAC) in Barcelona.

There are, however, good copies in both churches of the principal paintings, as I wrote earlier. These come from the central apse of each of them. In **Sant Climent**

Sant Climent, Taüll

East end of Sant Climent, Taüll

there is a powerful and moving depiction of Christ in Majesty. He is sitting in a mandorla with his right hand raised in blessing and his left holding a book with the words 'EGO SUM LUX MUNDI' (I am the light of the world) written on it. Around him are angels together with the lion, the calf, the eagle and the winged man that represent the four evangelists. Below are standing figures of the Virgin Mary and several saints.

The church also has a few fragmentary paintings that have only been discovered in recent years and are still in place. They include one high up on the right-hand side of the apse that shows Cain's murder of Abel in vivid style.

In **Santa Maria** it is Mary, with the infant Jesus on her lap, who is the central figure, and she has the three Magi approaching her with their gifts from either side. Interestingly, they are made to represent the three ages of man. Melchior, who is coming from the left, is elderly; Gaspar and Balthazar, on the right, are respectively young and adult. Down below there are well-preserved portraits of St Peter, St Paul and St John, also standing, and fragments of the paintings of several other saints.

One unusual fact about these two churches is that they were built at exactly the same time, and in the same style. Sant Climent was consecrated on 10th December 1123, and Santa Maria the following day. It seems that this can be attributed to

Santa Maria, Taüll

funds from the Erill family, who had fought with Alfonso el Batallador, the Fighter of Battles, king of Aragon, in his successful campaigns against the Moors in the early twelfth century, and used the booty they won to finance the rebuilding of churches in the Vall de Boí, much of which they owned.

They generally combine the simplicity of traditional country churches with the greater sophistication presumably brought in by stonemasons from Italy – and by some master painters and sculptors. In Taüll, for example, both Sant Climent and Santa Maria have timber ceilings rather than the stone vaults that were common elsewhere at the time, and their interiors are very plain.

They have a nave and two side-aisles. But in each church there are round arches resting on round columns with almost no carved decoration that divide the nave from the aisles – in Sant Climent the columns have just a serrated band near the top – and apart from the apses there are almost no windows.

By way of contrast, however, each of them has an accomplished east end, which was decorated with the paintings on the inside and Lombard bands on the outside. And each has its bell-tower. In Sant Climent the tower is separate from the body of the church, standing at the south-east corner, and it soars into the sky with its six tiers of arched windows, each covered by a frieze of tiny blind arches. In Santa Maria the tower is based in the south side-aisle, and though it only has four tiers of arched windows, their design is the same.

Several of the other churches in the Vall de Boí have tall bell-towers, and it appears that their role was not just decorative. The times were dangerous, and they were also useful as watch-towers and for communications between the villages.

The church in **Boí** is a few years earlier, dating from the late eleventh century. It too has a bell-tower, though its upper levels were much modified in later years; and it has lost much of its central apse, which was replaced by a flat wall. But the two smaller apses are still in place, and like the others it stands out well when seen against the mountain backdrop.

Its interior is different. It too is very simple, with a timber ceiling over its nave and side-aisles, but most of its walls have been plastered white, and they have numerous copies on them of paintings that were once in the church but, like those from Taüll, are now in the museum in Barcelona.

They are an amazing collection. They include a scene of the stoning of St Stephen and another in which two men are engaged in a dance with swords, one standing on a rock and the other flying through the air upside down. There are also paintings of some exotic-looking creatures, among them an elephant ('lifan'), a dromedary, a fish with a bird's head and a dog-like animal that has hooves, flames emerging from its mouth and a tiny head at the end of its tail.

Sant Joan, Boí

Bell-tower of church of Erill la Vall

There is another copy of a painting over the north doorway on the outside of the church, a Christ in Majesty with angels.

Erill la Vall, which is a little further down the valley, has a tall bell-tower that is well preserved – and visible from far away. Like the tower of Sant Climent, it is structurally separate from the body of the church, and it has six tiers of arches each covered by a frieze of tiny blind arches. Below it are three apses, undecorated except for one or two small windows, and, running along the north side of the church, a porch formed by four round arches.

Erill la Vall is another plain country church enhanced by its splendid bell-tower. Inside, it has no more than a single nave covered by a timber ceiling, the main apse, and the two smaller apses that lead off the nave on either side. But as I have recorded, it also has, or had, a special feature, a group of seven sculptured figures dating from the first half of the twelfth century that make up the scene of the Deposition from the Cross.

These figures are now split up; some are in the MNAC in Barcelona, others in the Museu Episcopal in Vic. But there is a complete set of copies in the church in Erill la Vall, where they are splendidly placed at the east end and dominate the little nave.

The church in **Barruera**, also in the valley, has only a short bell-tower. But it is

Barruera, from east

Durro, from west

a charming, well-proportioned Romanesque structure that stands a little outside
the village. It was built in two phases, as can be seen in its two apses. The smaller
one, to the south, is plain with roughly cut stonework, and dates from the eleventh
century. The larger, central one is from the twelfth and is altogether more accomplished, with well-cut stonework and Lombard bands.

A porch runs along the west side, covering an arched doorway into the church.
The interior too is simple, without any carved decoration, but satisfying. It has a
stone barrel vault that rests on transverse arches and leads to a short choir and,
beyond it, the main apse. There is a short transept, also barrel-vaulted, that is
linked to the nave by round arches on each side.

The village of **Durro**, which is on the mountainside above Barruera, has
another church with a tall bell-tower; it has four tiers, some with arches, some
plain, and each is topped by a frieze of tiny blind arches. The church stands in the
heart of the village, and it too dates from the twelfth century.

There is a porch along the south side and inside it a carved doorway leading
into the church. It has carved capitals, quite worn, on the columns on either side,
and up above a chequerboard semicircle and a chi-rho symbol set into the wall.

Durro was for a time a prosperous village, and so modifications were made over
the years to the original Romanesque structure. There is a small apse on the south

side, but the main apse has been largely demolished; and there are two chapels in Gothic style inside the church, as well as a baroque altarpiece and sacristy.

But the nave retains its slightly pointed barrel vault, and there is still the bell-tower, as well as the porch. So enough is left of the Romanesque church to place it among the distinctive creations of the period in the Vall de Boí.

Terrassa

The industrial town of Terrassa, on the outskirts of Barcelona, has an ancient site that, as I have described, has no less than three churches. Two of them are largely Romanesque but have parts that are earlier, the third is wholly pre-Romanesque, and together they form a group that is interesting both for its architecture and for its history.

The exact dating of the churches is controversial. What is known for sure is that the site, on a ridge between two streams, has been occupied continuously since the days of the Iberians, who were there before the Romans arrived. Christianity had reached the area by the fourth century, when the Romans were still there, and Egara, as it was known then, became the seat of a bishop in 450.

Collegiate church of Santa Maria, Terrassa

Over the centuries after that a succession of churches was built there, one replacing the other. Egara lost its status of bishopric in the confusion that followed the Arab occupation of the eighth century, but building revived after the Carolingians took over much of Catalonia in the late eighth and early ninth century.

So Santa Maria, which belonged to a college of canons and was consecrated in 1112 after being largely rebuilt in Romanesque style, was only the latest of several. It still has a fragment of a mosaic of a peacock that is dated to the fourth or fifth century and is thought to come from one of the earliest churches. A baptismal pool found under its transept is believed to have been linked to a basilica of the fifth century.

The foundations of that basilica lie partly under the floor of Santa Maria and partly beneath the pavement to the west of it. Excavation is still continuing.

The three churches have a picturesque setting, with a little park down below and a seventeenth-century bridge which you cross on foot to reach the site from the centre of the town. Santa Maria stands out most strongly when you arrive. Its west front is quite plain but is decorated with Lombard bands, and so are the outside wall of the nave and the polygonal cupola which rises above the transept crossing and supports the bell-tower. Its east end, which contains an apse, is rectangular on the outside, with two sloping roofs.

Next to it is Sant Miquel, which is pre-Romanesque and, as evidence of the fact, has a horseshoe arch over a window on its west side. It is square apart from the polygonal apse that extends out from its eastern side, and is given interest and style by the different levels of its stretches of roof, low at the four corners and rising to a peak in the centre. It is reminiscent of the mausoleum of Galla Placidia in Ravenna.

At the top is Sant Pere, a long building whose most prominent feature is the two turrets, one at each end, for hanging the bells. It has little decoration apart from a line of corbels under the cornice along its south side, but its east end is most appealing, with a central apse closely ringed by three smaller ones.

It is generally accepted that the east ends of the three churches, though very different from each other, are all pre-Romanesque, and that since they are aligned with each other, they were in all likelihood built at about the same time. Sant Miquel as a whole would also have been built then.

What is in dispute is when that was done, whether it was during the days of Visigothic rule, which ended as a result of the Arab invasion of 711, or later, after the Carolingians had taken over.

Whatever the answer, the churches are well worth visiting. **Santa Maria** is small, with only a short, barrel-vaulted nave. But it has a good sense of space, and its transept crossing is imposing, with four substantial arches that support the cupola. Beyond it is the oldest part of the church, the apse. Its vault is an almost complete hemisphere, with traces of early painting that recount the life and passion of Christ, and the floor plan is horseshoe-shaped.

One of its most interesting features is a niche at the end of the south arm of the transept which has well-preserved paintings of the assassination in 1170 of Thomas à Becket, the archbishop of Canterbury, who was subsequently canonized. The paintings, which date from the late twelfth or early thirteenth century, have Christ in Majesty in the apse above and three scenes showing Thomas being attacked, his murder, and the ascension to Heaven of his soul.

Sant Miquel is the most original of the three churches, and a building of great charm. Its floor plan is basically a Greek cross, which has arms of equal length, and there is a stylish arrangement at the centre: a square space that is framed by eight columns, one at each corner and one in the middle of each side, and tall round arches. Above it is a dome that rests on squinches and has four tiny windows set deep into its stonework.

The columns are all different from each other, and clearly were taken from earlier buildings, with the more robust ones put at the corners of the central square. The capitals too have come from elsewhere; some of them are late Roman, others from the Visigothic period. Many of them are variations on the Corinthian-style acanthus.

Sant Miquel and Santa Maria, Terrassa

Murder of Thomas à Becket, in Santa Maria

It was once thought that Sant Miquel was a baptistery, and during restoration a baptismal pool was put into this central space. This is not now accepted by everyone, but the pool is still there.

The arms of the cross extend out beyond this square, and that has created four more square spaces, each covered by groin vaulting. In the four corners between the arms the outer walls are curved, and there is rounded vaulting overhead.

On the east side of the church a round arch frames the apse, which also has traces of early painting. It has three round-topped windows and, like that of Santa Maria, has a horseshoe-shaped floor plan. And down below there is a tiny crypt, which is shaped like a clover-leaf, with three rounded niches, each of which also has a horseshoe-shaped floor plan.

Sant Pere too was rebuilt in Romanesque style, but late in the twelfth century, some while after Santa Maria. It has a single nave from that period, covered by a slightly pointed barrel vault. Its transept and apse survive from the earlier, pre-Romanesque building, and the apse, like that of Santa Maria, is an almost complete hemisphere.

Apse above story of Thomas à Becket: Christ in Majesty

La Tossa de Montbui

The church of **La Tossa de Montbui**, which stands nearly alone on a remote hill-side near Igualada, north-west of Barcelona, is well worth visiting, and not just for the splendid views of the valley below. It is a small, intriguing church which illus-trates the changes in architectural style introduced by the Lombard builders who were so influential in Catalonia in the eleventh century.

The body of the church dates from the late tenth century and is dark and atmos-pheric, with only small windows. It has a rectangular shape, made up of a nave and two side-aisles that are covered by low barrel vaulting without transverse arches. Between the nave and the aisles are arches that are slightly horseshoe-shaped and rest on squat round columns.

The three apses at the east end were built onto this early church in the first half of the eleventh century, and reflect the style brought in by the Lombards. The west end was also extended at the same time, and the tall belfry which is now so promi-nent was subsequently constructed over the extension. A chapel was added onto the north side of the church in the sixteenth century.

The church is not quite alone on its hillside because only a hundred yards or so

away are the remains of a massive defensive
tower; and this reflects the turbulence in the
area around the time both church and tower
were built. It was land that was largely abandoned after the Arabs marched into Catalonia
in 714 and that continued to be disputed by
Christians and Moors long after the Carolingians had occupied much of northern Catalonia in the eighth and ninth centuries.

In the late tenth century efforts were made
by the Christians to establish a firm frontier
to the south, not least by resettling the area,
and the tower was one of several on which
construction was set in motion then. Work
was begun on the church at the same time,
using the style of the day. But both tower and
church had to be abandoned before they were
completed because of a catastrophic drought
around 990; and there was a serious Moorish
incursion in 1003.

Nave of church of La Tossa de Montbui

It was only some years later that the Moorish threat receded, largely as a result
of the weakening and eventual collapse of the caliphate in Córdoba, and resettlement could resume. Sometime after 1023 work began again on building both the
tower and the church, and the church was finished, complete with the features in
the new Lombard style, in about 1032, when it was consecrated.

A line of cypresses provides a setting for the church today, and you see the three
apses, with their Lombard bands, when you drive up to the church from the valley
below. Beyond them is the rectangular shape of the body of the church, with
stonework that is noticeably more rustic; and towering above the whole building
is the belfry.

It is the inside of the church, however, that displays its originality. The low,
plain vaulting shows that by the late tenth century Catalan churches were no
longer being built with timber ceilings, so vulnerable to fire. At the east end the
transition from the nave and the aisles to the apses is clearly visible, with the central apse framed by a round arch that rests on two engaged half-columns; and at the
west end a solid pillar shows where the extension began.

Simplicity is the mark of this little church. Even the three apses have only a
single round-topped window in each.

Aragon

The kingdom of Aragon came to play an important part in European history. Its union with Castile in the fifteenth century created what is now Spain; and there was the ill-fated marriage a few years later of Henry VIII, king of England, to Catherine of Aragon. But its beginnings were very much simpler, and it is not hard to picture them when you travel round the towns and villages, often set in splendid mountain scenery, in the north of the province.

In the eighth century, and for some time after that, Aragon consisted of no more than a few scattered communities grouped around the various branches of the Aragón river in the foothills of the Pyrenees. They were Christian, and like the Asturians and the Basques to their west they held to their religion and their independence after almost the whole Iberian peninsula had been occupied by Arabs and their various Muslim subjects.

They organized themselves, and little by little they drove the Muslims south, eventually advancing into the plains and taking over such Moorish strongholds as Huesca and Saragossa. By the middle of the eleventh century Jaca had become relatively prosperous through its position on the trade route over the Pyrenees, and a cathedral was built that became one of the most influential Romanesque churches in Spain. It has been modified over the years, but its basic Romanesque form, and its superb carved capitals, are still there to be seen.

Other churches reflect the turbulent conditions of earlier days, when fighting with the Muslims continued and there was always the possibility of raids from the south. The monastery of San Juan de la Peña is in remote, hilly country south-west of Jaca, and is built deep into a tall cliff, with a huge mass of rock overhanging it.

Further to the south is the castle of Loarre, which stands on a rock that had been seized from the Muslims and fortified against them, and has an elegant royal chapel at its heart. Much of the castle survives, surrounded by a turreted wall, and it is one of the most spectacular sights to be seen anywhere in Spain.

Other small towns, such as Sos del Rey Católico, Uncastillo and Alquézar, are also in eye-catching positions, perched high up on hillsides – and as well as their

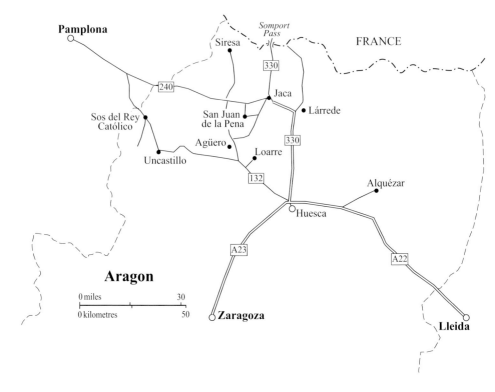

churches, they still have the remains of their fortifications. Siresa, in a remote
Pyrenean valley, has a church largely built in the twelfth century, but the monastery
to which it belonged had probably been there since before the Arabs arrived.

Agüero too, which is west of Loarre, has a mountain setting and the twelfth-
century church of Santiago, though it was never completed.

Some of the earlier churches in Aragon show the influence of the first southern
Romanesque style that was brought to Catalonia by Lombard stonemasons and
spread from there. That is true of the chapel of San Caprasio in Santa Cruz de la
Serós, the village below San Juan de la Peña. Others, such as Lárrede, have horseshoe arches that suggest Mozarabic influence.

The more ornate style of Jaca cathedral, however, derives from the far side of the
Pyrenees, and is an indication of influence from France, which supplanted the
earlier styles. It is interesting to note that the small monastic church of San Adrián
de Sásabe, which is in a remote setting north of Jaca and was completed towards
the end of the eleventh century, has something of Jaca and something of Catalonia.

This little monastery was for a time the seat of a bishop. The church's east end, which has a single apse ringed by tiny blind arches set between pilasters, is in Lombard style. The doorway at the west end has an arrangement of receding arches, including an archivolt which rests on a pair of columns topped by capitals, that is reminiscent of Jaca.

The capitals in the cloisters of San Juan de la Peña and Huesca, which are thought to be partly the work of the same sculptor, are later still, from the late twelfth century. So are the carvings on the south doorway of Uncastillo. And very fine they all are.

Agüero

The little town of Agüero, north-west of Huesca, is surrounded by some dramatic mountain scenery, with a stretch of sheer rock, reddish in colour, immediately above it and other peaks in the distance. It has the church of San Salvador, which dates from the twelfth century and has a carved doorway from that time, in a central square. Even more impressive is the church of Santiago, that stands alone on a hillside about a mile away.

San Salvador is largely Gothic in style. But its doorway is Romanesque, and it has a tympanum, set in a slightly pointed arch, with an appealing presentation of

Tympanum of San Salvador, Agüero

Christ in Majesty. Christ is sitting in a mandorla, a serene figure with his right hand raised in blessing, and the four symbolic creatures that represent the evangelists are around him: the lion of St Mark, the calf or bull of St Luke, the eagle of St John and the winged man of St Matthew.

Four of the archivolts are decorated with various patterns, and there are capitals on the columns on either side of the door that have carvings of imaginary birds and animals on them, as well as a pair of human figures.

Santiago also has a doorway with good carvings, but it is different from San Salvador in other ways. Work on it began in the second half of the twelfth century and continued in the first third of the thirteenth, with the intention of creating a large and imposing church, and though it was not completed, for reasons that are not known, it dominates the surroundings when you see it from a distance.

It consists of three apses and a transept, with no nave or side-aisles. The apses are exceptionally tall on the outside, and largely plain, with narrow windows and a tiny frieze, showing men fighting monsters, that circles round the central apse under the windows. The numerous columns that run up from the ground to the cornices, some engaged, some almost completely round, give them great style.

Capital on doorway of Santiago, Agüero

Capital on doorway of Santiago, Agüero

There are more such columns on the south end of the transept, and in the middle of them is the doorway. Investigation has shown that initially this only had the two inner archivolts, and that the other two were added later. But the doorway as a whole is perfectly unified, with a tympanum in the centre, capitals on the four columns that flank it on either side, and a line of corbels beneath the ridge of stonework above.

The tympanum has the Adoration of the Magi as its subject. Mary is seated in the centre, with the child Jesus, who is holding out his right hand in blessing, on her lap. One of the Magi is kneeling and kissing the child's foot, while the other two are in the background, holding their gifts. Joseph is seated on the far side of Mary, his head resting on one hand and his eyes closed.

The capitals have a mixture of very different themes. Some show monsters back to back, others a pair of lions devouring a deer. There are also centaurs. But two of the capitals present a dancer who is similar to carvings of Salome elsewhere. She is in different positions. In one capital she is standing and looking at a person with a harp-like instrument, apparently about to dance. In the other she is in full flow, twisted over backwards with her hair flying, while a different musician plays a wind instrument.

Below the tympanum are two large heads of monsters. One has a naked woman in its jaws; the other has one foot of a fully-clad man, but the man is stabbing the monster between the eyes with a sword.

Inside the church it is possible to imagine how it might have been if it had been completed. A wall has been built across the west side of the transept, shutting off what would have been the nave and side-aisles. But the three apses are there, and over the transept two pointed arches that would have supported a cupola or lantern tower over the crossing. The only incongruity is in the fact that the barrel vaulting over the three sections of the transept runs east-west rather than north-south, as was presumably the original intention.

The central apse has a simple but stylish arrangement. At the lower level there is a semicircle of narrow blind arches that have good capitals on the columns. They are divided into three parts by a pair of tall engaged columns, and so are the three pairs of tall and narrow windows that are above them. The tops of the two en-gaged columns mark the beginning of the apse, and two ribs spring from them to support it.

The north apse has only a simple frieze of fleurs-de-lys running round it. But the south one has a delightful frieze, quite narrow but full of life, that depicts the life of Christ from the Nativity to the Flight into Egypt. The journey of the Magi is treated with verve, and it can be observed that a scene in which they are lying side by side in bed, all wearing their crowns, and are woken by an angel telling them they must leave immediately, is similar to one in Autun cathedral in Burgundy.

There are also carved capitals on the columns supporting the arches of the transept – although one has been left unfinished. Some of them have formalized plant designs, but one shows two eagles pecking the head of a small boy who rep-resents innocence; and there are some with harpies and other such creatures of the medieval imagination.

Alquézar

The ancient village of Alquézar, in empty, rolling country east of Huesca, has only a few survivals from the Romanesque period: principally six capitals in the cloister of its collegiate church. But the capitals are original and interesting, and the village is worth visiting for its own sake because of its spectacular setting.

It was once a Moorish castle, as indicated by its name, and the remains of the castle walls still circle the rock on which it stood, enclosing the church and its cloister. Down below are the houses that have been built up the slopes, and walking through the narrow streets before climbing up to a gate in the walls is a pleasure in itself.

Alquézar: capital in cloister – John the Baptist admonishing Herod and Herod's feast (with Salome dancing under the table)

Driving there from Huesca you cross vast open stretches of countryside, with views of the Pyrenees in the distance, and then take a country road that winds through fields and little woods. It brings you to a high point from which you see the village laid out before you. In the foreground, on rising ground, is another, later monastic complex, and beyond it the castle.

You have to leave your car in a car park on the edge of the village, some way from the foot of the castle rock, and walk from there. But it is not a hardship.

Alquézar was a Moorish strongpoint for centuries, but was captured by Sancho Ramírez, king of Aragon, in 1067, with the help of Crusaders from north of the Pyrenees. It withstood a siege by the Moors a few years later, in 1075. Sancho Ramírez had already taken steps to encourage Christian settlers, and soon after that he established a college of Augustinian canons who set about building a church. It was begun in 1083 and consecrated in 1099.

The **church** that is there today dates from the sixteenth century, and the tiny cloister, which is irregular in shape and has a cypress tree in the centre, from the fourteenth. But the north side of the cloister has the six Romanesque capitals, which were carved for an earlier structure and are thought to date from the first half of the twelfth century.

They are naive and often crude in style, and fascinating for that reason. The strangest of them is a depiction of the creation of Adam. It shows a figure with three heads who is standing in a mandorla and represents the Trinity. He is holding Adam, who is lying horizontally across his waist. Four angels are supporting the mandorla, two of them upside down.

Another capital has the story of Adam and Eve, two simple figures who are standing on either side of the Tree of Knowledge, while a scaly serpent curls round it and reaches out towards Eve. On the other three sides is the story of Cain and Abel. It culminates in Cain's murder of Abel, presented dramatically, but on either side are rustic scenes. Cain is ploughing, while Abel is standing with his shepherd's crook by what look like two piles of sheep, but are in fact his flock.

Noah's Ark occupies another capital, a complex structure with three rows of openings: in the middle one are human faces representing Noah's family; in the bottom one, pairs of animals, badly worn; and in the top one, pairs of birds.

Then there is Abraham. There is a simple but powerful carving of his sacrifice of Isaac, halted by an angel bringing a ram to take Isaac's place, and under it a very different scene. A young man is roasting a calf on a spit for a feast, while on one side of the capital Abraham's three visitors are approaching and on the other Sarah is also preparing food for them.

The only New Testament story is that of John the Baptist. There is a small scene in which he is denouncing Herod, and then on the main face of the capital an engaging version of Herod's feast. Six people, crudely carved, are standing behind a table while under it, bent over backwards to

Alquézar: capital in cloister – Sarah preparing meal for Abraham's three visitors

Alquézar: capital in cloister – Herodias and head of John the Baptist

form an almost circular shape, is the tiny figure of Salome dancing. To one side are Herodias and the head of John the Baptist, both surrounded by snakes.

The most mysterious of the capitals is one that is ringed by ten standing figures, including St Peter, a bishop, four men who could be Apostles, and two who are dragging along the Devil, a rope round his neck. It is thought that this might refer to the consecration of the church in 1099. It was conducted by the bishop of Barbastro, and was presented as an important political event by Pedro I, king of Aragon; hence, perhaps, the presence of St Peter.

Huesca

The church of **San Pedro el Viejo**, which dominates a small square in the old part of Huesca, is a simple, harmonious structure that dates back to the first half of the twelfth century, not long after the city had been captured from the Moors. Its outstanding feature is its cloister, which was built later in the same century and has a wide range of subjects, Biblical and allegorical, on its capitals.

The cloister was thoroughly restored in the nineteenth century and only about half of the capitals – eighteen out of thirty-eight – are original. The others were badly damaged and were replaced by copies; they can be seen in the Museo Provincial. But the eighteen originals, which are thought to have been the work of the same sculptor as the historiated capitals of San Juan de la Peña (see page 141), are full of life. So are the copies, and the overall effect of the cloister is impressive.

The originals include Joseph bringing Mary and the infant Jesus back from Egypt, the Temptation of Christ, his appearance to Mary Magdalene after his Resurrection, Doubting Thomas, Pentecost. There are men fighting dragons and other monstrous creatures that are devouring some prey. There is a dancer giving a dramatic performance, one leg kicked high and her hair flying, to the accompaniment of a harpist.

There are also two unusual capitals which have a number of scenes on them that may, it is thought, represent the events in Huesca after its capture from the Moors: a king riding in on horseback escorted by soldiers, a bishop arriving in a carriage, elaborate baptism ceremonies.

The capitals run all round the cloister, with the originals and the copies easily distinguishable. Just over half have scenes from the New Testament, in a sequence that begins in the middle of the east side and continues along the northern and western sides. The others have a mix of subjects, all vigorously treated. There are two with Old Testament scenes – Samson fighting a lion, the story of Cain and Abel – while the others range from the allegorical to the historiated.

Cloister of San Pedro el Viejo, Huesca

Monastic church of San Pedro el Viejo, Huesca: tympanum over north doorway

Not the least noteworthy are the abaci that form the upper part of the capitals. Most of them are plant designs, entwined to form some delightful patterns.

Huesca stands on high ground above the river Isuela, a tributary of the Ebro. It is surrounded by good agricultural land, and its known history goes back to Roman times, when it was called Osca. After the Arab occupation of most of Spain it became one of the fortified cities that guarded their northern frontier just south of the Pyrenees. Remains of the walls built by its Muslim rulers can still be seen on the north-eastern stretch of the road that circles round the old city, following the line of the fortifications that once protected it.

Huesca was a tough nut to crack for the mountain men of Aragon as they gradually extended their power south from the Pyrenees in the course of the eleventh century. Sancho Ramírez, the second king of Aragon, was killed under its walls in 1094 as his army laid siege to it. But Pedro I, his son and successor, finally took the city two years later, in 1096, and moved his capital there from Jaca (see page 130).

The principal mosque was converted into a cathedral and eventually replaced by the present cathedral, which is largely Gothic. But there was also a church in Huesca which belonged to the community of Christians, or Mozarabs, that had lived in the city throughout the centuries of Muslim rule. It was on the site of this Mozarabic church that San Pedro el Viejo, 'the old', was built – so called because

Capital in cloister of San Pedro el Viejo, Huesca: priests before Herod

the new cathedral was also dedicated to St Peter – and it became the centre of an important monastery.

Ramiro II, king of Aragon, who had been a monk before succeeding his brother, Alfonso I, in 1134, returned to monastic life at San Pedro in 1137, and is buried there. He is known as 'the Monk'. His remains are in a Roman sarcophagus placed in the chapel of St Bartholomew, a Romanesque building which leads off the cloister and was once the chapterhouse.

So are those of Alfonso I, a very different man who captured Saragossa from the Moors in 1118 and is known as el Batallador, or the Fighter of Battles. Alfonso's remains were brought to San Pedro from Montearagón in the nineteenth century.

The most prominent feature of the church as you see it across the little Plaza San Pedro is its massive hexagonal tower, added in the late thirteenth century and largely plain, but with arched windows in Romanesque style at a lower level. Behind it is the east end, and to one side a decorative doorway with the circular chi-rho symbol on its tympanum. Two angels support the circle, which has the Lamb of God complete with cross in the centre and a tiny figure of St Vincent, who was baptized in this church, fitted into the empty space at the top.

Inside, the church has been modified and added to over the centuries, but it still has the nave and two aisles, as well as a short transept, that derive from its

Romanesque beginnings. They are all covered by barrel vaulting. The central apse is now filled by a reredos, but the two side ones can be seen.

A door in the south aisle leads to the cloister and above it, on the cloister side, is another tympanum with some lively carved figures. It is in two parts: the upper section has, once again, the chi-rho symbol supported by two angels; the lower one the Adoration of the Magi.

Jaca

The cathedral of **Jaca**, which was briefly the capital of the kingdom of Aragon, was one of the first large Spanish churches to be built in the more ornate version of Romanesque which followed that of the early churches of Catalonia. Whereas Cardona, for example (see page 44), makes its effect with its pure lines and the interplay of arches, but has no carved decoration, Jaca has round columns topped by carved capitals, some set into many-sided pillars, and is altogether more elaborate.

Seen from the outside, it is a long, well-proportioned building that is chiefly remarkable for the tall, open narthex at its west end, topped by a short, stocky tower, and for the decorative apse on the south side of the east end, the only one that survives intact of the three that were originally there. The interior was also much modified in later centuries, principally by building late Gothic vaulting over the nave and the two side-aisles and by replacing the sanctuary and the central apse with a much larger structure.

But the form, the proportions and the sense of space of the Romanesque structure are still there.

Above all, there is the carved stonework, both inside the cathedral and on the outside. The Jaca style of decoration was widely copied, for its vigorous sculpture and also for its use of chequerboard patterning, and the cathedral has some outstanding capitals: above the columns of the nave, in the narthex at the west end, and in the porch that was built onto the south side in the sixteenth century, using capitals that came from other parts of the cathedral.

There are differences between Spanish historians over the date at which the building of Jaca cathedral began – whether it was before or after 1063, the year in which Ramiro I, the first king of Aragon, died and was succeeded by his son, the dynamic Sancho Ramírez. But it is generally accepted that the first phase can be dated to the second half of the eleventh century, and that there was a second phase at the beginning of the twelfth century.

The building of the cathedral was the culmination of a long process that had begun in the ninth century. That was a time when most of Spain was under Muslim rule. But in the foothills of the Pyrenees there were communities of farmers and shepherds, as well as a few small towns, that were determined to preserve their independence, and Jaca became the most important of these towns.

Aznar Galíndez, count of Aragon from 809 to 839, was for some years the local leader. He maintained friendly relations with Frankish lords north of the Pyrenees, and his little county not only provided protection for the local people but offered a refuge for Christians fleeing from the Muslim-ruled areas to the south.

Aragon came under the rule of the kings of Navarre in the tenth century. But Ramiro I broke free after inheriting the county from his father, Sancho el Mayor, in 1035, and proclaimed himself king of Aragon. Jaca was the main town of this new kingdom, and its status as capital was formally confirmed by Sancho Ramírez, who did much to enhance its standing. In 1077 he issued a proclamation giving rights to its existing citizens and offering incentives to foreigners who decided to settle there.

By then Jaca was becoming increasingly wealthy thanks to its position at the foot of the Somport pass over the Pyrenees and the other roads that converged there. There was a flow of traders of all sorts, who had to pay customs duties as they came down from the pass, and there were also the pilgrims making their way along what was one of the main routes to Santiago de Compostela.

The Jaca region had had its own bishop for some time, perhaps since the tenth century, and Jaca itself already had one or more churches. But it was decided to construct a new, more splendid cathedral in the Romanesque style that was being introduced from across the Pyrenees. So whether or not building had begun before he succeeded his father, Sancho Ramírez, who was king from 1063 to 1094, pursued the project as part of his policy of promoting Jaca.

In the event Jaca only continued to be the capital for a few years, because in 1096 Pedro I, the son of Sancho Ramírez, captured the ancient city of Huesca, as we saw (see page 128), from the Muslims, and he transferred the capital to that city, larger and more important than Jaca. But though it was delayed, and the more ambitious plans may have been abandoned, work on the cathedral continued under Alfonso I el Batallador, the Fighter of Battles, who ruled from 1104 to 1134.

Today Jaca is a tranquil market town, dominated in the south by the sheer rock of Mount Oroel, more than 5,000 ft high. Its most prominent feature is a vast, five-sided fortress surrounded by a moat which is on its western edge and whose construction dates back to the end of the sixteenth century.

The cathedral is not far away, and it is worth stopping to look at the apse on the south side of the east end. It has an arched window complete with capitals, three bands of the chequerboard patterning that is characteristic of Jaca, and under the cornice not just a succession of corbels, largely decorated with a variety of animal heads, but in between them little scenes of humans and animals, several of them mythical.

Round the corner, with a little square in front of it, is the south porch and within it a doorway which is original and has two good capitals. On one side is Abraham's planned sacrifice of Isaac, in which Isaac is an athletic, almost classical, nude figure who stands poised at one corner, while Abraham, who is wielding a large knife on one side, is being restrained by an angel. On the other is Balaam riding his ass towards the angel who is stopping him with a sword.

The origin of the other capitals in the porch is not known. It is possible, but far from certain, that they came from a choir which used to stand in the nave but was dismantled. In any case they too are magnificent. One has David sitting and playing a stringed instrument in the middle of a group of other musicians all playing different instruments, so lively that one can almost hear the music. Another has scenes from the life and martyrdom of St Sixtus.

The narthex at the western end of the cathedral leads to a formal doorway.

Capital in south porch of Jaca cathedral: scene from life of St Sixtus

Capital in south porch of Jaca cathedral: David and musicians

Above it, on the tympanum, is a carving in relief of the chi-rho symbol, so
often found in northern Spain, and it is
a particularly lively example. There is a
lion on each side. One of them is walking over the figure of a man who is,
according to the Book of Revelation,
being pardoned, and who is grasping
a serpent while the lion tramples on it;
the other lion is trampling on a bear
and a basilisk.

There are also four capitals, three of
them with human figures on them, that
are carved in near-classical style. Who
they are is hard to know. But one capi-

*Capital in south porch of Jaca cathedral: David
and musicians*

tal has two contrasting scenes: in one a man appears to be threatening another
with a knife, in the other two men seem to be good friends. Another capital
has a debonair angel. A third shows a young man apparently carrying a large
snake.

Inside the cathedral, five round arches line each side of the nave, dividing it
from the side-aisles. Single columns and composite pillars alternate, and there are
capitals high up on either side. They are hard to see without binoculars, but they
too have a range of subjects – from elaborate compositions made up of plant patterns and entwined tendrils to scenes with humans and animals. Art historians have
detected Islamic influence.

One of the most striking is interpreted as representing the purification of souls
in the rivers of Paradise. A naked figure is shown in the middle of swirling water
while a young man indicates the direction to go and a winged cupid plays a double
flute at the corner. Others have human figures caught in tendrils or consorting with
lions.

The nave and the side-aisles were originally covered by timber ceilings, which
were replaced many centuries later by the Gothic vaulting. But the transept, which
does not extend beyond the aisles, still has its original barrel vaulting, and over the
crossing there is one of the distinctive features of the cathedral: a cupola in
Moorish style in which four arches criss-cross to form a star pattern at the top of
the dome, which rests on four squinches.

A small chapel that opens out of the south arm of the transept has the apse
which is visible from the outside and is also in the original Romanesque style.

A museum has been created on the north side of Jaca cathedral, in the area once occupied by the cloister, and it has an exceptional collection of Romanesque wall-paintings taken from churches in the surrounding region, as well as stone carvings. But it has been closed for refurbishment for some years.

Lárrede

The church of **Lárrede**, a village in the valley of the river Gallego a few miles east of Jaca, has a fine silhouette, particularly when seen against the distant backdrop of the Pyrenees. It has a tall and relatively plain tower, with sets of three small horseshoe arches near the top, and it makes a striking ensemble with the apse and the nave, both of which have some unusual decoration.

Inside, it has the proportions and the atmospheric quality of early Romanesque: a single nave with plain stone walls, barrel vaulting supported by transverse arches that rest on pairs of columns set against the walls of the nave, a hemispherical apse, and a short transept both of whose arms have barrel vaulting that runs across the line of the nave.

There is some doubt about the date of Lárrede. It has even been suggested that it was built by Mozarabs at a time when the area was still under Muslim rule. What is certain is that while it has Romanesque characteristics, it also has Mozarabic features, not least the horseshoe arches in the tower and elsewhere. It is built of roughly cut stone, and one conclusion is that it dates from the first half of the eleventh century.

The south side of the church is the most decorative, in a simple and satisfying way. At its centre is the main doorway, which has a deliberately false horseshoe arch: in other words, a piece of stone protrudes on each side at the base of the arch, making it seem at first sight like a horseshoe. This device has been traced to Islamic style, and the same is true of the double rectangle, carved in the stone and known as an *alfiz*, that frames the doorway.

Above the doorway are three narrow windows, each surrounded by an arch and, framing that, a single *alfiz*. There is another double *alfiz* surrounding a more elaborate window further east: this has two small openings each topped by a horseshoe arch.

Lárrede's apse, too, is simply decorated, and no less appealing for that. It is encircled by seven blind arches, all rounded, and above them is a complete ring of tall semi-cylindrical stones standing upright beneath a horizontal line of stonework. They give one more distinctive touch to this country church.

Nave of church of Lárrede

Loarre

Loarre castle, which stands in the wild, hilly country between Jaca and Huesca, dominates its surroundings for miles around. It is built on a steep outcrop of rock which made it inaccessible from the north and west, while a long semicircular curtain wall that contained eight round towers – and is still largely in place – protected the approaches from the south and east.

High up on the castle's south-eastern corner, and flanked on either side by the defensive walls, is an elegant Romanesque **chapel** built in the second half of the eleventh century by Sancho Ramírez, king of Aragon, who chose the castle as his residence and founded a college of Augustinian canons there. This royal chapel is worth visiting both for its architecture and for the carved capitals which were an important part of it.

Loarre was always a natural fortress, situated in the frontier zone between the Christians of upper Aragon and the Muslims of Huesca and the surrounding plains. It came early into Christian hands, and played an important military role in the tenth century, when Aragon was for a time part of the kingdom of Navarre. It appears to have been recaptured by the Muslims of Huesca in the eleventh century, but was recovered in 1070 by Sancho Ramírez, who set about both fortifying and embellishing the castle.

Loarre's preeminence was short-lived, because a few years later, as the Aragonese pushed further south, a new royal chapel was established in the monastery of Montearagón, a short way east of Huesca; and after the capture of Huesca by Pedro I in 1096 Loarre lost its importance as a strategic base. But the evidence of its days of glory is still there to be seen.

One of the most fascinating features is the technical ingenuity of its architects. The oldest part of the castle is the level space at the top of the rock, where there is a plain but well-built early Romanesque chapel dating from the first half of the eleventh century, as well as two imposing towers and the remains of other structures.

When they were given the task of designing a new, larger chapel at a lower level, the architects had to build out from the castle rock, over the void, as well as providing a means of access to the upper level. They solved these challenges by, first, building a crypt that is set into the rock and supports the new chapel, which is above it; and by then constructing a covered stone staircase that climbs up directly under the chapel and emerges at more or less the level of the entrance to it, providing access both to the chapel and to the level above it.

Today's visitors enter the castle through a gate in the curtain wall, and then

Loarre castle, with domed chapel

walk up an inclined slope towards the heart of the castle, passing by a tall, free-standing watchtower. Straight ahead of them is the east end of the crypt, and immediately above it that of the chapel itself. Together they produce a stylish structure that is a contrast with the rougher walls of the castle. It has a unified semicircular form with engaged columns running all the way up and two levels of arched windows, one marking the crypt, the other the chapel above.

The entrance into the centre of the castle is through a formal, arched doorway that is damaged but still has some decorative features. Across the top is a mutilated frieze which probably once showed Christ in Majesty; on either side of the door an impeccably carved capital. One capital has floral decoration in the middle of which is a man who is about to strike another person with a sword, the other crouching monkeys.

Then comes the staircase that runs up under the chapel. It is wide and barrel-vaulted, with a chequerboard frieze on each wall. On one side a doorway leads into what is thought to have been the guardroom. On the other is the entrance to the crypt, which has the chi-rho symbol carved into the stone above it.

The crypt is a well-built structure that has a semicircular apse and below it a ring of round arches. Some of the arches have deeply embrasured windows in them, some are blind; they are linked by chequerboard friezes.

Further up, the staircase emerges into a small triangular space between the wall of the chapel and a section of the castle rock. Here is the formal doorway into the chapel, and also the outside of one of the chapel windows, both of which are arched and have good capitals. Those on the doorway have plant designs. On the window one capital has children riding lions; the other is more complex. A pair of birds are poised with their heads turned towards each other, while above them are a snake apparently emerging from a flower and a procession of three smaller, mythical birds, two of them with the heads of lions, who are marching towards it.

The chapel itself is magnificent. It is tall and spacious, with a succession of rounded forms. In the middle is a square space with a cupola high above it; it rests on an arrangement of double squinches, one above the other, and has four tiny round windows in the stretches of wall between them. West of that is a short stretch of nave, which has a barrel vault and ends in a plain wall. To the east is the semicircular form of the sanctuary, with an apse above and two rings of round arches below.

The upper ring has five arches and tiny chequerboard friezes that run above and below them: three of the arches have windows in them, while the other two are blocked by the castle walls. There are more arches in the lower ring, which are smaller and blind, and they rest on columns that are topped by a number of out-standing capitals.

Many of the subjects are ornamental, and intricately carved: there are elaborations on the theme of the Corinthian-style acanthus and entwined plant patterns that derive from Muslim designs. Others have human figures in them, vigorously presented.

They are not always easy to interpret, however. One capital is often understood to represent Daniel, for instance, because it has a man standing between two lions and holding a book. But another interpretation is that the subject derives from Muslim beliefs. In this case the man is not Daniel, but a believer who is holding a book that recounts his good works, and the two animals are a lion and a wolf, who are the guardians of Paradise.

Another capital has a man throwing up his arms in dismay as two serpents, one on either side and sharing a single head, set about devouring him; on one side is another man who is holding on to one of the serpents, while on the other is a third man being devoured by another serpent. It is suggested that the central man might also be Daniel and the scene might refer to his encounter with the Serpent of Baal. But it is far from certain.

A third capital has a man with his arms open, apparently praying, while on

Capital inside the chapel of Loarre

either side is a crouching lion with a human figure astride it. This too, it is suggested, could represent Daniel.

There are other carved capitals in the chapel, and some at least are easier to interpret. High up on an engaged column that supports the arch which frames the apse, for instance, are Adam and Eve with the Tree of Knowledge and the serpent between them, quite crudely carved. Many others are allegorical. Close to Adam and Eve is one that has an intriguing combination of humans, birds and animals, full of movement, but mysterious.

San Juan de la Peña

The church of **San Juan de la Peña**, built into a sheer rock-face in the wild mountainous country a few miles south-west of Jaca, is exceptional in several ways. It is in a superb position, with views of the valley below, the Pyrenees in the distance and reddish cliffs up behind.

It is also a vivid reminder of the early history of Aragon and of the basic and precarious life led by Christian communities in the foothills of the Pyrenees as late as the tenth century.

There is still a small church, dating from about 920, that was built into a natural hollow of the rock by a monastic community made up of Mozarabs. Above it is a Romanesque church, dedicated in 1094, that is a little larger, but is also built into the rock and has the rock overhang as part of its vaulting.

Its outstanding feature, however, is the remains of a cloister at one side of the upper church, with the bare rock immediately above it and views out from it over the valley. It has a colonnade of arches that has been extensively restored, but contains an exceptional array of carved capitals dating from the twelfth and thirteenth centuries.

It is possible that there were once hermits living in this remote place, though there is no firm evidence for it. There is only a colourful legend according to which a young nobleman called Voto was hunting in the surrounding area and was chasing a deer which jumped, or fell, over the edge of the cliff. Voto followed, not having seen the drop, and as he fell he prayed to St John the Baptist for help. Miraculously, he landed safely.

As he looked around he found a path leading into a cave and came upon the corpse of a hermit who had lived there. He decided to sell all his possessions to give money to the poor and, with his brother, moved into the cave to live as a hermit himself.

What is known for sure is that by the early tenth century the counts of Aragon had extended the territory that they controlled as far as this mountainous area, and Galindo Aznárez II founded the Mozarabic monastery, which was dedicated to St Julian and St Basilisa. This was partly an assertion of sovereignty, partly a way to bring in people and develop the area's economy.

Not least, the remoteness of the site was a protection at a time of raids by Moorish forces from further south. There is at least one account of an occasion when a large number of people took refuge there.

The monastery flourished thanks to support from both the counts of Aragon and the kings of Navarre, who had extended their rule to Aragon at the beginning of the tenth century. In the eleventh century it became a purely Aragonese Royal Pantheon, in which Ramiro I, the first king of Aragon (1035-63), and his two immediate successors were buried, as well as prominent nobles who had made donations to the monastery.

It was also reformed. The Benedictine Rule had already been introduced in the time of Sancho el Mayor, king of Navarre, early in the eleventh century. Under Sancho Ramírez, the second king of Aragon (1063-94), the monastery was put into the hands of monks from Cluny, the great Burgundian abbey, and in 1071 a big step was taken when the monastery gave up the use of the old Mozarabic rite, which dated back to the days of the Visigoths, and adopted the Roman one.

It was Sancho Ramírez who decided to build the new, Romanesque church, dedicated to St John the Baptist. He died in 1094 while besieging Huesca (see page 128) with his army, but the church was finished by then and it was consecrated a few months later by Pedro I, his son and successor.

This ancient site eventually lost much of its importance as the kings of Aragon extended their activities, and territory, further to the south. But the monastery continued to exist for centuries, and several of its older parts survive. One is a vaulted chamber of the eleventh century, thought to have been the monks' dormitory, that you walk through to reach the Mozarabic church.

This church is quite small: it has two short barrel-vaulted aisles with horseshoe arches between them each of which leads to a little sanctuary, also barrel-vaulted, that is built into the rock. The sanctuaries were decorated in the twelfth century with mural paintings in Romanesque style, and fragments of these survive; one of the angels is particularly appealing, and it is possible to make out a Crucifixion and the martyrdom of St Cosmas and St Damian. The tiny church was given an extension to the west, down two flights of steps, in the eleventh century.

Up above are the Romanesque church and several other parts of the monastery, also largely dating from the eleventh and twelfth centuries. One of the most striking is the Nobles' Pantheon, a courtyard that has a line of blind arches along one

Cloister of San Juan de la Peña

wall, each decorated with chequerboard carving and supported by tiny female figures. Each arch commemorates one of the nobles buried there, and they have a range of carved reliefs, some with formal designs, some with little scenes.

The Romanesque church is another simple structure, with only a single nave. But it is spacious and it has an attractive arrangement of its east end. There are three round arches, each resting on a cluster of engaged columns and each framing a sanctuary that has been carved out of the rock. The sanctuaries each have a short stretch of barrel vaulting, an apse and under the apse a ring of blind arches resting on columns and capitals.

Leading off one side of the church is a very different monument: a Royal Pantheon built in the eighteenth century, when Aragon had long been part of Spain. It commemorates the history of the early kingdom and in particular the three kings who were buried at San Juan de la Peña; the site of their original tombs is behind the wall on the right-hand side, under the rock.

On the other side of the church, as if to draw attention to the antiquity of San Juan, is a Mozarabic horseshoe arch from the tenth century which must have been moved to the upper church from somewhere in the older part of the monastery.

Beyond that is the jewel of San Juan de la Peña: the cloister. This has two chapels which are built into the rock and lead off it, one in Gothic style, the other neo-classical. But it is the Romanesque capitals and their beautifully carved little scenes that are exceptional. Their subjects are very largely Biblical, drawn from

Capital in cloister of San Juan de la Peña: Christ and Mary Magdalene

both the Old and the New Testament, but there are also some capitals with the fantastic birds and animals that so often featured in those days.

The historiated capitals are thought to have been the work of a sculptor known as the Master of San Juan de la Peña who was active in the late twelfth century and also worked in the cloister of San Pedro el Viejo in Huesca (see page 126) and at Sangüesa (page 180); the others of a different artist who worked in the early thirteenth century – or possibly earlier; the experts disagree.

There is a great range of subjects, all treated with freshness and verve, and it is worth taking the time to look at them all. From the Old Testament is the story of Adam and Eve and their expulsion from the Garden of Eden; and also Cain's murder of Abel. From the New Testament are many more: the Annunciation, the Nativity, the Miracle of Cana, the Raising of Lazarus, the Entry into Jerusalem, to name just a few.

You see Joseph being woken by an angel before the Flight into Egypt, Christ instructing the fishermen on the Sea of Galilee, Christ comforting the woman taken in adultery, and St John resting his head on Christ's shoulder at the Last Supper.

There is a poignancy about these little scenes, and the cloister is an unforgettable place. That is true of San Juan de la Peña as a whole, with its wonderful setting and its sense of the passage of the centuries.

On the way down from the monastery it is well worth stopping in the village of **Santa Cruz de la Serós**, which is in the valley below and has two Romanesque churches. One is the little chapel of San Caprasio, that was built in the early eleventh century and is a simple, well-proportioned example of the First Southern Romanesque style, with a line of Lombard bands along the outside of its single nave.

Nearby, and clearly visible from the viewpoints up on the cliffs above, is the larger church of Santa María. This is an impressive building with a tall and distinctive bell-tower that is built over the south arm of the transept. The tower is largely plain at the lower level, but has pairs of round, open arches placed one above the other high up on three of its sides, and an octagonal turret at the top.

Alongside the bell-tower at the east end of the church is a single apse with three windows framed by round-topped arches. Over the west door is the carved design often found in churches in the Pyrenees, the chi-rho symbol, with a lion on each side.

Inside the church, there is a single nave that has round barrel vaulting and, unusually, a small upper room covered by an apse that is set over the transept. The apse is supported by ribs that rest on columns set against the wall, and one of them has a carving of the Annunciation on its capital.

Siresa

Siresa is a village that is tucked away in the Hecho valley, a remote corner of the Pyrenees north-west of Jaca. It has probably had a monastery since the days of the Visigoths, and it still has a sizable and handsome church, **San Pedro**, that was largely built in the twelfth century on the site of earlier buildings. It stands out strongly against the surrounding mountains.

Its interior is particularly memorable. It has only a single nave, but it is a wide one that is covered by a round barrel vault, and when you stand at the western end, there is an effect of both height and space, emphasized by a succession of round forms. Three transverse arches lead your eye to the transept and beyond that to the single apse, which has a ring of five round arches below it, three of them enclosing windows and two blind.

Behind you is a tribune that is built over a long entrance corridor and is flanked by two tall pointed arches, one on each side. The tribune and the open doorway beneath it that leads to the corridor both have round arches; and so the west end of the nave has a distinctive mixture of forms.

That part of San Pedro is the oldest. The tribune and the corridor were part of an earlier, pre-Romanesque structure, and were incorporated in the new building when work on that was carried out at the beginning of the twelfth century.

Interestingly, there is no carved decoration in the church, which must have been the result of a deliberate decision, possibly influenced by the austere views of the Cistercians, though there is no other evidence of their style. The various arches – all of them round except for the two at the west end – rest on pilasters that run up from floor level, which contributes to the sense of height; and each of them culminates in a plain stone impost.

That arrangement is especially obvious in the transept crossing, which has a cluster of pilasters below it at each of the four corners. Here for some reason a barrel vault running from north to south has been constructed in recent years, though photographs taken as late as the second half of the twentieth century show that it used to have groin vaulting.

The two arms of the transept also have barrel vaulting that runs from north to south. The arches that lead to them are elongated, and both arms have pairs of arches high up on each of their three sides; they are blind on two walls and frame

Monastic church of Siresa

windows on the third. There are tiny vaulted niches, like mini-apses, built into the walls at floor level.

The outside of San Pedro is imposing, with walls that are built in red stone and tower over the houses of the village. It is rather lacking in unity, but it is interesting to see the west front, where the walls of the tribune and its corridor protrude. A succession of arches covers the entrance into the corridor, leading to a tympanum that has the chi-rho symbol carved on it.

At the east end there is a good view of the apse, the transept, and the substantial tower over the transept crossing that marks the newly-built vault.

Sos del Rey Católico

The small town of **Sos del Rey Católico** stands on a hilltop from which there are commanding views of the surrounding countryside and the mountains in the distance. This position gave it strategic importance in the Middle Ages, and the town still has remains of its medieval walls, as mentioned earlier, as well as a tower at its highest point, reached by walking up through the narrow, winding streets.

It also has a fine church that was constructed alongside the town's fortress in the course of the eleventh and twelfth centuries and that, with the tower, dominates the skyline. It was built onto the face of the rock on two levels, with a crypt, or lower church, down below and above it the main body of the church.

The sharply pointed bell-tower is the most prominent feature. But the two churches each have three apses at the east end, and together they form a tall, well-proportioned structure that rises above the rooftops of the town and is visible from far away, particularly from the neighbouring hillside. Much of it is plain, but there are narrow slits for windows at the lower level, and at the upper arched windows. The cornices above have corbels.

Sos was in a region that was conquered from the Moors by Sancho Garcés I, king of Navarre, early in the tenth century, and it became one of several fortified citadels. As the different Christian kingdoms took shape, it came sometimes under the rule of Navarre, and sometimes that of Aragon, but ended up as part of Aragon.

It has its name because years later, in 1452, it was the birthplace of Ferdinand, the king of Aragon who married Isabella, queen of Castile, and united their two kingdoms, the two of them being known as *los reyes católicos*. The house in which Ferdinand was born, the Palacio de Sada, still stands.

There are differences of opinion over the dating of the two levels of the church. What is known is that in 1055 Queen Estefanía, widow of García de Nájera, king of Navarre, gave her support to the building of the upper church, and documents show that work on it must have begun between 1059 and 1081. It continued for some years after that, much of the church not being completed until the middle of the twelfth century or even later.

It was extended by new building on both the north and south side in the sixteenth century.

The lower church had originally been intended to be little more than a crypt providing structural support to the main church above. But it was made a church in its own right, with its three apses, a short nave and two side-aisles, and the two levels are well integrated.

The challenge that was presented by building onto sheer rock was similar to that at Loarre (see page 137), and as at Loarre it was decided to have a passageway under the church. At Sos the passageway is level and passes under the main church. It is well vaulted, with a sequence of round arches, and has an arched doorway on one side, complete with columns, capitals and archivolts, that forms a formal entrance into the lower church.

After walking through this passageway you climb a few steps and come to one of the outstanding features of the upper church: the formal doorway on its north

Sos del Rey Católico: church in the middle of the village

side. It is now covered by vaulting built over it in the sixteenth century, but the doorway itself is Romanesque, and decorated by an array of sculpture: on the tympanum, on the archivolts and, above all, on either side. Much of it is badly worn, but there are some splendid figures to be seen.

The tympanum is devoted to Christ in Majesty. He is a benign presence sitting in a mandorla and flanked by the figures representing the four evangelists – the lion of St Mark, the calf of St Luke, the eagle of St John and the winged man of St Matthew – as well as two angels and two people praying. Above in the archivolts are numerous little scenes that, tantalizingly, are mostly too badly preserved to be identified, though humans and animals can be made out.

It is the tall, elongated figures on either side, particularly on the left, that are arresting. As at Sangüesa (see page 180), which is not far away, they take the place of columns, with formal carved capitals above their heads. There are several smaller figures in the spaces between them, and they all have an extraordinary serenity.

On the left are St John the Evangelist carrying his gospel, an unidentified bishop with mitre and crozier, and a martyr carrying a miniature grill, who is perhaps St Vincent. On the right, and less well preserved, are King David, Queen Estefanía and St Pelagius.

The presence of St Pelagius is an indication of the link between Sos and the pilgrimage to Santiago de Compostela (see page 27), because it was Pelagius, a hermit, who reportedly discovered the tomb of St James in the early ninth century and himself founded a church in Compostela.

The upper church is relatively short, with the three apses, a transept and only two bays in the nave and the side-aisles. It seems that it was originally intended to extend it further to the west, but this was never done, and a gallery was built over the western bay of the nave.

The church is, however, tall and well-constructed, with a pleasantly spacious feel. The apses make a fine trio, each of them framed by a slightly pointed arch and each having a ring of smaller round arches, some containing windows, some blind, in its outer wall. And there are more pointed arches in the barrel vaulting over the nave and the two arms of the transept, while the transept crossing has a rib vault, indicating a relatively late date.

There are also good capitals, some historiated and some with formal designs. Those in the nave and the transept crossing are high up and sometimes difficult to make out. There are some exquisite floral patterns, however, often showing Islamic influence. One of the composite columns at the entrance to the central apse has a capital in which two men are grappling with an animal.

The capitals in the three apses are largely formal, but one behind the main altar has Adam and Eve, dressed in skins and contrite, being expelled from Paradise.

There are two outstanding capitals in the lower church, which you reach by walking down a spiral staircase. This level too is well and solidly built, with massive pillars supporting groin vaulting in the nave and side-aisles. The capitals are on columns that stand on either side of the entrance to the central apse (which has Gothic paintings of the fourteenth century).

On the left are two birds with their necks entwined, each biting a claw-like leg, and in the abacus above entwined plants that echo this posture. On the right are two crouching women, each pulling on her hair and straining as she leans forward. The message that they convey is mysterious, but powerful, and comes from the heart of the ancient town of Sos.

Uncastillo

Uncastillo is one of several small fortress towns, all surrounded by wild rolling scenery, that are to be found in Aragon. As I have already written, it still has the remains of its castle, a reminder of turbulent times in the Middle Ages, as well as a number of churches, both inside and outside what is left of its walls, that date back at least partly to those days.

The best of them is **Santa María**. Its floor plan is not elaborate – just a single nave and apse, which are quite wide, and no transept or side-aisles – but it has a splendid formal doorway on its south side that is covered by lively and original carving.

High up in the stonework above the doorway proper are two large works: a powerful Christ in Majesty, staring almost fiercely ahead of him, and an Apostle. Below them even the columns on either side of the door are decorative: four of them twisted and the other two covered by patchwork patterns.

The columns are topped by six capitals with scenes that all tell a story, each one full of drama; and in the archivolts above them are several sequences of small figures, both human and animal, vigorously engaged in a range of activities.

Uncastillo was conquered from the Moors by Sancho Garcés II, king of Navarre, in about 940, and fortified soon after that. There was an earlier church dedicated to the Virgin Mary, but in 1135 funds were provided by Ramiro II, king of Aragon, for the construction of a new one, and that is the one that still stands.

Its formal consecration is reported to have taken place many years later, in 1246, but much of the church, not least the south doorway, is thought to have been completed some time before that, in the middle of the twelfth century or soon afterwards.

You walk up to Santa María through narrow, paved streets lined with old buildings, and as you approach it from the east you see the broad semicircle of the apse, decorated with arched windows and corbels. At the far end, beyond the south doorway, is a bell-tower that is Romanesque at its base, but has an upper level that was built on in an elaborate, and incongruous, Gothic style.

The body of the church is Romanesque, however, and the corbels on the outside of the apse are a lively collection, mainly of human figures. They include acrobats, and also some explicit sexual couplings. In one, a monk is locked in an embrace with a woman, and both are being attacked by serpents – an indication that they are damned.

The interior is spacious and well-proportioned. The nave, which is relatively wide, as already mentioned, has a barrel vault supported by slightly pointed transverse arches. It leads to a short choir bay and an elegant apse that is ringed by a succession of round arches, wide ones that frame windows alternating with narrow ones that are blind.

There are capitals throughout the church, some of them with formal designs made up of foliage, fruit or other traditional elements, others with some very active scenes. One of the capitals in the nave has a group made up of a contortionist, a woman and a violinist. Another, on the north side of the choir, shows devils

Uncastillo: south doorway

tormenting sinners, one of whom is being prodded with a pitchfork while the flames beneath him are fanned.

It is the south doorway that is the outstanding feature, however, and there is so much detailed work on it that it needs time to take it all in. The six capitals include the expulsion of Adam and Eve from Paradise, the Flight into Egypt, a horseman being attacked by two men on foot, and another version, similar to the one inside the church, of the torments inflicted on sinners in hell.

The archivolts above have a lively collection of little figures. Those in the innermost ring are small but lovingly carved, and range from a harpy and a mermaid to eagles, a bear, a man with

Detail of Uncastillo doorway

a lance, a money-lender, a man blowing a hunting horn, a griffin pinning a man to the floor and a she-goat suckling a kid.

The next archivolt is unusual in that the various figures, who are mainly men and women, but include a wolf cub and a monkey, appear to be looking out from behind the moulding, with the upper parts of their bodies above it and their legs below. Two of them seem to be actors on a stage.

The outermost archivolt has the largest figures, and some of the most accomplished. Here, as elsewhere in the church, there is an emphasis on show business. There are acrobats going into contortions and musicians playing a variety of instruments: flutes, harps and other stringed instruments. There are also a man grappling with the head of a monster, a man tending a sheep, and another repairing a pot, as well as two women holding a plate, a ram, a wolf and two birds with their necks entwined.

The masons of Uncastillo must have enjoyed their work.

Navarre and the Basque Country

Navarre was the setting for one of the early Christian kingdoms in Spain, as we have seen. It also lay across the route taken by most of the pilgrims coming from what is now France and heading for Santiago de Compostela, whether they had crossed the Pyrenees by the Roncesvalles pass or the Somport. The two groups joined up at Puente la Reina (see page 29), and from there followed the route laid out by Sancho el Mayor, king of Navarre from 1004 to 1035 (see page 29).

So several of the region's surviving churches are on or near the pilgrim routes. One route passed through Pamplona, the capital, and though the Romanesque cathedral that once stood there has long gone, replaced by its Gothic successor, the Museum of Navarre has a collection of superb twelfth-century column capitals that were once in its cloister. Some of them are historiated, with Biblical scenes carved on them, some purely decorative.

West of Navarre is the Basque Country, which is related to it since Navarre too has a sizable Basque population and was originally founded by them. The Basque Country is bypassed by the pilgrim route laid out by Sancho, but Vitoria, its capital, stands on the site of a Roman town served by a Roman road. It was prosperous in the twelfth and thirteenth centuries, and there are some fine Romanesque churches in the surrounding area: Armentia, Estíbaliz and San Vicentejo.

In Navarre, one of the most fascinating churches belongs to the ancient, and still active, monastery of Leyre, that was once used for the burial of the kings of Navarre; it is a few miles north of the pilgrim route that leads west from Jaca. South-west of there, on the other side of the pilgrim route, is Sangüesa, which has a magnificent porch.

Some way to the south is Tudela, a city that was only taken from the Moors in the first quarter of the twelfth century, whose church has some late Romanesque carving, particularly in its cloister.

There are also churches in Navarre that show a strong Islamic influence. This is particularly marked in two small octagonal chapels, at Eunate and Torres del Rio,

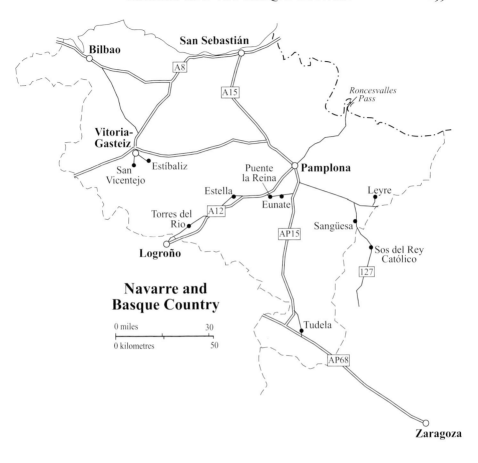

which both have Moorish-style cupolas. Both are near the pilgrim route and are thought to have been used for burials.

There is more Islamic influence to be seen in the church of San Pedro de la Rúa in Estella, which has a cusped doorway that dates from the early thirteenth century. Estella is a town that was specifically founded in the eleventh century to serve pilgrims, and it has two churches, San Pedro and San Miguel, which are partly Romanesque and have good carving in that style. It also has a secular Romanesque building that has carved capitals on its front.

Armentia

The church of **San Andrés** in Armentia, a district on the outskirts of Vitoria (or Gasteiz), the Basque regional capital, has a fine position on rising ground above a small park. Sadly, there is little of the original twelfth-century structure to be seen from there, apart from a stylish apse at the east end, but this is amply made up for by the quality of the carvings both outside and inside the church.

Not least, there is an exceptional collection of sculpture, most of it dating from around 1200, to be seen in a porch-gallery on the south side. The sculpture was originally part of an ornate façade on that side of the church. The gallery was built to display the various works at the end of the eighteenth century when the whole church was being extensively restored and the façade was dismantled.

Armentia has a long history that goes back to the early days of the *reconquista*. It was the seat of a bishop from the ninth century until the end of the eleventh, when its place was taken by Calahorra. Nothing is left of the cathedral that it had in those days. But a college of canons was installed on the site, and the present building was erected for their use between 1146 and 1190.

The canons moved to Vitoria, which had grown to be much bigger and more important than Armentia, in 1498. San Andrés became a parish church, and over the years much of it and its dependencies, including the cloister, fell into ruin. So it was decided in 1776 that rather than put up a new church the existing one should be restored.

The restoration is very visible on the outside: San Andrés, which originally had the shape of a cross, is now virtually rectangular. At the east end a plain extension has been inserted on each side of the apse in the angle between it and the transept; on the south side there is the porch-gallery, and the space above it has been filled by another extension, originally designed to provide a chapterhouse and a lodging for a priest. The space on the north side of the nave has also been filled, and both the lantern tower over the crossing and the bell-tower have been rebuilt.

On the inside the single nave now has groin vaulting supported by two round transverse arches, an arrangement that was installed as part of the restoration process.

In spite of all this, however, the choir at the east end of the church has retained its Romanesque form, and so has the apse, both inside and out. Above all there is the sculpture, which is the product of work carried out at three different periods, and has exceptional power and originality.

The first period was around the middle of the twelfth century, when the column capitals on both the inside and the outside of the apse are thought to have

been carved. They are vivid, but crude.
There are animals and monsters, humans confronting animals or each other,
an eagle, various horsemen; and the
humans have strange, frog-like faces, as
if they came from outer space.

The next period was between 1170
and 1190. By then the sculptors were
more accomplished, and they carried
out work in different parts of the
church. One ambitious project was the
carving of four life-size statues that
represent the evangelists and are placed
high up above the transept crossing,
one at each corner. Each has the head
of the creature traditionally associated
with him – a lion for St Mark, an eagle
for St John, a calf for St Luke and a
winged man for St Matthew – and each

Collegiate church of Armentia: capital on east end

has an angel above his head who is blowing a trumpet to announce the end of the
world.

Down below them, on the engaged columns that support the four pointed
arches of the crossing, are capitals that date from the same period, and they too
are impeccably carved. Some have intricate arrangements of foliage. On one there
are griffins confronting each other in heraldic poses. On another two horsemen are
battling a pair of centaurs armed with bows.

There is more work from those years to be seen on the capitals of two free-
standing pairs of columns at the western end of the nave. They were originally part
of the support of a choir which was dismantled during the restoration process.
They have the same subject, but the one on the north side is the more successful.
It is a dramatic scene in which two lions are tearing apart young asses while in the
centre the head of a monster is shown devouring a human.

The sculptors of that period were also active on the outside of San Andrés.
There is a line of corbels on the south side which may not be in the same position
as they were before the eighteenth-century restoration, but are full of life. Again,
there are animals and humans, and scenes such as a goat playing a harp, a person
pulling a thorn out his foot, and a siren holding a fish in her arms.

Finally, there are two works from that time in the porch-gallery: an Annunci-

Armentia: St Mark in angle above transept crossing

Porch-gallery of Armentia: Entombment of Christ, Resurrection and visit of Three Marys

ation and a tympanum that has the Lamb of God standing in a circle in the centre with John the Baptist and Isaiah crouching on either side. They are sensitively carved, as are the two angels who are holding a circular chi-rho symbol below, and it is thought that the original doorway into the south side of the church was under this tympanum.

The other works in the porch-gallery were produced during the third period, which was around 1200, and were taken down, as recounted earlier, when the south façade was dismantled in the eighteenth century. They focus on events surrounding the Resurrection, and they have a dramatic quality, coupled with decorative features, that makes one long to have seen them in their original setting – though it is not known how they were arranged.

There is a second tympanum, much larger than the earlier one, that gives a distinctive version of the Ascension. Christ stands in the centre, a towering figure who is more than twice the size of the Apostles, who are standing in two groups below him, one on either side. The lower half of the tympanum represents the Earth. The upper half, in which because of his height Christ is already present, is Heaven.

Flanking him are two angels, some tiny buildings representing the celestial Jerusalem, and a pair of human figures thought to be the two who were killed and brought back to life as described in chapter 11 of the Book of Revelation

On the far wall of the gallery are two other scenes, that have been set side by side with a pair of pointed arches above them, and are also dramatic. On the left the subject is Christ's descent into Hell, and he is shown taking Adam and Eve away with him, while behind them are the standing figure of Satan and the gruesome heads of various monsters, one of which has a human in its mouth.

On the right three events are shown or at least evoked: the Entombment, the Resurrection and the visit to the empty tomb by the Three Marys. Nicodemus and Joseph of Arimathea are covering the dead body of Christ; above them are two angels who are raising their hands in a symbolic gesture that suggests the Resurrection; and at the side are the statuesque figures of the Three Marys together with an angel who is talking to them.

There are other works to be seen in the gallery: a horseman trampling an enemy under his horse's hooves, Abraham preparing to sacrifice Isaac, and two mutilated, but serene figures on the columns that support the arches which frame the two scenes on the far wall. It is an unforgettable display.

Porch-gallery of Armentia: Christ rescuing Adam and Eve from Hell

Estella

The town of Estella, built on the banks of the river Ega south-west of Pamplona, was an important stopping-point on the pilgrim route to Santiago de Compostela. So numerous churches were erected there over the years, and two of them have outstanding features that date back to the Romanesque period.

San Pedro de la Rúa has two surviving sides of a cloister that was built in the second half of the twelfth century and has a notable set of capitals. San Miguel, on the other bank of the Ega, has a porch on its north side that is a few years later, from the late twelfth or the early thirteenth century, and is covered with carving, not only around the doorway itself, but on the walls on either side.

There is also a rare secular building from the same period, a palace that is said to have belonged to the kings of Navarre and that has some especially vigorous capitals. It stands in the old part of the town, just below San Pedro de la Rúa, which was itself built on the rocky slope that leads up to the site of a former citadel.

The town of Estella was founded in 1090 by Sancho Ramírez, king of Navarre. He chose the location, then known by the Basque name of Lizarra, because it was well placed on a bend of the river Ega, at the heart of a mountainous region; and he decreed that the pilgrim route should pass through it.

This was an important consideration because, by the time it reached Estella, the route served the two main groups of pilgrims: those who had crossed the Pyrenees by the Roncesvalles pass and travelled on through Pamplona and those who had used the Somport pass and come on through Jaca (page 130). The two routes joined at Puente la Reina, a few miles east of Estella, where pilgrims who had used both crossed the river Arga by an elegant arched bridge that dates from the eleventh century and still stands.

Until the foundation of Estella this single route had passed further south, and the decision to redirect it was opposed by the monks of the important monastery of San Juan de la Peña (see page 141) because it took the pilgrims by a smaller monastery at Zarapuz that they also owned. But they were compensated financially, and Estella became a flourishing town that attracted a great number of immigrants. Many of them came from France.

The **palace of the kings of Navarre** is a handsome structure whose two lower floors date from the twelfth century; the upper ones were built on later. There are open arches at ground level and a line of four windows, each filled with four narrow arches, on the first floor. At each end of the building are pairs of engaged columns, one above the other, and each of the columns has capitals on it.

One of them depicts a battle scene in which Roland, on horseback, is toppling the giant Ferragut, also on horseback, with his lance. Another has a grisly view of Hell: two dejected sinners, clearly misers because of the bags of money they are carrying, are chained by the neck and being pulled along by a snarling devil, while other devils are thrusting sinners into a cauldron.

San Pedro is opposite, and the approach to it is a rewarding one. You walk up a long flight of steps flanked by trees and bushes, and at the top is a splendid doorway that leads into the north side of the church. It is set deep into the wall, with receding archivolts that rest on columns on either side. Most strikingly, the innermost archivolt, which frames the door itself, is cusped and gives a markedly Islamic touch to the whole structure.

The doorway is dated to the beginning of the thirteenth century, a time of transition when Romanesque was evolving into Gothic. Most of the capitals that top the columns have formal decoration, as do the archivolts above them. But there are carved figures on the capitals at the base of the cusped arch: on the right, harpies and a centaur with a bow and arrow aimed at a siren; on the left, bearded griffins.

The interior of San Pedro is also in transitional style. It has rib vaulting over the nave and the two side-aisles, and its three apses all have a pointed profile. The central apse is particularly elaborate. It has a short choir bay and beyond that three smaller apses, all with pointed arches, that radiate out from it at floor level. On the

Estella: cloister of San Pedro de la Rúa

Estella: capital in cloister of San Pedro de la Rúa

level above that are three windows with round arches complete with columns and capitals, and above them three plain, narrow window openings.

When you go out into the cloister you go back some years and are well in the twelfth century. At the time that this was originally built it had four sides, but those on the east and south were destroyed in the sixteenth century when the citadel on the cliff above was being demolished. The explosives used were so powerful that a great part of the cloister crumbled as a result of the shock.

It was lovingly restored – and in part rearranged – and today it is a most attractive place, with a tree and bushes in the centre and the rock-face up above. The two surviving arms both have excellent capitals. Those on the north side are historiated, with scenes from the New Testament and the lives of saints; those on the west have formal designs.

The historiated scenes include the Nativity and the events surrounding it; a vivid presentation of the Massacre of the Innocents; and scenes from the Passion of Christ, among them a serene version of the Entombment, with angels flying down from above with incense in their hands – and plant patterns on either side. Other capitals are devoted to the lives and martyrdoms of St Lawrence and St Andrew, vividly shown, and the imprisonment and liberation of St Peter.

They are an impressive collection, and the same is true of the formal capitals on the west side of the cloister. They are immaculately carved, and include several decorative compositions made up of birds, harpies and other monsters. They are shown confronting each other in heraldic postures and surrounded by intricate patterns.

In the middle of the west side is a strange arrangement, found elsewhere in Romanesque cloisters – in Santo Domingo de Silos (see page 264), for instance – in which four columns are twisted around each other and together support a capital, in this case consisting of plant patterns.

Like San Pedro, **San Miguel** is built on rising ground, above the centuries-old site of the market, and this too you reach by walking up a flight of steps. By the time the church had been completed the transition from Romanesque to Gothic was largely complete, at least in the interior, which is early Gothic. But the north porch is still Romanesque, and a very good example of the style.

It has five receding archivolts, each resting on a pair of columns, and both the capitals of the columns and the archivolts are covered with carving. There is more carving on either side of the doorway itself, and the various figures and scenes there are one of the outstanding features of San Miguel.

On each side of the arch is a line of four saints, all robed and bearded and all staring serenely ahead with almost identical expressions; St Peter is carrying the keys that mark him out, and the others have either a book or a scroll. Above each line of four is a small arch complete with carved decoration – and with two smaller figures who are also carrying a scroll or a book.

Down below them are some very different scenes. On the left, St Michael is shown twice. First, he transfixes a dragon with his spear, to the admiration of another angel. Then he presides over the weighing of souls, with a devil on one side, and on the other a seated Abraham who is holding the souls of the righteous, in the form of young children, on his lap; while down below is a view of the torments inflicted on sinners by other devils.

The scene on the right is also dramatic, but more peaceful. It shows the Three Marys, visibly moved, as they visit the empty tomb after the Resurrection of Christ. One angel is sitting on the tomb, which has its lid raised, while another explains to the three women what has happened.

The doorway itself is also richly decorated. In the centre is the tympanum, which has Christ in Majesty on it. He is a benign figure who is sitting in a slightly cusped mandorla and surrounded by the four creatures that symbolize the evangelists: the lion of St Mark, the bull or calf of St Luke, the eagle of St John and the winged man of St Matthew. They crane their necks to gaze at him, while two robed figures, a man and a woman, look on from either side.

Estella: saints on north doorway of San Miguel

San Miguel, Estella: Three Marys visit the empty tomb and encounter two angels

At a lower level and on either side, the column capitals recount the events surrounding the Nativity, step by step. The story begins on the left with the Annunciation and includes the Visitation, the Announcement to the Shepherds, the Adoration of the Magi, the Presentation in the Temple and the Flight into Egypt. It ends with the Massacre of the Innocents. There are then two other capitals on the right with scenes that show hunters in thickets spearing birds.

The carved figures up above in the archivolts are also small and also full of character. Each archivolt has its own theme. The innermost one shows angels scattering incense, and the next one a theme often found in Romanesque sculpture: the Elders of the Apocalypse. As always, they are engaging old men carrying musical instruments, and at San Miguel they are shown sitting together in pairs.

The third archivolt presents various prophets and patriarchs, and the fourth and fifth have numerous tiny scenes taken from the Bible and the lives of saints. On the left a man, perhaps John the Baptist, is being beheaded, and a woman, perhaps Salome, appears to be holding his head on a plate. Just above is St Martin giving half of his cloak to a beggar, and further up St Lawrence being roasted to death on a grill. On the other side is St Peter being crucified upside down.

Each scene is graphically shown, making San Miguel – and Estella as a whole – a place in which it is worth spending time.

Estíbaliz

The church of **Estíbaliz**, which has a beautiful setting on a hill a few miles east of Vitoria, has a particularly fine façade on its south side, with carving round its doorway that is both fanciful and highly skilled. It also has some good capitals inside.

The façade dominates an open space that is surrounded by trees, through which there are views of the valley below. The doorway is its central feature, and it is known as the *puerta speciosa*, or beautiful door, because of its decoration.

This decoration is not only on the capitals that top the four columns – two on each side – but on the stonework on either side of the door, on the little frieze that runs above that and the capitals, and on the archivolts that support the arch. Even the four columns have patterns carved into them.

Much of the carving is of plant designs, very imaginatively done and sometimes with little human heads emerging from the foliage. But there are two tiny portraits, on the pillars on either side of the door, that are of special interest. On the left, at the head of some largely decorative designs, is a seated figure with one hand raised in blessing and the other holding a book who is thought to be Christ.

On the right, the pillar has several human figures framed in circular or spiral

Detail of Estíbaliz doorway, including the figure of Christ

Monastic church of Estíbaliz: south doorway

shapes one above the other, and at the top the bust of a person who is pointing with an elongated right index finger. He is thought to be John the Baptist.

Estíbaliz was for many years a military and trading centre, from the days of the Romans and into the Middle Ages. It was also known for the worship of the Virgin Mary. In 1138 its church was presented to the monastery of Nájera, some way to the south, by the local family that owned it, and construction of the present building is presumed to have begun at about that time, replacing the one that had been there before.

Like several other Spanish monasteries, Nájera was linked to Cluny, the powerful Burgundian abbey, and Cluniac influence is visible both in the design of the church at Estíbaliz and, especially, the carving of the capitals.

Building continued over a number of years, with modifications being made to the original plan. So though the layout is basically the one that it had from the beginning, with a single nave, a transept and three apses that are set a short way apart from each other, it appears that plans for the vaulting evolved in the course of the work.

The main innovation, carried out towards the end of the twelfth century, was to increase the height of the transept crossing and cover it with rib vaulting, though the style was still late Romanesque rather than Gothic. So the crossing is supported by four tall pointed arches, and pointed arches predominate in the church. But it can be seen that the chapel in the south apse – which has a carved Romanesque font – still has a round arch at its entrance, and the same may once have been true of the central apse. The north arm of the transept was rebuilt a century later in Gothic style, and the westernmost bay of the nave added on much later still.

The capitals in the nave and at the entrance to the central apse are dated to the earliest phase of building, in the mid-twelfth century. Those in the nave have largely formal and often intricate designs: a mask and animals in the midst of foliage, for example. The four capitals at the entrance to the nave, on the other hand, are historiated and in some cases noticeably similar to capitals that survive in Cluny.

They are a lively collection: Adam and Eve and the serpent in the Garden of Eden; their expulsion; the torments in Hell of those guilty of lust and avarice; and, by way of contrast, the Annunciation. The Annunciation is interesting because the Holy Ghost is shown as a dove attached to the Virgin Mary's head, a reference to the doctrine that she conceived through her ear.

The façade on the south side of the church was built at the same time as the rib vaulting over the transept crossing. It now has three levels, which combine to make a well-proportioned whole. At ground level is the *puerta speciosa*, which is the main

Capital in church of Estíbaliz

entrance into the church, and it is interesting to note that while the innermost archivolt is slightly pointed, those further out are less pointed and the outermost is round.

Above it is a formal arched window, set deep into the stonework with columns, capitals and rounded archivolts. At the top is a stretch of free-standing wall with two arches in which the bells are hung.

It seems that there was once a fourth level above that, but that it was dismantled.

The *puerta speciosa* has a line of corbels above it, and some little scenes set into the stonework on the corners on either side. They include a small bearded man crouching under the weight of a capital on the left; and on the right a larger, stylish presentation of the Annunciation, with the Angel Gabriel and the Virgin Mary each standing under an arch.

A final point of interest is the corbels on the outside of the central apse. They consist mainly of animals, vigorously carved, and include a donkey playing a wind instrument, a fish, lions and a siren with a double tail.

Eunate

The chapel of **Eunate**, octagonal in shape and surrounded by a ring of open arches, also octagonal, is one of the little jewels of the Romanesque period in Spain. It stands almost alone in the middle of fields, with low hills nearby and villages in the far distance, and its unusual form and the balance between its different parts create an enchanting effect. (See page 28.)

A five-sided apse complete with arched windows and corbels extends from the eastern face of the octagon. Rising from the roof is a simple bell-tower consisting of a flat wall of masonry with two round-topped openings for the bells; and on one side there is a turret that gives access to the roof. All round are the arches, several of them resting on columns and capitals, which form a sort of open cloister.

Inside, the chapel has a Moorish-style cupola for a vault. Four separate arches spring from eight different points at ground level and they criss-cross high overhead, making a star-shaped pattern at the top.

Nothing is known for certain about the origins or purpose of this shrine, well-constructed though it is. It is generally thought to date from the second half of the twelfth century, and at one time it was considered to have been built by the Templars, with the Church of the Holy Sepulchre in Jerusalem, also octagonal, as a model.

But there is no evidence for that, and the chapel is now believed to have been intended as an imposing burial place for people who had died on the pilgrim route

Moorish-style vault in Eunate chapel

to Santiago de Compostela, which passes by not far away. The same would have been true of the similar chapel at Torres del Rio (see page 188), further west along the route.

The octagonal ring of arches is one of the distinctive features of Eunate. It is not thought that they were ever linked by roofing to the main body of the chapel. Rather, they would have been linked to buildings that surrounded the chapel and have now disappeared.

The main entrance to the chapel was by the doorway on the north side, and it is the three sides of the octagon that are nearest to that which have the columns, set in pairs and topped by capitals. There are fourteen capitals in all. They include masks with the tendrils of plants emerging from their mouths, lions confronting each other, and a scene which appears to depict the Crucifixion, including a group of people that could include the Apostles.

The north doorway itself also has carved decoration. There is a succession of human figures, masks and monsters in the outer archivolt; two of the inner ones have formal plant patterns. The capitals are generally worn, but one that is well-preserved has the head of a man whose beard forms a spiral pattern on each side.

The inside of the chapel is a marvel. Up above is the cupola, and set into one of the sides is the apse, which has similar vaulting on a smaller scale. The arches that support the cupola rest on pairs of columns and capitals, one above the other, and they mark the eight points at which the sides of the octagon meet. Between them, in the walls surrounding the central space, there are five windows framed by columns and capitals, three of them open and two blind.

The apse has two semicircular rings of round arches, the lower one plain and the upper quite ornate, with arches resting on columns and capitals. They surround the sanctuary and provide a decorative backdrop.

Many of the capitals of Eunate are fairly elaborate. There is one on the right side of the arch framing the sanctuary that has the masks of monsters and tendrils emerging from their mouths to form patterns – as well as a small human face. But nearby, on the far side of the arch, is one that is very different. It is simple and quite primitive: a crudely carved person is playing a string instrument and another is apparently dancing.

Leyre

The monastery of **Leyre**, which stands alone on an empty hillside south-east of Pamplona with some rugged mountains overlooking it, has a church that is inter-esting in several ways. Its east end is an early and stylish example of Romanesque, both outside and in; its crypt is one of the most impressive to be seen anywhere; and it has a west porch with twelfth-century carving of great charm and variety.

The monastery has been there for a long time. It is known from the writings of St Eulogius of Córdoba that it was well established in 848, when he visited it; so it had presumably been founded well before that. In 924, because of its remoteness, it provided a refuge for the king of Navarre and the bishop of Pamplona when Abd al-Rahman III, the great Muslim caliph, came north and sacked Pamplona.

Leyre had long been seen as a special place by the kings of Navarre. Many of the earliest ones were buried there, and for some years the bishops of Pamplona were chosen from among the monks of Leyre. Sancho el Mayor (1004-35), the most powerful of the Navarrese kings, gave the monastery strong support, and it became influential and rich.

It lost its privileged position in 1134, when a new dynasty was installed in Pamplona, and there were years of power struggles and decline. But Leyre continued to be an important presence on the Navarre scene.

In 1307 the Cistercians were finally the victors in a long battle to take over control from the Benedictines who had run the monastery until then. Troubled times continued, however, and it was only in the early years of the sixteenth century, with the Cistercians still in charge, that extensive reconstruction work was completed, including the fine Gothic vaulting that now covers the nave.

Much of the rest of the church is Romanesque, however, and dates from the first half of the eleventh century when, with the support of Sancho el Mayor, it replaced an earlier building on the same site. It was consecrated in 1057, when Sancho's grandson, also called Sancho, was king of Navarre, and that makes it older than many of the other great Spanish churches of that century – in Jaca (see page 130), Frómista (page 220), or León (page 295).

There was more building in Romanesque style in the second half of the eleventh century, followed by the Gothic work that was carried out by the Cistercians centuries later. But the Cistercians did not touch the east end or the crypt, both of which date from the earliest phase, in the first half of the eleventh century, and they retain their distinctive character.

The west porch is also Romanesque, but its sculpture is from different periods, most of it from the twelfth century, some possibly earlier, and it is thought to have been assembled in its present form by the Cistercians.

The east end is the most prominent feature when you look at the church from the outside. It has three apses that are relatively plain, with just small, round-topped windows on two levels and a line of corbels under the cornices. But they are tall, well-built and well-proportioned, and the overall effect is most pleasing, with a Romanesque bell-tower behind them that was built at the same time as they were and up above the peak of the sixteenth-century nave.

The interior, too, is one to cherish. There is a single nave, wide and covered by the Cistercians' Gothic vaulting, and it provides a perfect setting for admiring the Romanesque east end. Three tall, round arches stand at the end of the nave, the wide one in the centre framing the entrance to the choir and the two narrower ones the aisles on either side. Beyond each of the arches are two barrel-vaulted bays that lead to an apse, and there are more round arches between the choir and the two side-aisles.

It is an original arrangement that has height and is at the same time three-dimensional. And it is enhanced by the capitals at the springing of the arches that indicate just how early in the story of Spanish Romanesque Leyre's church was. They are decorative but very simple, consisting of a few lines that are like sketches in stone, with patterns that are derived from the forms of plants and flowers.

There are similar capitals in the crypt, and this part of the church makes an immediate impression when you enter. It is low and massively built, with three apses and, leading to them, a nave that is divided in two and an aisle on either side of it, making four narrow aisles.

The outstanding feature, however, is the capitals which, instead of being at eye

East end of monastic church of Leyre

Monastic church of Leyre: crypt

level or higher, stand dramatically in isolation only a few feet up from the floor.
They have the various arches springing from them and just a short, round column
below.

The crypt had to be solidly constructed in order to support the weight of the
east end of the church above it. Its arches, the barrel vaulting and the three apses
are certainly imposing, built as they are of large blocks of stone, and the crypt is an
atmospheric place. The capitals and their designs, many of them ultimately derived
from the Corinthian-style acanthus, give it its extra, highly original, appeal.

The entrance to the crypt is through a doorway that seems simple at first sight,
but is carefully built with three receding arches; and there are other Romanesque
doorways to be seen in Leyre. An arched doorway with two of the early capitals
leads into the north side of the church from what was once the cloister. Another,
more ornate one, which dates from the second half of the eleventh century and has
carved capitals and the chi-rho symbol in its tympanum, links one of the chapels
with the nave.

The porch at the west end of the church is an ambitious creation with sculpture
that, though it is in a variety of styles, combines to make a splendid ensemble.
At the centre is a tympanum with some serene, rather archaic figures standing in
a line, their feet resting on animals. Two are badly damaged and one is missing

Monastic church of Leyre: evangelist on west doorway

altogether, but four of them are intact: in the centre Christ, with one arm raised in blessing and the other holding a book; on one side the Virgin Mary, who is wearing an elaborate dress, and beyond her St Peter with his key; on the other St John carrying his gospel and beyond him one of the damaged figures, perhaps another Apostle.

It seems that the tympanum was originally smaller, and was enlarged by the addition of the ring of palm-leaf patterns around the top. So it is likely that it and the standing figures were brought from some other part of the church and, given their archaic style, they may be older than the rest of the porch.

The main framework of the porch, with three columns on each side each topped by capitals, three archivolts and an outer arc that is also carved, is thought to date from the very beginning of the twelfth century. The style of the capitals and of the innumerable little figures in the archivolts is distinctive, and has been linked with Esteban, the sculptor from Santiago de Compostela (see page 374) who is known to have been working in Navarre at that time.

The six capitals are full of life, including lions, crouching women and birds pecking at their own legs; and there is a seventh one on the central column of the door that shows seated figures and may or may not be from the same time. The carvings on the archivolts are a riot of animals, humans, monsters and much else, some of them grotesque, some naturalistic, displaying the full range of the sculptor's imagination.

Finally, there are the many carvings around the outer edge of the porch, most of them in the space above it. Here, it is thought, the people reassembling the porch, perhaps many years after the Romanesque period had ended, put the various pieces into position unsystematically, without any linking theme.

There are, however, some very fine pieces to be seen – though the sloping roof built out to protect the porch from the weather means that the higher ones are in shadow. There is a saint, perhaps an evangelist, pointing to a book on the left of the doorway, and above him another saint, perhaps an abbot, together with an entwined pattern and a tiny head. Opposite is another similar pattern made up of a vine, grapes and, in the centre, another tiny face.

Across the top is a sequence of scenes. They include Christ and Apostles, the martyrdom of St Nunilo and St Alodia (whose relics Leyre had received), a grimacing mask, a *danse macabre*, and on the far right the Annunciation and the Visitation. Beneath them are two angels with trumpets who are announcing the Day of Judgment.

It is quite a collection, and its quality demonstrates the important place that Leyre once had in the life of Navarre.

Sangüesa

The church of **Sangüesa**, a town built on the bank of the river Aragón south-east of Pamplona, has one of the finest Romanesque porches to be seen in Spain. It has a tympanum with a dramatic treatment of the Last Judgment, some exquisitely elongated figures that are reminiscent of the *portail royal* at Chartres, and an array of other sculpture that goes from saintly figures to musicians, acrobats, simple craftsmen and monsters.

Sangüesa is younger than most Spanish towns. In the days when there was still the threat of armed incursions by the Moors to the south the main Christian settlement was on a hilltop some miles to the north, then called Sangüesa but now known as Rocaforte. By the early twelfth century this danger no longer existed, and under Alfonso I, who was king of both Navarre and Aragon and was known as el Batallador, Fighter of Battles, a new town was founded beside the bridge over the Aragón.

This too was a strategic position, and the town was walled – though by then any fighting was between the two Christian kingdoms of Navarre and Aragon. But the principal role of the new Sangüesa was as a convenient stopping point for the many pilgrims who had crossed the Pyrenees by the Somport pass and travelled through Jaca (see page 130) on their way to Santiago de Compostela. So numerous churches and hospices sprang up.

Many of the pilgrims came from far away, and it is believed that one of them was St Francis of Assisi, who visited Rocaforte and founded there the first community of Franciscan friars in Spain.

The church of Santa María la Real, which stands in the 'new' town not far from the bridge over the Aragón, near the site of what was a royal palace, is the main survivor of those days. It belonged to the Knights Hospitaller from 1131, when Alfonso formally handed over both the church and the palace to them, and they continued to own it until the middle of the fourteenth century.

Not all the church is Romanesque. The upper levels of the bell-tower are Gothic, and so is much of the interior. This is relatively small, with a nave and two side-aisles of two bays each, all covered by rib vaulting from the period of transition from Romanesque to Gothic; and there is an early Gothic cupola from the thirteenth century over the short transept.

But the three apses at the east end are pure Romanesque of the first half of the twelfth century, and they can be appreciated from both inside and outside. Inside, the central apse is largely hidden by a splendid sixteenth-century altarpiece. However, it is possible to look behind it and see the arched windows in the curve

Sangüesa, from south-east

of the wall below the hemisphere of the apse proper. They have some well-carved capitals, including one showing the Flight into Egypt. The smaller apses on either side are in the same style.

On the outside, the apses have the distinctive form of their period, with more arched windows and corbels underneath the cornices. And close to them is the south porch with its sculpture, which was part of a second phase of building and is dated to the end of the twelfth century and the beginning of the thirteenth.

This splendid creation has so much to look at and admire that it is worth spending time in front of it. There are thought to have been two main sculptors, together with their teams of assistants, who worked here: one who was responsible for much of the carving around the doorway itself, and a second who created the two rows of arches, each framing a small statue, that form the top level.

In between, in the triangular wall spaces on either side of the main doorway, are a number of pieces which are individually full of life and vigour, but seem to have been placed there almost randomly. And there are a few pieces on the pilasters that flank the porch.

First perhaps should be the six tall figures that flank the door, three on either side. They are all very fine, but those on the left are particularly arresting. Stylized and serene, they represent the Virgin Mary, who is in the centre, Mary Magdalene on the left, and the other Mary, the mother of St John and St James, on the right.

On the other side of the door are St Peter, St Paul and, most surprisingly, Judas Iscariot, who is shown hanged from the tree with the rope round his neck.

Over each of these figures there is a carved capital. Three are historiated: above Mary Magdalene are the Annunciation and the Visitation, above the Virgin Mary the Presentation in the Temple, and above St Paul the Judgment of Solomon. The others have formal, and decorative, designs.

The name of the sculptor who carved the statues, or some of them, is known – Leodegarius – because he inscribed it on the book held by the Virgin Mary. He is thought to have been a Frenchman, who must have known Chartres, and the belief is that he and his team of masons were responsible, not only for the six statues and the capitals above them, but also for the Last Judgment on the tympanum and some of the little figures in the archivolts.

The tympanum has a powerful figure of Christ in the centre: he has his right arm raised and is surrounded by four angels blowing trumpets. The devout are standing, calm and fully robed, on one side, the sinners falling back naked on the other. Down below is a row of arches, with the Virgin Mary seated beneath the central one, the infant Jesus in her arms, and standing on either side of her the twelve Apostles, each also beneath an arch.

South doorway of Sangüesa: Mary Magdalene, Virgin Mary and Mary, mother of St James

Sangüesa: tympanum of south doorway

There is a vivid little scene in the panel below the sinners in which St Michael is holding the scales on which souls are weighed. A dove is on one side of the scales, representing a soul's good works, and there are three people who appear to have passed the test. But a gruesome-looking devil in the form of a reptile is pulling at the other side of the scales, and above it are two naked figures, presumably sinners, and a stack of grimacing faces.

There is more fascinating carving in the archivolts, some of which could be the work of Leodegarius and his team. There is some formal decoration, but what is outstanding is the array of tiny figures that are to be found there. Some of the subjects are traditional in Romanesque sculpture: monsters, a mermaid, a woman paying the penalty for lust. There are also Apostles and monks. Mixed in with them are people engaged in a great range of different activities: a warrior, a shoemaker, a blacksmith, a butcher, a man playing a stringed instrument, and many others, all graphically presented.

There is an even more exotic mix in the triangular wall spaces on either side of the main arch. Here too are harpies and other winged monsters, another representation of the punishment for lust, a pattern of entwined tendrils, and various animals and birds. But there are also three of the creatures that represent the evangelists, a lion for St Mark, a bull for St Luke and an eagle for St John; and there

Detail of Sangüesa doorway

are some Biblical scenes: Adam and Eve being expelled from Paradise and Cain's murder of Abel.

Interestingly, one of the subjects is thought to derive from Nordic myth – and to indicate how themes from distant countries could be brought by pilgrims travelling along the route to Santiago de Compostela. A warrior stabbing a dragon on the right-hand side is believed to be Sigurd, the hero of Icelandic myth. The scene below of a blacksmith at his anvil represents the making of his sword, and there are other scenes from his story.

The two rows of arches at the top of the porch, with their benign statues of the Apostles, form a contrast to these scenes of frenzied activity and imagination. They are the work of the other principal sculptor who worked at Sangüesa, who is known as the Master of San Juan de la Peña (see page 141) because of the capitals he carved in the cloister there – and who also worked in San Pedro el Viejo in Huesca (page 126).

In the centre of the upper row is Christ in Majesty, surrounded by the four evangelists: the winged man for St Matthew and the three 'beasts' for the others. On either side is an angel. Beyond them and in the lower row are the twelve Apostles, each carved individually and standing composedly in an arch.

Overall, the porch forms a perfect entity. But there are differences between the various parts, and it is thought that it consists of works taken from two separate doorways that were brought together when a single porch was being constructed.

The tympanum, for example, is framed by a pointed arch that encroaches slightly on the figures at the far left and far right of the line of Apostles underneath the main scene, and this suggests that there was once an arch of a different form.

Also the various animals, monsters and tiny scenes on the triangular spaces to the left and right of the arch appear to have been put there without any specific theme or plan. So they may well have been brought from elsewhere, rather as was done on the west porch of Leyre (see page 174).

It is surprising, for instance, to see the three creatures representing evangelists, the lion, the bull and the eagle, placed at random among the other pieces. So the presumption must be that they were once part of a group, together with a winged man representing St Matthew, that surrounded a Christ in Majesty on another doorway.

But none of this detracts from the splendour of Sangüesa.

San Vicentejo

The chapel of **San Vicentejo** stands on the top of a small hill a few miles south of Vitoria with a few houses to one side and beautiful rolling country all round. It is an immaculate example of late Romanesque, with some slightly pointed arches both inside and out and a number of exquisitely carved capitals.

It is not known for sure when and for whom this chapel was built, since there is another church that serves the tiny parish. But a surviving inscription gives 1162 as the date of its dedication, and though it is simple, it is a building of high quality.

It consists of a single nave of two bays, a short choir bay and an apse. The nave has pointed barrel vaulting supported by two transverse arches, and the choir bay is similarly vaulted. The apse has three windows, all set within pointed arches, in the semicircular wall below it.

You can appreciate the charm of the chapel when you approach it from below. The outer wall of the nave is relatively plain, apart from an arched entrance doorway at the western end and a small circular window. But the apse has an unusually elaborate design, and it stands out strongly.

Engaged pilasters with an angular cross-section divide it into five panels, and within each of these there is a pointed arch that rests on engaged columns, the two outer ones blind and the other three framing the windows. Above the arches and just below the cornice is one of San Vicentejo's distinctive features, blind cusped arches, Islamic style.

Chapel of San Vicentejo

There is an array of carved capitals, some on the main pilasters, some on the shorter columns that support the five arches. Most of them are of intricate plant patterns, though there is the occasional monster's head to be seen spewing out tendrils; and there are two quite crude carvings of a pair of humans that were presumably brought from elsewhere, one on a pilaster, the other inserted sideways high up in the central panel.

The three apse windows are set deep within the pointed arches, with a pair of smaller, round arches over them. In each of them the innermost arch has an intricate plant and tendril design.

The most intricate, and exceptional, designs are to be seen inside the chapel, on the capitals immediately below the two transverse arches, one placed in the middle of the nave and the other dividing the nave from the choir bay.

Their arrangement is a complex one. On each wall of the nave each of the arches rests on an angular pilaster similar to those on the outside of the apse together with two engaged columns, one on each side of it. The capitals of all three are linked, and the sculptors have taken advantage of this space to create some particularly ambitious designs.

One of the four arrangements, on the south side of the nave, was never completed. But the other three are both fanciful and delicate, displaying an

Capitals in San Vicentejo

extraordinary degree of expertise. They all have a combination of leaves and flowers, imaginatively worked. One, on the north side, has a human face at the centre. The other one on the same side also has a human face, but this one is spitting out tiny dragons.

There are other features of San Vicentejo that are worth looking at. On the south side of the choir bay is a niche covered by a pair of small round arches, both of them decorated with more fanciful plant designs.

Finally, there is a line of stonework that runs all round the chapel, including the apse, at a level just above the capitals, and it has a number of tiny, but carefully worked corbels beneath it. There are dragons, snakes, a toad and a harpy. There are also human faces, not least one that has two snakes entering through the mouth and leaving through the eye sockets.

Torres del Rio

The village of **Torres del Rio**, just off the road that runs south-west from Pamplona towards Logroño, has a small church, or chapel, that is both original and exotic. It is octagonal in form – with an apse built out from one of its sides – and

Funerary chapel of Torres del Rio

in its interior it has a magnificent Moorish-style cupola that creates the effect of a bursting star.

The cupola is an elaborate construction which must have been the work of Moorish or Mozarabic builders, using techniques that had been developed in Córdoba and elsewhere in Islamic Spain. Its vault is supported by eight slightly pointed arches that each spring from the middle of two of the sides of the chapel and cross over each other overhead. Eight more ribs rise from the corners where the sides of the octagon meet, and at the centre of the arches is an open circular space that is filled by a small dome: a cupola within the cupola.

It all combines to form a complex and intriguing pattern.

Like Eunate (see page 172), which is not far away, the chapel of Santo Sepulcro in Torres del Rio was long thought to have been built by the Templars, and modelled on the Church of the Holy Sepulchre in Jerusalem, also octagonal. There is no evidence for that, however, and it is now believed that it too was essentially a funerary chapel for pilgrims who died on the route to Santiago de Compostela, which passed through Torres.

It has a tower which is built over the cupola and which, like the chapel itself, is octagonal; and on one of its sides it has an unusually sturdy turret that contains a staircase leading up to the roof. So it is thought that the tower would have been a feature often found in cemeteries of the Romanesque period: a 'lantern of the dead' in which a fire was regularly lit, symbolizing the eternal life of the soul.

Little is known of the chapel's origins. But it has been dated to the end of the twelfth century or the beginning of the thirteenth, and there is some evidence that it belonged to the Knights of the Holy Sepulchre, one of the military orders created in the course of the Crusades, which was active in Spain at that time.

It is a harmonious structure, both inside and out. On the outside engaged columns run all the way up to the cornice between the faces of the octagon, and each of the faces has three levels, divided from each other by strips of stonework that run round the building. The uppermost level is the most decorative, with arched windows complete with columns, capitals and archivolts in seven of the eight faces (the eighth is occupied by the staircase). The simple corbels under the cornice are, like the cupola, Moorish-influenced.

Up above, the tower is virtually a miniature version of the main body of the chapel. Together with the apse that protrudes from one side of the chapel and the staircase on the opposite side it makes a satisfying ensemble.

Inside the chapel the lower part of the walls is plain, as if to provide a contrast to the flamboyance of the cupola above. The apse too, which is slightly pointed and framed by a pointed arch, is quite simple. But there are good capitals beneath

Moorish-style vault in chapel of Torres del Rio

the arch – the Deposition from the Cross and the Visit of the Three Marys to the empty tomb. There are more on the arched windows on either side of the apse and at the top of columns which, like those outside, run all the way up to the base of the cupola.

There are also more signs of Islamic influence. It is interesting that in the capitals on either side of the apse the women's dress is distinctly Moorish. And up in the cupola there is a narrow space in the middle of each pair of arches at the point where they spring from the centre of one of the sides of the octagon. In these spaces are narrow windows that are filled by Moorish-style patterned stonework and have tiny cusped arches above them.

Tudela

The city of Tudela, roughly halfway between Pamplona and Saragossa, was taken from the Moors by Alfonso I, el Batallador, the Fighter of Battles, king of Aragon and Navarre, in 1119. This was a relatively late date in the story of the *reconquista*, and the building of what is now the cathedral of **Santa María**, which was erected on the site of the principal mosque, only began towards the end of the twelfth century. It continued into the thirteenth, and the cathedral is, therefore, predominantly Gothic in style.

The basic plan, however, is Romanesque, and there are several features in that style. That includes the doorways at each end of the transept and not least the splendid west doorway, which was some years later and already showing Gothic tendencies. It has a large pointed arch filled by no less than eight archivolts, all of them covered with tiny carved scenes.

Above all it includes the cloister, also begun in the twelfth century and completed in the thirteenth, which has carved capitals on all four sides. They are placed on sets of two or three columns that have round arches between them, and have a wide range of subjects, mainly stories from the New Testament, but also incidents from the lives of saints and scenes in which birds or monsters are caught in tendrils.

The cathedral was originally built as a collegiate church for the use of Augustinian canons. It became the seat of a bishop in 1783, and has been a cathedral ever since – though the diocese of Tudela was abolished in 1851 and it came under the authority of the bishop of Tarazona, a few miles to the south-west.

The west doorway is known as the Doorway of the Last Judgment. Much of the detail on it is quite small, but it is well worth a careful look. The capitals of the

Tudela cathedral: capitals in cloister

columns that support the archivolts have stories from the Old Testament. Adam and Eve are shown being expelled from the Garden of Eden, for instance, and Cain and Abel with their respective offerings of a sheaf of corn and a sheep.

The carvings on the archivolts are broadly divided into depictions of the bléssed on the left and the sinners on the right, though that is not an invariable arrangement. Those on the left look generally serene, while there are scenes on the right of sinners being thrust into a fire by devils.

Even more time is needed for the cloister, given the number of capitals, and it is time well spent. The New Testament stories begin in the northern and eastern sides, the first to be constructed, and range from the Annunciation to the Resurrection and Ascension. The south side has the death of the Virgin Mary and her Assumption, as well as the lives of various saints, among them John the Baptist and St Paul. The symbolic designs of animals, birds and plants are on the west side, the last to be built, as well as the story of the rich man and the poor man at his gate.

The faces are full of feeling whether the scene is the Marriage at Cana, the resurrection of Lazarus or the Entry of Christ into Jerusalem. The Last Supper is shown, with the head of St John resting on Christ's chest. So is the Descent of Christ into Hell: he is grasping Adam by the arm in order to take him out, while

Eve is just behind and various faces, both of devils and crowned heads, are looking on.

There are other churches in Tudela that are at least partly Romanesque. The
church of **San Nicolás**, for example, was rebuilt in the eighteenth century, but
retained a Romanesque tympanum on its façade. It shows the Trinity by presenting God the Father sitting in a mandorla and holding the Son in his arms while a
dove representing the Holy Ghost is overhead among some floral decorations.

Around the outside of the mandorla are the four figures symbolizing the
evangelists – a lion for St Mark, a calf for St Luke, an eagle for St John and a
winged man for St Matthew – and two seated saints, one of them St Nicholas.

Tudela cathedral: capital in cloister

Cantabria

Cantabria is a fairly small region that, like Asturias and the Basque Country, stretches from the mountains of the Cantabrian range to the north coast of Spain. There are links through the mountains to the south, and this was one reason why Mozarabs, with the support of some local aristocrats, decided in the tenth century to build a church in Lebeña, at the beginning of the Liébana valley. It is a good example of their style in a lovely setting.

Near the coast is a later and very different church, Santa Juliana in Santillana del Mar. Santillana was at one time a pilgrimage centre, and its inhabitants became prosperous on the money that this brought in. Santa Juliana was constructed in the late twelfth century and, though it has been added to since, much of it is unchanged and it has some good late Romanesque carving.

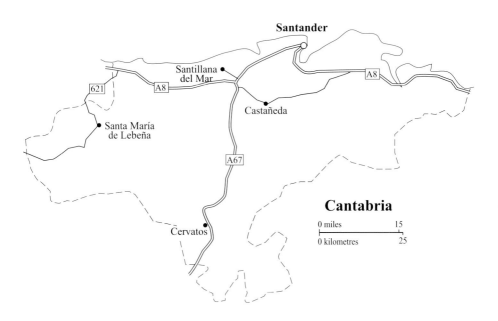

Not far away, but already in the foothills of the mountains, is the village of Castañeda, which also has a church of the late twelfth century. It too was modified in later years, and it too has good late Romanesque carving.

Cervatos is completely in the mountains, with lovely scenery around it. This was the sort of setting that often appealed to monks, and Cervatos's church was at one time part of a monastery. Like those of Santillana and Castañeda, it dates from the late twelfth century, and like them is worth visiting both for the building itself and for the range of its carvings.

Castañeda

The village of Castañeda, some miles south-west of Santander, has a good example of the small Romanesque churches built in northern Spain in the late twelfth century. The village is in the foothills of the Cantabrian mountains, known as 'La Montaña' by the people of those parts. The church stands alone on a gently sloping hillside not far away, a chunky but well-proportioned structure made up of several different elements, all built in yellowish stone.

Like Santillana del Mar (see page 203), **Castañeda** was initially the site of a monastery, but in the eleventh or twelfth century it was turned into a college of canons, and the church was constructed under that regime.

Not all of it is Romanesque, but it has a deep-set Romanesque doorway which stands out from the wall at the western end of the church and has a succession of round archivolts that recede far inwards. They rest on columns that are topped by capitals with pairs of animals on them, though many of them are badly worn.

Beyond it, on the south side of the church, is a bell-tower that is also Romanesque. Most of it is quite plain, but it has a pair of open round-topped arches on each face near the top, and above them a cornice decorated with corbels.

The east end has a large central apse with three arched windows and another array of corbels; and there is a smaller, plainer apse on the north side. There was once a second side apse to the south, but it was pulled down in the eighteenth century to make way for the neo-classical chapel that is still to be seen inside the church. Above the central apse is another, stocky tower that rises over the transept crossing and encloses the cupola.

Inside the church, there is a excellent view from the body of the nave. You see the rounded form of the cupola rising above the crossing, supported by squinches that each consist of four small arches; and beyond it the semicircle of the apse, ringed by two sets of round arches, one above the other. The broad round arches

Collegiate church of Castañeda

that support the weight of the cupola are decorated with capitals, and there are more capitals in the apse.

The arrangement of the sanctuary is similar to that of other churches in the region, and an appealing one. There is first a short bay that is barrel-vaulted and has blind arches complete with capitals at floor level on either side. Beyond it is the apse. This has four more blind arches which also have capitals and are more ornate but continue the line of those in the bay; above them three plain arches that frame windows.

It is interesting that at Castañeda the Romanesque form of the sanctuary has not just been preserved, but has been left clearly visible. In some other churches that form has been obscured by the introduction of a reredos of later date.

There are numerous capitals and, as so often, they add life to the ensemble. The subjects are largely animals, birds and plant designs – a pair of lions with a single head, eagles with spread wings, a lion crushing a human head – but there are also human figures. Adam and Eve are depicted on one of the capitals of the transept crossing, and another shows a man who could be Samson struggling with a lion.

On one of the capitals of the apse there are three scenes which are perhaps related and open to interpretation: two of them have men fighting, in one hand to hand, in the other with swords, while on the third a man and a woman are embracing.

There have been some post-Romanesque additions to the church. On the north side a Gothic aisle was built on some years after the original church was completed. On the south is the neo-classical chapel. But the nave is original: it is short, consisting of three bays, and covered by a barrel vault. So are the small apse on the north side and the arm of the transept to which it is attached.

The essentially Romanesque character of Castañeda has been preserved.

Cervatos

There are often Romanesque churches to be found in remote corners of the Spanish countryside, in areas that used to be more densely populated than they are now. One such is the little church of **Cervatos**, which was once at the heart of a monastery, and then a college of canons, but now stands alone on the edge of a small hamlet.

The setting is an attractive one, among rolling hills not far from the source of the Ebro. The church, which is thought to date from the late twelfth century, has the fine lines of late Romanesque and some good, and original, carved stonework.

Its best feature is an elaborate doorway on the south side. It has a line of six snarling lions, possibly showing the influence of Persian design, across the lintel; and above them a tympanum consisting entirely of interwoven leaf and stem patterns. It is like embroidery, and it too could derive from a Near Eastern or Arab original. It is in any case unique in the world of Spanish Romanesque.

The church stands on a slope above the hamlet, and its various parts, all built in a yellowish stone, stand out clearly as you approach it: a tall apse with three arched windows, each containing two columns topped by carved capitals; the rectangular body of the church, made up of a single nave with the doorway and two other arched windows on its south side; and a stocky but well-proportioned bell-tower at the west end, its upper levels decorated by two rows of arches.

There are capitals on the outside of the church, as well as inside. High up on the bell-tower a centaur is apparently firing a bow and arrow at a man on horseback. In one of the windows on the outside of the apse there are two that are unashamedly obscene, and there are corbels under the cornice above that are also suggestive. Clearly the sculptors were given a free hand in demonstrating sin – and the importance of avoiding it.

The south doorway is a deep one. It has three columns on each side, all with

Collegiate church of Cervatos: tympanum over south door

capitals carved with animals, and above them seven receding archivolts. At their
centre is the tympanum, with the row of lions below it, and below them the lintel
itself, which has the same carved patterns, leaves and stems, as the tympanum.

On either side of the doorway are more carved figures, badly worn. The most
prominent are Adam and Eve on one side and Daniel in the lions' den on the other.
Above Adam and Eve are the Virgin and Child and St Michael; above Daniel an
angel and St Peter.

Inside the church the nave has lost its Romanesque vault, which was replaced by
rib vaulting in Gothic style in the fourteenth or fifteenth century. But the sanctuary is intact, and characteristically Romanesque. It opens out of a tall, round arch
at the east end of the nave, and is encircled by two rings of smaller round arches,
one above the other, under the spherical form of the apse. The ten lower arches are
blind, their columns topped with capitals. The three higher ones frame windows,
and are linked at top and bottom by a string course with a chequerboard pattern.

The capitals inside the church are as lively as those outside. The sculptors clearly
had a predilection for lions, and there are several of them to be seen. The capital
on the north side of the large arch leading into the sanctuary has a heaving mass
of lions together with a few human faces, and there are others in which humans
and lions are intertwined.

Cervatos: lintel over south door

There are also eagles, standing with their wings spread on the opposite side of the large sanctuary arch, for instance; and the capitals on the ring of blind arches have a range of subjects, from animals caught in thickets and birds confronting each other to purely decorative patterns. One has a little figure of St Peter carrying his crozier and his keys, and on the other side a naked woman whose breasts are being gnawed by serpents – the traditional representation of lust and its punishment.

The remote little church of Cervatos has a character of its own.

Cervatos: saintly figure on outside wall

Santa María de Lebeña

Deep in a remote Cantabrian mountain valley south-west of Santander, and surrounded by towering peaks, is **Santa María de Lebeña**, a small but sophisticated church built in the middle of the tenth century by Mozarabs. Largely plain on the outside, though with an appealing pattern of roofs, cornices and corbels, it has a complex arrangement of horseshoe arches, each supported by columns topped by Corinthian-style acanthus capitals, in its interior.

The capitals are set at slightly different heights, and the arches run both east-west and north-south. So there is a three-dimensional effect, and almost a sense of movement as the arches spring from clusters of columns and rise at right angles to each other.

The church is best approached from the north, because the road runs through some spectacular scenery in the narrow La Hermida gorge, which is several miles long and has the river Deva flowing down below and bare mountains up above. This is the edge of the Picos de Europa range, which is on the western side, and there are more mountains to the east.

The Liébana valley opens up as you drive south, and the church can be seen on rising ground near the handful of houses that are the hamlet of Lebeña,

Santa María de Lebeña from south-east

Moorish-style corbels on Santa María de Lebeña

surrounded by trees and with jagged rock-faces soaring up into the sky behind. It has been given some later additions, a bell-tower at the western end, and an arcade running along the north side, but they do not conflict with the clear lines of the original structure.

There is an interplay of the tiled roofs that cover the various parts of the church and are set at different angles. Most interesting are the distinctive corbels that can be seen under the cornices. They are carved with simple but decorative plant and star designs, and their form is characteristic both of Islamic work in the south of Spain and of the style brought north by the Mozarabs. A narrow frieze, also with formal patterns, runs beneath them.

It is known that the founders of the church were Alfonso, count of Liébana, and his wife Justa, and it is thought that they may have been immigrants from Andalusia, perhaps Seville. The Liébana valley had its attractions because, though it was remote, it had links both to the north, to Asturias and Cantabria, and to the south to León and Castile; and by the tenth century the process of *reconquista* had extended the control of what had become the kingdom of León beyond the Cantabrian mountains onto Spain's central *meseta*.

Seen from the outside, the church has an almost rectangular floor plan, with just a slight protrusion in the middle of the east end that marks the sanctuary. Inside, it is carefully divided up: there is a modified version of a Greek cross, with arms of equal length, in the centre, and the spaces between the arms are all filled.

The sanctuary forms the eastern arm, and is flanked by two side-chapels, all three having square ends. West of it, instead of a single bay that would have marked the centre of the cross, are two bays, each of which has a horseshoe arch, one pair higher than the other, on either side; and beyond each arch is a square or rectangular space like the arm of a transept. Further west is the single bay that forms the fourth arm of the cross and has a walled-off chamber on either side.

The two bays at the centre each have an open rectangular space above, and the two spaces are linked to form a tall feature visible on the outside of the church. They are covered by a single barrel vault, and there is barrel vaulting over every other part of the church – though you can see that the various vaults are at different heights and even run at right angles to each other; those over the arms of the two 'transepts' go from north to south.

This variety is a feature of the little church, and clearly deliberate. It is also seen in the clusters of columns and capitals that support the various arches. The most elaborate are the two in the centre of the nave, each of which has four more or less free-standing columns around a square central pillar; their capitals are at different heights. The same is true of the two clusters to the east, each of which has three columns and capitals of different heights.

Santa María de Lebeña is predominantly Mozarabic in style, with features brought north by immigrants. But it is also possible to identify earlier influences: Visigothic in the floor plan and the formal designs of the external frieze, and Asturian in the layout of the east end, with its three more or less rectangular chapels, the central one slightly protruding. Alfonso's architect made a most successful synthesis.

Santillana del Mar

The collegiate church of **Santa Juliana** stands on the outskirts of Santillana del Mar, a picturesque little town not far from the coast to the west of Santander. Parts of it are post-Romanesque, but it has some superb late Romanesque capitals in both the church itself and the cloister, and in spite of the mixture of styles it looks distinctive and commanding as you approach it down a cobbled street lined with old houses.

The formal doorway which stands out prominently on the south side of the church is largely Romanesque, though it has been much restored. The pediment at

Collegiate church of Santillana del Mar: view from village

its top, with a statue of St Juliana in the centre, was put there in the seventeenth century. Also from the seventeenth century is the row of round arches that runs along the outside of the nave above the doorway.

But the circular tower with a small double window at the top is Romanesque, and so is the crossing tower behind it. So too is the east end as a whole, although you have to walk round the back of the plain building that contains the sacristy to see it. It has three apses, the central one much larger than the two others, all with decorative windows and carved corbels under the eaves. Above them is the square crossing tower, its effect lightened by a pair of windows on its east face and two pairs of blind arches higher up.

The stonework on the south doorway is badly worn, but at the centre, above the receding archivolts, is a carving of Christ in Majesty. He is seated in a mandorla that is being supported by four flying angels, all horizontal. On either side are the twelve Apostles, though they are hard to identify.

Santillana is a corruption of Sancta Iuliana, the name of a young woman who was martyred in Nicomedia, now the Turkish city of Izmit, in the late third or early fourth century. The monks who founded a monastery in this remote region of Spain, perhaps in the eighth century, claimed to have her bones. This made

Santillana del Mar: carving on south doorway

Santillana an attractive pilgrimage centre, and since in addition it was on an early pilgrim route that ran along the north coast of Spain to Oviedo and then on to Santiago de Compostela, it became an increasingly prosperous place.

In the eleventh century, or perhaps later, the monastery was turned into a college of canons which was not just rich, but politically influential. The town's wealth continued for several centuries, and the many fine townhouses, or *casonas*, which are still to be seen in Santillana, some built with money made in the Spanish colonies in the Americas, are an indication of the resources its inhabitants once had.

The church was built in the second half of the twelfth century, presumably over an earlier structure: there is a window in the choir that is surrounded by two horseshoe arches, and this could be a surviving part of an older, Mozarab-influenced, church. The new building appears to have been modelled on the church of San Martín in Frómista (see page 220). It has a nave and two side-aisles, a transept with an unusually high cupola over the crossing, and the three apses.

There have been changes since the twelfth century. There is now Gothic-style rib vaulting over the nave and aisles, put there in the thirteenth century after the original wooden vault had collapsed. In the eighteenth century a choir and organ

Cloister of Santillana del Mar: St Michael fighting monster

were installed over the west part of the nave, together with an ironwork screen, and that has had the effect of shortening it. Also in the eighteenth century the cupola was remade after it too had collapsed.

The sarcophagus under the transept crossing with the carved figure of St Juliana was put there in 1453, and the splendid reredos which fills the central apse – and now contains the remains of St Juliana – also dates from the fifteenth or sixteenth century.

But the form of the three apses and the barrel vaulting over both arms of the transept are Romanesque, and the basic structure of the church has been retained. Not least, it still has the original columns and no less than sixty-three capitals. They are an outstanding collection that includes not just formalized designs of plants, birds and animals, with a snake here, human masks there, but several descriptive scenes.

There are horsemen charging each other with lances, others attacking a wild beast, two men fighting with huge swords and, interestingly, a group of builders at work. Adam and Eve are there, and St George slaying the dragon, but it is noticeable that there are no Gospel scenes.

There are also a few pieces of late Romanesque sculpture that have been removed from their original positions, perhaps on a doorway that no longer exists.

Santillana del Mar: capitals in cloister

Carved reliefs of four saints – Peter, Paul, John and James – have been placed on the front of the altar, and there is the figure of Christ in Majesty in the chapel under the bell-tower at the west end of the church, above a simple twelfth-century font.

The cloister is one of the glories of Santillana. This is because of the exceptional quality and variety of its capitals, which were installed on three of its four sides, and because, unlike the church itself, it is uniformly Romanesque or very largely so: two arches were rebuilt in Gothic style, and a few others are pointed. The columns are generally grouped in pairs, or sometimes in clusters of four, and this means that each of the capitals extends over two columns.

Like those inside the church, they date from the late twelfth and early thirteenth century, and like them they include many of the characteristic subjects of the Romanesque period: abstract patterns, entwined plants and flowers, animals caught in thickets, and a wide range of Biblical and other subjects.

There are Old Testament scenes: Daniel in the lions' den, Nebuchadnezzar's dream, Samson struggling with a lion. There are also, unlike the capitals inside the church, a good number of Gospel scenes. On the south side of the cloister, which runs along the church and was probably the first to be built, are Christ in Majesty, the Baptism of Christ, the beheading of John the Baptist, the Crucifixion and the Deposition from the Cross.

The north side has only abstract designs based on plant motifs. On the west side there is a mixture of historiated capitals and abstract designs. The abstract designs are, as so often in Romanesque sculpture, extraordinarily beautiful, with plant tendrils weaving in and out, and the alternation of these intricate works with scenes of great human or angelic activity creates an unforgettable effect.

One capital has the Last Judgment, in which St Michael is weighing souls on a set of scales that Satan is trying to tilt in his direction – a subject that was taken from the mythology of ancient Egypt, in which souls were weighed in the presence of Osiris, and became common in Romanesque art. On another Paradise is represented by two rows of tiny heads sheltering under the wings of an angel. Elsewhere there are angels engaged in a struggle with monsters.

The cloister at Santillana is a place to spend time and to walk around slowly, in order to take in everything that is there to be seen.

Castile and La Rioja

Castile was one of the most dynamic parts of Spain in the Middle Ages and for some time afterwards, as we have observed. It consisted of territory that had to be resettled after being won by force of arms from the Moors, and in the process several of the most remarkable Romanesque churches in Spain were built there.

The well-preserved church of St Martin in Frómista, west of Burgos, was one of the earliest, dating from the late eleventh century, when Romanesque was beginning to be widely used in Spain. A new church was erected at about the same time at Santo Domingo de Silos, south of Burgos, and though the church itself has been almost entirely demolished, its lovely cloister has survived.

Segovia, further south, has an exceptional array of Romanesque churches, as noted earlier, and they are a fascinating aspect of a generally fascinating city. One of the earliest is San Justo, which is unusual in having some well-preserved frescoes; while San Millán is one of the best examples of a slightly later style. And there are several others that have great appeal.

There are also some exceptionally interesting churches in pre-Romanesque styles in Castile. I have already mentioned that there is the Visigothic church of San Juan de Baños de Cerrato, near Palencia, that dates from before the Arab occupation of the eighth century; and there is another one, less well preserved but with some outstanding carvings, at Quintanilla de las Viñas, a few miles north of Santo Domingo de Silos.

Many Mozarabs settled in Castile some centuries later when they moved north from the Muslim-ruled part of Spain; and they were responsible for a number of churches that have the distinctive characteristics that they brought with them. The shrine of San Baudelio de Berlanga, south-west of Soria, is an unusual, and intriguing, example, with an ambiance of its own. West of Valladolid are two churches that also have great charm: San Cebrián de Mazote, which is wholly Mozarabic, and Santa María de Wamba partly.

There are more Mozarabic features in San Millán de la Cogolla, an ancient monastic church west of Logroño in the small neighbouring province of La Rioja.

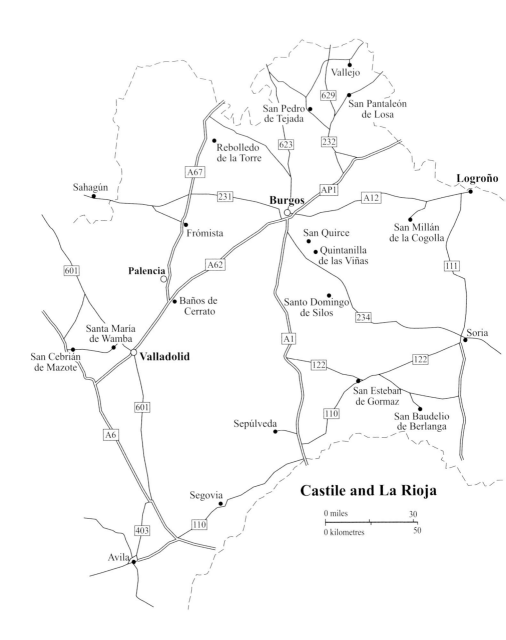

Vallejo

629

San Pedro
de Tejada

San Pantaleón
de Losa

232

623

Rebolledo
de la Torre

Logroño

A67

Sahagún

231

Burgos

AP1

A12

Frómista

San Quirce

San Millán
de la Cogolla

601

Palencia

A62

Quintanilla
de las Viñas

111

Baños de
Cerrato

Santo Domingo
de Silos

234

Santa María
de Wamba

A1

Soria

San Cebrián
de Mazote

Valladolid

122

122

601

San Esteban
de Gormaz

110

San Baudelio
de Berlanga

Sepúlveda

A6

Castile and La Rioja

Segovia

0 miles   30

403

110

0 kilometres   50

Avila

This is particularly interesting because it also has parts that date back to the Visigothic period, and others that are Romanesque.

Castile, or rather Old Castile, which is now part of the region of Castilla y León, is a vast area that extends across the *meseta* from the Cantabrian range in the north to the mountains west and north of Madrid. Down in the south is the impressive walled city of Avila, which has several Romanesque churches, while up in the north are others that are built in the foothills of the Cantabrian range.

They include San Lorenzo de Vallejo in the Mena valley north-east of Burgos, which has a wealth of carvings, and the enchanting chapel of San Pantaleón de Losa, perched high up on top of its outcrop of rock. Further to the west is San Pedro de Tejada, built in a commanding position on the slope of another valley and also rich in carvings.

North-east of Burgos is the church of Rebolledo de la Torre, which also stands in a valley far out in the country and has an attractive feature that is found in a number of Castilian churches, but not usually so far north: a porch-gallery.

Most of the porch-galleries are part of churches in Segovia and the surrounding region. They consist of a line of open arches that is decorated with capitals and corbels; and in some ways they resemble one side of a cloister. They were most often built onto the south side of a church, but they sometimes extend to the west end, and there are a few on the north side.

There are good examples in San Esteban de Gormaz and Sepúlveda, both north-east of Segovia, as well as in Segovia itself.

Avila

The massive walls that surround Avila, a mile and a half long and punctuated by no less than eighty-eight towers, are one of Spain's most spectacular sights. And they can be regarded as Romanesque, as I have written, since they were built at the end of the eleventh century, at the same time as many of the churches in that style.

Avila also has some of those churches, and some good ones. The largest is San Vicente, an imposing building that stands just outside the walls, near one of the main gates. It was completed in later styles, but it was initially Romanesque and its basic structure dates from that time, as does some very fine carving.

Two smaller ones are the enchanting San Andrés, which was built at the same time as the walls and stands in a small park not far from San Vicente, and San Pedro, which has a stylish west front that can be seen at the far end of a square that extends out from the walls.

Avila's cathedral is inside the walls and largely Gothic, but it has some Roman-esque features. The most notable is the apse at its east end, which is heavily re-inforced and battlemented, and forms part of the walls.

This fortified city is a symbol of the turbulent conditions of life in the tenth, eleventh and twelfth centuries, when much of Castile was still being fought over by Christians and Moors. The city's origins go back to Roman times, but it had been virtually abandoned during the centuries of Muslim rule, and it was only at the end of the eleventh century that positive steps were taken to revive it by encouraging people from elsewhere to come and settle there.

The new policy followed the capture of Toledo by Alfonso VI, king of Castile and León, in 1085, and the need to have proper support, in the form of established population centres, for the new frontier to the south. Avila, Segovia and Salamanca were among the places to which settlers were directed, and in Avila the new population was put to work building the walls. It is said that they were completed in nine years between 1090 and 1099.

The foundations of **San Vicente** were laid at that time. The site was the place at which, according to tradition, three young martyrs, St Vincent, St Sabina and St Cristeta, a brother and two sisters, had been put to death in the early fourth century. Their relics were preserved for several centuries in a church that was erected there.

But Avila, like other northern Spanish cities, suffered from the devastating raids by al-Mansur, the Muslim leader, at the end of the tenth century. So early in the following century it was decided to move the greater part of the relics to a safer place, the monastery of San Pedro de Arlanza, south of Burgos.

The relics were returned to Avila from San Pedro, now a ruin, in 2000. But San Vicente has an ornate memorial, in the form of a cenotaph, that was put up in the twelfth century to commemorate the martyrdom of the three saints; and there is some excellent carving to be seen along its sides.

It is the view from the east that gives the best idea of the basic Romanesque structure of this church. There is a splendid east end, with three tall apses, that was a product of the first phase of building. Each of the apses is decorated with arched windows and an array of corbels under its cornice. Behind them are the two arms of the transept, which were left plain apart from another line of corbels at the top, and a square tower over the crossing.

By way of contrast the view from the west shows the mix of styles in the rest of the church. It seems that after that early phase, which included the lower parts of the nave and side-aisles, there was a break in the work. When it resumed in the second half of the twelfth century there was a new master-mason, thought to have

San Vicente in Avila

been called Fruchel, and the style had changed to one that was closer to Gothic.

So there is a sizeable narthex at the western end of the church, with a tall pointed arch in the centre and on either side of it a substantial but uncompleted tower. Over the northern end of this façade is a curious bell-tower with pointed windows and a serrated design on all four sides that was built on in 1440.

The porch-gallery that runs along the south side of the church was also added relatively late, at the end of the thirteenth or early in the fourteenth century. Its arches are round at the top, but they are tall and more Gothic than Romanesque in style.

One of the best features of San Vicente is the carving on its external doorways, and particularly those in the narthex and under the porch-gallery on the south side of the church. The carving in the narthex is thought to have been the work of Fruchel, or whoever was the master-mason in the second phase of building, and is one of the masterpieces of the Romanesque period.

On the central pillar is the seated figure of Christ, while on either side of the doors are five elongated and immaculately carved figures representing Apostles. The two nearest to Christ are also seated and are presumed to be St Peter and St Paul, who was often treated as though he was an Apostle. The others are standing and are presented as talking to each other in pairs, giving animation to the whole doorway.

The doorway is also richly decorated. There are two bulls' heads above the figure of Christ, and lions' heads over St Peter and St Paul. Above, in the archivolts, is an array of ornate and intricately carved designs, mainly of formalized plants. A frieze of tiny carved figures, set in arches like a line of corbels, runs along the top.

Much of the tympanum is plain, but there are two small semicircular scenes set into it. Though they are in bad condition, they can be seen to illustrate the story of Dives, the rich man, and Lazarus, the poor man at his gate. On the left are Dives sitting at his table and Lazarus standing outside, with dogs licking his feet. On the right are the events after their deaths, the soul of Dives being grabbed by devils and that of Lazarus being carried up to Heaven by angels.

The south doorway is less decorated, but it also has full-length figures and they too are outstanding. They date from different periods. There are two saints, probably St Sabina and St Vincent, on the right-hand side which are full of charm and have a simplicity that indicates work of the first half of the twelfth century, as do the capitals above their heads.

Opposite is the Annunciation. The figures of the Angel Gabriel and the Virgin Mary have flowing robes and a greater sense of movement, and are thought to date from the second half of the twelfth century. The same is true of the seated king, perhaps Alfonso VI, who is next to St Sabina to the right of the door.

San Vicente: saintly figures on south doorway

The interior of San Vicente gives a further illustration of the combination of styles. The three apses at the east end are clearly Romanesque in form, but the reredos behind the main altar is much later, as are the baroque altars in the two sidechapels. And the two arms of the transept have Romanesque-style barrel vaulting, although there are pointed arches on all four sides of the crossing, and the octagonal cupola above it is Gothic from the late thirteenth century.

Most striking is the nave. The lower part is Romanesque, with its round arches and simple capitals, mostly consisting of formal plant designs. So are the side-aisles, which have groin vaulting over each bay. But there is Gothic-style rib vaulting over the nave and, while there is only a little light, coming in from small windows high up in the clerestory, this vaulting gives a sense of height to the whole interior.

Standing under the south arch of the transept crossing is something that is unique to Avila, the memorial to the three young martyrs, St Vincent, St Sabina and St Cristeta. One's first sight is of the tall, flamboyant structure, resting on four columns and topped by a pointed roof, that was built over it in the fifteenth century. But beneath that is the original empty tomb, or cenotaph, dating from the late twelfth century, and it is an unforgettable work.

It is rectangular in form and constructed on two levels. At the lower level are cusped arches that are supported by patterned columns and have little carved figures in the spaces between them. The upper level is even more striking because, as well as carvings of Christ in Majesty and the Adoration of the Magi at its two ends, it has a sequence of little scenes, five on each side, that vividly illustrate the events that led to the deaths of the three saints, their being taken up to Heaven and their eventual burial.

The story begins with the young Vincent before Dacianus, the Roman prefect, and later shows him and his sisters escaping to Avila, with soldiers in pursuit. They are shown being stripped of their clothes after being arrested and then being tortured to death. Finally a Jew who had mocked them is attacked by a snake, as a result of which he converts to Christianity and builds a church in their memory. The last scene is the construction of their tombs.

Like much else in San Vicente, the memorial is more Gothic than Romanesque. And like the other features it demonstrates the transition from one to the other.

San Andrés is a contrast because it is a small and simple church, and is wholly Romanesque. It too has a well-shaped east end with three apses, similar on a smaller scale to that of San Vicente. It also has pretty arched doorways both at its west end and on its south side; they have carved animals on the capitals and rosettes and other formal plant patterns on the archivolts.

There are more capitals inside the church. The nave and the two side-aisles have timber ceilings, and so the nave is relatively wide, leading to a pleasing sanctuary area with a short choir bay and the rounded form of the apse. The chapels in the two side-apses are different from each other; the one on the north side is similar on a smaller scale to the main one, that on the south has an unusual cusped arch that shows Islamic influence.

Avila: San Andrés from south-east

The capitals are particularly vigorous: savage-looking lions, a man being
attacked by two snakes, a mounted
warrior charging a winged monster,
and several other dramatic scenes. And
there are some original abaci above
them. They give an extra edge to the
appeal of San Andrés.

San Pedro is also an old church,
and an appealing one. Building began at about the same time as that of
San Vicente, and as happened with San
Vicente it extended over a long period.
So the basic form is Romanesque, and
it has the proportions and volumes of
that style. It too has an east end with
three apses, a transept with a square
tower over the crossing, and a doorway

Capital in San Andrés

Avila: west front of San Pedro

on the north side that is decorated with capitals and formal plant designs in the archivolts.

Like San Vicente, however, San Pedro has much that is Gothic in its interior, not least the vaulting of the nave, the side-aisles and the transept.

The most visible sign of the combination of styles is in the west front, which stands prominently at one end of the Plaza de Santa Teresa. Its form is Romanesque, with the ends of the nave and side-aisles clearly outlined and a rounded doorway complete with archivolts at the centre. But above the doorway is a fine rose window that is purely Gothic – and demonstrates the interaction of the two styles that is characteristic of Avila.

Baños de Cerrato

The little basilica of **San Juan de Baños de Cerrato**, in a village a few miles south of Palencia, is a delightful example of a church of the Visigothic period, as I wrote earlier. It is known that it was consecrated in 661, having been sponsored by King Reccesuinth, and though it has been modified over the years, it retains the distinctive character of the architecture of the seventh century.

Baños de Cerrato, Visigothic period

Seen from the outside it is quite plain, a long, low building constructed with large, well-cut blocks of stone. But the entrance is through a horseshoe arch at the western end which still displays much of its decorative stonework. Beyond that is an elegant nave, which is lined on both sides by columns supporting more horseshoe arches, and at the far end a larger horseshoe arch that forms a barrel vault over the sanctuary.

The design is in many ways a small version of the basilicas of the early Christian period – though the horseshoe arch is a specifically Spanish feature. It shows how much continued as before after the Visigoths had taken over from the Romans. There are aisles on either side of the nave, and narrow windows filled with lattice patterns that form a clerestory above the arches of the nave and let in some light.

The columns are mostly of marble and, as elsewhere, were clearly taken from dismantled monuments of the Roman imperial period. They are topped by capitals in a stylized Corinthian style, each of them slightly different.

The sanctuary is an early example, for the medieval period, of a barrel vault. It ends in a flat wall which has a small window in the shape of yet another horseshoe arch in the middle, also filled with a lattice pattern. A sculptured frieze made up of formalized flower patterns runs along either side at the springing of the arch.

Nave of Baños de Cerrato

The origins of the church, and its village, can presumably be traced to the existence nearby of a spring, which is still there, covered by a horseshoe arch. Hence its dedication to John the Baptist. It is possible that Reccesuinth himself visited the spring, and that this prompted him to order the construction of the church.

The church's consecration and Reccesuinth's sponsorship are recorded in an inscription set into the wall above the arch of the sanctuary. It gives the date of 699, which corresponds to 661 in present-day chronology.

The church was originally slightly larger. It had a transept and chapels that extended from each of its arms.

Baños de Cerrato: lattice window

The spaces on either side of the sanctuary, now transformed into chapels, were left empty. The earlier chapels are no longer there, although signs of where they once were can be seen on the outside wall.

There have been other changes. The bell-cote over the west entrance is not original, nor are the lattice patterns in the windows. But the form of the church and its decorated stonework, inside and out, demonstrate some of the achievements of the Visigothic period.

Frómista

The small town of Frómista, set in the flat plains some twenty miles north of Palencia, has one of the most imposing and best-preserved Romanesque churches in Spain. It was built over a very short period, probably in the last third of the eleventh century, so that it is all of a piece in its style, and there are almost no later additions to speak of. (See page 4.)

Dedicated to **San Martín**, it stands prominently in an open square on the edge of the town, displaying the three-dimensional quality and the harmonious balance between its component parts that are the mark of Romanesque. It is all in honey-coloured stone, and each part stands out clearly: the nave and two side-aisles; the transept, octagonal crossing tower and three apses which together make up a fine view of the east end; three formal doorways; and an uncommon feature, two plain cylindrical towers which frame the west front.

The only sign of later building work is a small doorway with a pointed arch which provides an entrance into the south arm of the transept. But it is not conspicuous.

These outside features are richly decorated. There are round-topped windows in the apses, the crossing tower and the two side walls, all with carved capitals, and an exceptional array of corbels all round the church which mark out the lines of the various tiled roofs. And there is more carved decoration inside. The nave and the aisles, all three barrel-vaulted, have capitals of high quality, some historiated and some with animals, birds or formalized plant designs, along their whole length.

Not all the capitals are original, and it has to be said that the church was extensively restored between 1896 and 1904, with results that are criticized by some specialists. Several additions that had been made over the centuries were removed at that time, not least an additional tower built on top of the transept crossing in the fifteenth century. In the process a number of corbels and capitals that were in poor condition were repaired or removed to the Palencia museum and replaced with copies.

Frómista: corbels on outside

That restoration accounts for the immaculate condition of the church today. It also means that for some critics it is now no more a wholly authentic Romanesque church of the eleventh century. But there is no denying that the restoration, both of the structures of the church and of its sculpture, was convincingly done.

San Martín was founded as part of a monastery by Queen Munia, or Mayor, the widow of Sancho, the powerful king of Navarre known as el Mayor, and this was recorded in her will of 1066. She was herself the daughter of Count Sancho of Castile, and it was through his marriage to her that Sancho of Navarre became Count of Castile himself. After his death in 1035 two of their sons became kings – García of Navarre and Ferdinand I of Castile and León – as did another, illegitimate son of Sancho's, Ramiro of Aragon.

The church was built soon after the cathedral of Jaca (see page 130) and San Isidoro in León (page 295). This was the time when the Romanesque style was just beginning to be adopted in Spain, as a result of influences from beyond the Pyrenees. Jaca, Frómista and León were all on the Camino de Santiago, the pilgrim route that led to Santiago de Compostela, and the stonemasons of Frómista were influenced by what had been done in the two larger centres, especially Jaca.

The result was a church which has the lines of early Romanesque style and the carved decoration that went with it. Before going inside it is worth taking time to walk round the outside and look at all the detail there. Figures vary, but there are more than three hundred corbels, combined with a typically Spanish feature said to have originated in Jaca, stone carved in chequerboard strips.

The corbels range in subject from plain geometric designs to animals, birds and humans in a variety of poses. Over the west door is a donkey playing a stringed instrument. Elsewhere are a hunchback, a female contortionist and Samson struggling with a lion.

There are fewer capitals, but they too are varied in subject-matter. About half of them have formalized plant designs, with intricately entwined tendrils. The others include lions, a scene in which monkeys have snakes whispering in their ears, pelicans and a number of historiated scenes with humans in them. They are often not easy to make out or interpret, but there are people grasping snakes, a couple embracing and another scene of Samson and the lion.

Many, perhaps all, must have been intended to convey a message or point a moral. But they are irresistible today for the vitality of the carving.

The inside of the church is just as compelling. The nave is a well-balanced creation in which a succession of round arches – the transverse arches of the vault and the two arcades which separate the nave from the aisles – leads the eye to the rounded form of the apse and the three windows which are below it.

The light is not strong because there are no windows in the nave; such light as there is comes from the windows in the aisles. But the soft light in the nave contrasts, as so often in Romanesque churches, with the greater luminosity of the transept crossing and the choir at the east end. The crossing is formed by four arches that support a square, above which squinches, each decorated with a figure representing one of the evangelists, transform it into the base of an octagonal cupola.

Then there are the capitals. They were probably the work of a different artist or artists from those outside, but have an equal vitality. Here too there are elaborate formal designs made up of leaves, cones, flowers and abstract patterns, often showing the influence of Islamic art. Here too there are animals, birds and humans, often struggling with each other.

There are some Biblical scenes: Adam and Eve facing each other at the moment when Eve takes the apple from the serpent's mouth; their expulsion from Paradise; the Adoration of the Magi. There are others which, while not obviously related to Biblical stories, must have had symbolic significance: small human figures clinging on to the backs of large lions; pelicans fighting snakes; a naked, pregnant woman surrounded by lions.

One outstanding capital shows a group of people in the centre of whom someone is being arrested. It may represent the taking of Jesus in the Garden of Gethsemane, though that is far from certain.

Frómista: capital in interior

Perhaps surprisingly, there are references to classical literature. One capital appears to depict the fable of the fox and the crow. Another dramatic one, admittedly a copy of an original now in the Palencia museum, shows Orestes on the point of stabbing Clytemnestra, his mother, to death and already being threatened by Furies grasping snakes.

Not all the capitals are easy to see, or to understand when you do see them. But they are an exceptionally vigorous collection in a superb setting.

Quintanilla de las Viñas

High on a hillside south-east of Burgos, near the village of Quintanilla de las Viñas, lies what seems at first sight to be a plain stone building with a doorway but no windows. The ground around it has been cleared, and it has a fine position, with views out over the valley below.

When you get closer, however, you see friezes of carved stonework which run round the outside, with animals, birds, plants and much else set in some ornate tendrils; and these exquisite designs point to the origin of what is now such a simple structure. It is the surviving part of a church that is thought to date from the late seventh or early eighth century, when the Visigoths were still the rulers of Spain.

Inside are more carvings, also in relief, and they include some of the best from that distant time, stylized but moving. Two free-standing blocks of stone each show a human figure supported by angels who is looking fixedly out. One of them is carrying a cross and perhaps represents Christ. Two other blocks, which

Quintanilla de las Viñas, Visigothic period: carved designs on outside

are still in place on either side of a horseshoe arch, show figures representing the sun and the moon, each set in an almost circular frame and also flanked by angels.

Santa María de Lara, as it is now known, has had a troubled history, like so many other early Spanish churches. It survived the Arab occupation which began in the eighth century, and is known to have been restored late in the ninth century, probably by Mozarabs, after the region had been recovered by Christian forces. In the eleventh century it was donated to a neighbouring monastery, San Pedro de Arlanza, but after that went into decline.

The story of its rediscovery is a dramatic one. In the summer of 1921 a local parish priest, Don Bonifacio Zamora, was out walking when he came upon the ruins of the little church, hidden by trees and bushes. He had some difficulty in attracting the attention of experts, but before long Santa María de Lara was recognized for the fascinating survival that it is.

Excavations have shown that it was once much bigger. It had an entrance porch at its western end, a nave with two side-aisles, a transept and a rectangular east end. The east end is still there, as is most of the transept, and it is those parts that are decorated on the outside by the carved stone friezes. But the rest of the church has gone.

These outside friezes have a particular charm. They are quite shallow, but they include prancing lions, strutting peacocks and dangling bunches of grapes, as well as some mysterious clusters of letters which may well be acronyms or some other key to the identity of donors.

The inside of the church is quite dilapidated. But it still has some of the perfectly shaped stone blocks, similar to those visible on the outside, that were used to build the church. And the horseshoe arch, which frames the entrance to the

Quintanilla de las Viñas: carved designs on outside

sanctuary from the transept, is still impressive, with carvings in relief that are similar to those in the friezes on the outside.

Most impressive of all are the carvings of the sun and the moon – the latter, unusually, a grim-faced man with a beard, rather than a woman – and above all, the two commanding figures who look out from the free-standing blocks of stone. The angels in all four works have a special grace.

Rebolledo de la Torre

The village of **Rebolledo de la Torre** is in a remote and picturesque valley northwest of Burgos, and some distance from the area in which most of the churches with porch-galleries are found (see page 211). But it has one of the best of them, and you see it as you walk up to the church, standing as it does on rising ground on the edge of the village.

The gallery is in fact the only surviving part of a church that was built in the late twelfth century and largely pulled down years later. The body of the present building dates mainly from the sixteenth century, and it is of course incongruous to see a Renaissance-style tower at the western end, up above the gallery. But the gallery has survived, with all its intricate decoration, and the combination of the two styles is in no way jarring.

The gallery runs along the south side of the church, as was usual, and still provides the main entrance to the church. This is a formal arched doorway set into a section of wall that protrudes beyond the outer line of the gallery; it has archivolts above and columns complete with capitals on either side. The arch is slightly pointed, which is an indication of its relatively late date, while the open arches of the gallery on either side of it are rounded.

Porch-gallery of Rebolledo de la Torre

There are ten of these arches – a set of three to the east of the doorway, a set of four to the west of it and beyond that another set of three. Up above is a cornice decorated with corbels; and pairs of tall, slender columns run all the way up to it at either end of the gallery and also between the two sets of columns to the west of the doorway. There are vigorously carved capitals on the columns supporting the arches, as well as those on either side of the door. So altogether it is a well-balanced composition.

There is also another point of great interest in the gallery. At its western end is a tiny arched window that has carved decoration immediately above it on both its inner and its outer sides. The carving is worn, but on the inside it widens out into a cusped double arch that has an original, and delightful, rendering of the story of Adam and Eve.

Adam and Eve are each shown reclining over one of the arches. Adam is resting his chin on his hand, while Eve stretches out her hand towards the angle at which the two arches meet, where the serpent is emerging from the Tree of Knowledge. On either side is a tall formal tower; up above, a frieze of plant designs.

The outside of the window is also decorative, though less original. The window has a single column topped by a lion's head, while set into the stone around it is a larger arch that rests on two columns, each with a carved capital. Over the columns and in an archivolt are more plant designs.

What this outer face also has, however, is information about the origins of the church of which the porch-gallery was part. Specialists have deciphered an inscription indicating that it was built in about 1186, and that the gallery was the work of Juan de Piasca.

Such information is very rare, and nothing else is known about this talented builder and sculptor. There is a certain similarity to some of the subjects illustrated in the cloister of Santo Domingo de Silos (see page 258), but those of Rebolledo are thought to be later. In any case they have a distinctive character of their own.

Some of the capitals are largely decorative, with plants, leaves and entwined tendrils. But others recount stories. We see Samson struggling with a lion, St Michael and a devil confronting each over the scales on which a soul is being weighed, and two armoured and helmeted horsemen who are facing up to each other.

One capital describes the fate of the rich man who goes to Hell. On one side he is on his death-bed, his wife grieving behind his head, two lions under the bed and up above a person with a chain round his neck who must represent the rich man's soul. On another side he is standing in Hell with his bag of money round his neck and being tormented by a devil.

Rebolledo de la Torre: capital in porch-gallery   *Carved decoration in porch-gallery*

Other scenes are even more fanciful, or allegorical. A warrior is fighting a snake-like monster that has grabbed his shield in its jaws; two centaurs are advancing on each other, one armed with a bow, the other with a shield. Others are made up almost entirely of animals and monsters in various postures, usually with a background of formal patterns.

It makes for a lively collection, and it is enhanced by some decorative abaci – as well as the little figures up above in the corbels. Some are tiny winged monsters, others human beings playing musical instruments.

San Baudelio de Berlanga

Seen from the outside, the shrine of **San Baudelio de Berlanga**, south-west of Soria, is a simple box-like structure on an empty hillside, given interest only by the horseshoe arch that frames its main doorway. But when you enter it, you step into a world of fantasy and exotic forms that has few parallels, even among the Mozarabic churches of Spain.

In front of you is a single column that turns into an imaginary palm-tree, its branches formed by eight horseshoe arches that fan out from it and support the

'Palm-tree' in San Baudelio de Berlanga

vault. To the east is a doorway framed by another horseshoe arch that leads to a small chapel. Opposite is a small forest of columns, linked by yet more horseshoe arches, that is reminiscent of the great mosque of Córdoba.

These columns support a raised section or choir, reached by a flight of steps, on which there is a tiny shrine within the shrine, built up against the central column. Most extraordinary of all, there is another tiny space high up above the central column, resting as it were among the spreading branches of the palm-tree, and protected by them. It can just be seen through tiny horseshoe-shaped openings between the 'branches', and is covered by an Islamic-style cupola resting on arches that criss-cross.

It is not known what the purpose of this space was. It could have been a place for storing sacred objects or manuscripts, or it could have been the ultimate secluded spot for a hermit.

The origins of San Baudelio go far back into the past. It is clear that the setting was chosen long ago by a hermit or hermits because there was a cave in the hill-side and a spring nearby. The spring is still there, and so is the cave, whose open-ing can be seen in the south-western corner of the shrine. The mosque-like array of arches acts as an approach to it.

The building that is there today is thought to have been built at the end of the

San Baudelio de Berlanga: mosque-like interior section

San Baudelio de Berlanga: mural painting

eleventh century by Mozarabs at a time when the area around it had only recently been taken from the Moors, and life there was still precarious. It is a telling example of the extent to which Islamic ideas and architectural forms had been incorporated over the years into the culture of the Mozarabs.

The palm-tree held a special place in the thinking both of the early Christians and of Muslims. For Muslims, it was especially blessed, and it was sacred for some Christian writers too. So the palm-tree in San Baudelio could be seen as a link between Heaven and Earth, and the raised section with its tiny shrine a symbol of the Mountain of God on which a hermit lived and prayed.

Today it is not permitted, for reasons of safety, to climb the steps to the upper section. But it can be seen from below.

Not the least of the attractions of San Baudelio are the frescoes with which it is, or was, decorated. They are later than the building, mostly dating from the twelfth century. But there must have been a time when every stretch of wall or vaulting was covered by painting, and such a display in such a small space, in addition to the original style of the shrine, must have been overwhelming.

Such paintings do not often survive. In San Baudelio many of them did, and they include some unforgettable images, among them exotic animals, hunting scenes and episodes from the New Testament. Sadly, most of the best frescoes were sold by the owners of the shrine and stripped off the walls in the 1920s, in spite of a campaign to prevent this being done. Some of them are in the Prado Museum in Madrid. The majority are now in various American museums.

In spite of what has happened, however, enough of the frescoes remains on the walls to give an idea of what was once there, and to add colour to the overall effect. The various patches of painting that are still there have been restored. So there are two bulls head to head on the wall opposite the entrance, and the arches that spring from the central column to form the branches of the palm-tree have a range of designs on and between them.

The sections of the vault between the arches have lost much of their paint, and are in any case hard to see from below. But enough survives to make it possible to identify a sequence of Biblical scenes, from the Annunciation to the Flight into Egypt.

One interesting point is that the lower levels of San Baudelio had subjects that were not overtly religious – the animals and the hunting scenes, for instance – and even had similarities with subjects found in Islamic art, while the Biblical stories were in the upper parts.

A poignant feature is the surviving imprint of some of the frescoes that have been removed. The most striking example is the painting of a dromedary that is now in The Cloisters Collection in New York. The paint was so deeply embedded in the plaster covering the wall that even now, after the top level has been removed and transferred to canvas, the dromedary with its tall legs and long curving neck is still clearly visible. The same is true of a jumping dog just next to it.

San Cebrián de Mazote

The church of **San Cebrián de Mazote**, a village on the banks of the Bajoz river west of Valladolid, is one of the masterpieces of Mozarabic architecture. It has an eye-catching display of horseshoe arches, not just along the sides of the nave, but at both ends and even in the transept, and they create an ensemble that is both complex and evocative.

Basically, the church has the simple lines of an early Christian basilica. But the shape of the arches is reminiscent of the Islamic world of the south of Spain, and they give it an exotic character. It is worth walking round the church for the fine views to be had from every angle, not least of the often complex arrangement of arches and vaulting.

At the eastern end there are three chapels, all framed by the horseshoe arches.

Monastic church of San Cebrián de Mazote, from east

The two side chapels are rectangular, but the middle one, which contains the main altar and provides the central focus of the church, has a horseshoe-shaped floor plan. It is covered by an apse that is divided into segments and reflects that form.

There is a similar structure at the opposite end of the nave where, as in some early Christian churches, there is another apse, also framed by a horseshoe arch. Here too the floor plan is horseshoe-shaped, and there is a segmented vault overhead.

Then there is the transept, which also has a distinctive form. It is in three parts: the crossing at the centre that is formed by four arches and on each side an arm that extends a short way beyond the side-aisle and has arches that link the aisle with one of the chapels. The outer wall of each of the arms is rounded, and so is the vaulting over it, which is apse-like and, once again, split into segments.

San Cebrián is thought to date from the early tenth century. Like Santa María de Wamba (see page 253) and San Miguel de Escalada (page 309), it would have been part of a monastery established by Mozarabs. It too may well have been founded by an abbot and his community of monks from Córdoba, who dedicated it to St Cyprian (Cebrián), a bishop of Carthage martyred in the third century.

The monks came to a largely unpopulated part of Spain that was just north of

Nave of San Cebrián de Mazote

East end of San Cebrián de Mazote

San Cebrián de Mazote: carving of holy men, Apostles or evangelists

the Duero river, which provided a defensive line, and had not long before been taken from the Moors by Alfonso III, king of Asturias. Mozarabs were encouraged to settle there, and they brought with them their own distinctive style of architecture.

Today San Cebrián has a tall and ornate bell-tower built onto its western end many years later. But apart from that the outside retains its tenth-century style. It has a clear arrangement of its various features, which are all strongly outlined: the nave and the side-aisles, the transept and the crossing tower, and the three chapels at the east end.

The various apses are all contained within rectangular outer casings and, like the other features, covered by sloping tiled roofs. The roofs have different heights, and this diversity adds to the three-dimensional effect. Interestingly, it is not unlike that of San Pedro de la Nave (see page 313), a church built more than two centuries earlier in the Visigothic period.

Inside the church, it is the horseshoe arches which immediately attract your attention. It is worth looking carefully at the column capitals of the nave, however. They all derive from the acanthus motif of the Corinthian style, but with variations on the theme. The columns themselves are mostly of marble.

The nave is lit by two rows of small, round-topped windows, and covered by a timber ceiling, as are the side-aisles. The crossing has a segmented stone vault built onto it in the twentieth century.

Finally, there is a tiny block of carved stone displayed in the apse at the western end of the nave, that has the remains of two busts alongside a battlemented building and a decorative frieze. It is a haunting little piece which possibly represents two Apostles or evangelists. And it is certainly old, perhaps dating from the Visigothic period, but no one knows how old.

San Esteban de Gormaz

The small town of San Esteban de Gormaz, south-west of Soria, was once dominated by a Moorish castle, and its ruins can still be seen on the rock that towers over the roofs and the narrow winding streets. The town also has two small Romanesque churches, San Miguel and El Rivero, which are interesting for having early examples of porch-galleries, a feature often found in the area between Soria and Segovia, and especially in Segovia itself (see page 211).

The gallery in the church of San Miguel is thought to have been the earliest of them all, dating from the second half of the eleventh century. And though its stonework is worn, you can enjoy its orange-coloured stone and its well-balanced proportions when you walk up to it through the narrow streets of San Esteban.

The gallery is south-facing, as they most often are, and it has seven round arches, which was considered to be a significant number at the time, on its outer edge. The entrance is at the top of a flight of steps, through the central arch. The three arches on either side rest on relatively short, squat columns which have sizable capitals and abaci above them. Up above are two decorative windows in the wall of the church itself. To the east is an apse.

An unusual feature is that though the capitals are quite simple and are worn, so that it is often hard to make out their subjects, it has been possible to establish that some of the human figures on them are wearing Moorish dress – caftans and turbans – and so are some of those on the corbels above.

The same is true of several carvings in El Rivero, and the conclusion is that though San Miguel and El Rivero were clearly Christian churches being built in Romanesque style, the workmen were probably Muslims, who were skilled builders. It seems that it was not found shocking by church officials at the time that they incorporated scenes from contemporary life, including people wearing Moorish-style clothes.

San Esteban was in an area which was much fought over by Christians and

Moors in the ninth, tenth and eleventh centuries. A few miles away to the south-east is the village of Gormaz, which has a much larger Moorish castle, complete with its outer walls, sprawled over a hillside above it.

The frontier shifted back and forth, and there was a lot of contact between the two communities when they were not fighting each other. When a town like San Esteban finally came under Christian control it continued to have a Muslim community, and it has even been suggested that for a time its people dressed in Moorish style.

Apart from the gallery, **San Miguel** is a simple structure with a single nave covered by a timber ceiling, like many other country churches. The sanctuary consists of a short bay covered by a barrel vault and an apse with a single, narrow window in the centre. The church is now used to exhibit scale-models, documents and other objects that provide interesting information about its period.

But it has its gallery, which may have been built before the body of the church, and it is worth spending time to look at the capitals on it, damaged though they are; also the corbels on the two cornices above, over the gallery and under the roof. Apart from the human figures, the capitals have a camel, a peacock and a vicious-looking snake that is attacking some other creature. They also show Moorish-style fortresses, one of them with a line of defenders.

Among the corbels is a portrait of 'Magister Julianus', who was in charge of the building of the church, dated to 1081. He is a studious figure who is displaying a book that is open on his knees. There is also another coiled snake.

El Rivero is a larger church with a fine position on a high point on the outskirts of San Esteban. From it there are views both out over the rooftops – including San Miguel – and of the surrounding countryside.

Its porch-gallery is thought to have been a slightly later copy of San Miguel's, and it too is appealing when seen from below. But not all the original gallery survives. There are nine round arches, and only the five to the east of the entrance arch are completely as they were built in the late twelfth century. The entrance arch is partly original. The three arches to the west of it were built later; they rest on solid, square pillars and have no capitals.

The five original arches have columns topped by capitals, however, and a line of corbels above them. Their subjects are similar to those in San Miguel, and here too the capitals are badly worn. There are animals, birds, a man fighting a monster, and the people in Moorish dress.

There is also a decorative doorway leading from the gallery into the church itself; and it too has capitals, including another coiled snake that is devouring a bird.

But El Rivero also has two exceptional capitals that are better preserved than

El Rivero in San Esteban de Gormaz: men in Moorish clothes

El Rivero in San Esteban de Gormaz: window with carved capitals

El Rivero in San Esteban de Gormaz: porch-gallery

any of those in the gallery or in San Miguel, and that can only be seen from inside the church sacristy. They are on either side of an arched window that was part of the original east end and has a wealth of carving both above and below. It was covered over, and protected, when the sacristy was built.

Both capitals show people wearing turbans and flowing Moorish robes. One of them is particularly intriguing because of the way in which it depicts the Flight into Egypt. Mary is wearing a turban and caftan and is sitting side-saddle on a horse (though her legs are not clearly shown). Joseph, who is leading the horse, is smaller and is not dressed in the same impressive style. The infant Jesus features as a small head that appears to be emerging from the saddle, or possibly from between Mary's legs.

Like San Miguel, El Rivero has a simple structure inside, with a single nave leading to the sanctuary. The nave has been much modified in later years, as have other parts of the church, and only the apse, now filled by a reredos, remains of the twelfth-century structure.

San Lorenzo de Vallejo

The church of **San Lorenzo** in Vallejo, a village in the valley of the river Mena south-west of Bilbao, is a handsome example of late Romanesque style. It was built in two distinct phases, the sanctuary consisting of an apse and a short choir towards the end of the twelfth century and the main body of the church some years later in the early thirteenth.

The outstanding feature is its apse, which is most decorative and has a form that is unusual for Castile. Constructed in a golden-coloured stone, it is relatively tall, and is divided into five sections by engaged columns that run all the way up to the cornice. Shorter columns form clusters around those principal ones, and each of the sections has an arched window and above it a Lombard band – the line of small blind arches identified with northern Italy and often seen in Catalonia.

The central window is deeper than the others, and is the only one that opens into the church; the others are blind. But they all have capitals on their columns, and so do the other columns of the apse, with subjects ranging from formal plant designs to human masks. And there are corbels under the cornice which add to the effect.

The single bay of the choir is built in the same stone, and is flanked by even denser clusters of engaged columns that all run up to the cornice. Some have capitals at the top: one presents a complex scene in which a hunter carrying a falcon on his wrist stands at the centre while a horseman is trampling a human figure on one side, and Samson grappling with a lion on the other.

San Lorenzo de Vallejo from south-east

San Lorenzo de Vallejo: detail of west doorway

Not all the columns have capitals, however, and it is thought that these quite substantial clusters were originally intended to support a more ambitious structure, perhaps a cupola, which was abandoned in the interval between the two construction phases.

Between the clusters are the windows of the bay, one on each side of the church. They too are arched, with columns and capitals, and open into the church. But instead of a Lombard band they each have a smaller cornice complete with corbels set into the stonework above them.

There is also much to be seen in the main body of the church. This is constructed in a whitish stone that contrasts with the golden tone of the sanctuary, and has a single nave without side-aisles. It has three formal doorways, on the west, north and south, and it is significant that they all have slightly pointed arches, an indication of their late date.

They all have some carvings, but those in the archivolts of the western doorway are the most interesting, though several of them are damaged. There is a range of lively little figures: a centaur poised with bow and arrow to shoot a deer, pilgrims complete with staff, satchel and the shell representing the long road to Santiago de Compostela, a king on his throne, a musician, Adam and Eve and the Tree of Paradise, an angel, sphinxes and a few others.

Inside the church the difference between the two parts is less marked. The nave, the choir and the apse all have rib vaulting, another indication of their late date, and this makes for a good view along the length of the church, with a succession of round forms leading to the east end – even if a seventeenth-century tomb in Renaissance style breaks the Romanesque symmetry in the apse.

In the inside too there are clusters of columns, tall and fine, and they have good capitals that are placed at the springing of the arches and often spread across several columns. Several of them can be well seen from the gallery at the back of the nave.

The subjects include formal plant, tree and flower designs, but there are also winged monsters fighting, monsters with multiple heads, and armoured knights confronting each other. One scene has a little group of men in a boat, another shows people opening a coffin, and the corpse that is inside can be clearly seen. The sculptors of San Lorenzo were certainly not lacking in imagination.

Little is known about the origins of the church. A tombstone in the nave has an inscription saying that a certain Dona Endrequina de Mena gave 'this house' to Jerusalem, and that is almost the only indication of who founded the church.

But it is known that Vallejo was the site of a commandery of the Knights of St John of Jerusalem. So the inscription must be referring to that, and it is possible that the link with the Knights of St John led to influences from elsewhere, and in particular from Catalonia. That would explain the unusual form of the apse.

San Millán de la Cogolla

The tiny church of Suso, part of the monastery of **San Millán de la Cogolla**, is an ancient foundation which, like several other early Spanish churches, has a remote and beautiful setting. It is built into the rock face high above the valley of the little river Cárdenas, in the Rioja region south-west of Logroño, and from it there are views out over the valley and the thickly wooded hills that surround it.

Today there are two churches, both dedicated to San Millán. The monastery is still an active one, and the later of the two, known as Yuso, is in the valley down below, where the principal buildings now are. They are a large and impressive complex, mainly Renaissance in style, and they dominate the village.

Suso can just be seen from there, peering out from among the trees, and visitors have to travel up to it by minibus.

The little church is interesting for its long history and for the fact that it has features in three different styles: Visigothic, Mozarabic and Romanesque. It has

Monastic church of San Millán de la Cogolla

horseshoe arches in different parts of its double nave and, at one end, a pair of round, Romanesque arches which demonstrate the contrast between the two styles.

The oldest parts of the church go back to the sixth century, when a small monastic community formed around San Millán, or Emilianus, a local shepherd boy who became a hermit and was credited with numerous miracles. Emilianus seems to have been of Hispano-Roman, rather than Visigothic, stock. He lived for over one hundred years, from 473 to 574. *Cogolla* means a hood, and so he presumably became known for the one that he wore.

Emilianus and his companions settled near a spring in three cavernous spaces that they must have found or hollowed out from the rock, and that are still to be seen inside the church, along one side. This bare site was later enlarged, and the church built, when Emilianus's tomb came to attract large numbers of pilgrims. Then in the eleventh century his remains were taken down to Yuso in the valley below, and after some years monastic life came largely to an end in Suso.

The church is still there, however, and the entrance is an inspiring one, through an open gallery, once a simple cloister, from which the visitor looks far out over the valley. The arches that run along the outside were built in the nineteenth century, but the doorway into the gallery has a venerable horseshoe arch. So has the door that leads into the church itself, and it has some decorative capitals on one side.

Rough stone sarcophagi from the tenth and eleventh centuries – the tombs of local nobles and of three queens of Navarre – line the walls.

Once inside the church the visitor sees the three horseshoe arches which divide the nave in two, and beyond them the caves in which Emilianus and his followers lived. The central cave was once the site of Emilianus's tomb. Under a round arch complete with simple carved capitals it has a cenotaph that dates from the twelfth century: a lifesize carving of the saint, recumbent and surrounded by kneeling figures.

The cave to the left of it goes far into the rock and it was there that monks and others were buried; one account speaks of finding more than one hundred and twenty tombs. The cave to the right is framed by a horseshoe arch and was the focal point – the choir or sanctuary – of a small basilica-style church that can still be identified at the eastern end of the present church, running across the line of the nave. It has two bays, each framed by horseshoe arches and covered by a square stone vault formed by arches that cross each other in a star-shaped pattern.

San Millán has had a tumultuous history, and there is some doubt about the dating of its various parts. What can be said for certain is that the three caves were in use in Visigothic times. The central one has little niches in the wall that must have been used by Emilianus and his successors for their devotions. What is not certain is whether any of the surviving horseshoe arches also go back to the Visigothic period, or were built by Mozarabs several centuries later.

Like most of the rest of Spain, the region came under Muslim rule in the eighth century. The presumption is that monastic life continued at San Millán for the next two centuries, as it did elsewhere, though nothing is known about that. Then in 923 the region was recovered by Christian forces from Navarre and León, and the monastery took on new life. But in 1002 it was sacked by al-Mansur, the Muslim leader from Córdoba, in his last campaign into northern Spain and much of it was demolished; the marks of burning are still to be seen.

It is clear that the basilica at the eastern end of the church was built or, perhaps, rebuilt by Mozarabs in the first half of the tenth century, after the Christian forces had first recovered the region; there is a record of its consecration in 959. It largely survived the fire in 1002, and early in the eleventh century the church was extended by building the double nave onto it. It can be seen that the three horseshoe arches that run down its centre are different in form from those in the basilica. The nave was subsequently extended further by adding the two Romanesque arches.

Moving Emilianus's relics down to Yuso was not achieved without some controversy, as can be imagined. But from then on Yuso became the heart of the monastery of San Millán de la Cogolla. Its first church, built in Romanesque style in the middle of the eleventh century, was demolished, but it still has some treasures from the Romanesque period.

Two of the most compelling are the sets of ivory carvings that were originally made for the reliquaries of St Emilianus and of St Felices, his contemporary, in the eleventh century. They show scenes from the lives of the two saints, among other subjects, in a simple but vivid style. The reliquaries were largely demolished in the nineteenth century, when French troops sacked the monastery, and many of the carvings were dispersed. They are now in museums around the world.

But many others have been preserved at San Millán de la Cogolla, where new chests have been made for them. They are an engaging sequence of scenes, and a delightful demonstration of the artistry of the period.

San Pantaleón de Losa

The tiny, dramatically placed chapel of **San Pantaleón de Losa**, in the hills roughly halfway between Burgos and Bilbao, stands alone on its rock high above the valley of the river Losa. The village is far below, and the chapel can be seen from miles away.

Approaching it is strenuous, because you have to leave your car in the village and make your way up a steep slope on foot. But it is well worth every step, because apart from the stupendous views of the valley the chapel is a most original one; and though much of it is worn it has some good decoration.

Little is known about its history. Its style is late Romanesque, and it can be dated to the end of the twelfth or beginning of the thirteenth century when this part of Castile was being repopulated. It was formally consecrated in 1207. There are a number of legends surrounding it, but there is no firm indication of why this small but elaborate chapel, which was not part of a monastery, was built on a steep hillside above the Losa valley.

The original structure consists of two parts which stand out clearly as you walk up to it. The main body of the chapel is a single, square bay that is relatively tall and is covered on the inside by a cupola. Attached to it is the sanctuary, which consists of a short choir and an apse, and because of the slope stands on slightly higher ground. Rising over them and linking the two is the bell-tower, which is essentially a tall and sturdy wall with two arches in it for hanging the bells.

Sometime after the chapel was built it must have been decided that it was not large enough. It was not possible to have an extension to the west, which would have been normal, because of the downward slope. So an extra nave, Gothic in

Chapel of San Pantaleón de Losa

style and running north-south, was built onto the north side of the chapel, and is still there.

It is the Romanesque chapel, however, that is worth seeing. The west front has a decorative doorway with an arrangement of receding archivolts resting on columns and carved capitals. Above all, it has at one side one of the unusual features of San Pantaleón: a tall human figure carrying a bag over his shoulder. Up above is a window that is blind, but also has receding archivolts, columns and carved capitals.

There are more capitals, and several of them quite distinctive, in the windows on the south side of the chapel and round the apse; and there are also capitals inside the chapel.

But who is the tall, amiable man standing by the doorway? No one knows, and he is often referred to simply as 'the giant'. It is probable that the original intention was to have a matching figure on the other side of the doorway. So one theory is that he is Adam and the other figure would have been Eve. It is even suggested that the zigzag shape attached to a column on that side – a striking but unconventional feature – was intended to represent the serpent in the Garden of Eden.

In any case the tall man is an impressive presence, and an indication that there was something special about San Pantaleón.

Much of the sculpture of the doorway is damaged, including the large piece of stone above the man's head, though it is just possible to make out a she-wolf that is feeding either two infants or her own young, coupled with an animal mauling a human being. The two capitals on the right are better preserved, but mysterious. One shows three people seated, the other the heads of people in a boat and a shape in the water that could be a whale, suggesting that it might be the story of Jonah.

One of the archivolts has another mysterious motif. On either side there are small heads, each set in a tiny square frame, and below each of them a pair of legs in a similar frame. Once again this is hard to interpret, but it has been suggested that these are prisoners.

The two windows on the south side of the chapel have capitals that must have been designed to strike fear into anyone who saw them. In the first, which opens into the body of the chapel, two capitals have formalized plant designs, but alongside them are two with masks: one displaying a diabolical grimace and a formidable array of teeth, the other an expression of acceptance, suggesting that it was the victim.

There is a similar confrontation in the second window, which opens into the choir. But there the grimacing mask is even more ferocious and seems to be glorying in the fear it is causing, while the other one is open-mouthed and obviously panic-stricken. In that window too the other capitals have more peaceful plant designs, but there are also five human heads carved on the innermost arch whose eyes are closed, perhaps implying that they are dead.

The central window of the apse is not in good condition, but it also has its drama. It too is framed by receding arches resting on columns and capitals, and one of the surviving capitals has the face of a man who appears to have a thick gag over his mouth, and to be throwing up his hands in horror. Opposite him is a pair of dragons confronting each other.

Above, filling two of the archivolts, are more of the mysterious little openings that appear on the west front: alternately a head and, below it, a pair of legs, suggesting prisoners.

The window-frame on the north side of the apse is obscured by the Gothic addition, but the one on the south, although it is blind and also not in good condition, has some attractive carving. The capital on the left has a group of three figures similar to the one on the west front; opposite is a large bird, probably an eagle. The right-hand column has a formal flower design that runs all the way up it, and there is more carving, of tendrils and an interwoven pattern, on the arch and archivolt above.

The inside of the chapel is not normally open, but an arrangement can be made through the Burgos tourist office. It is worth visiting, if only to see the structure of this unusual building: the cupola over the body of the chapel and the sanctuary with its barrel vault and apse. Two points are interesting. Since the sanctuary is on a higher level it is reached by climbing a few steps; and the main arches are slightly pointed, as are some on the outside of the chapel, which is an indication of its late date.

The capitals are simple, but vigorous. There is one that is beautifully carved, with a design made up of formal plant patterns, high up on the south side of the choir. Others have pairs of griffin-like monsters with crossed beaks, dragons devouring prostrate humans, and more masks.

San Pedro de Tejada

The little church of **San Pedro de Tejada**, in the hills north of Burgos, is an enchanting sight, for itself, for its setting and for the fact that unlike many other churches of its period which have been partly rebuilt it has retained the purity of its Romanesque style.

It stands virtually alone on one of the slopes of the broad Valdivieso valley, with the river Ebro down below and a landscape of woods, rocks and a few fields on all sides. Once it was at the heart of a monastery, and the most important one of the region, with several others dependent on it. Today there is just one rustic structure at its side, once part of the monastic buildings, but the church is still standing, with its formal west doorway, its tower and its single apse, all built in a yellowish stone that glows in the sunlight.

Above all, it still has its carved stonework, much of it restored, but perfectly conveying the artistry of the sculptor or sculptors of the twelfth century. The west doorway has a range of engaging figures, each with their own individuality; and there are many more on the corbels that run round the church under the eaves. There are also good and well-carved capitals inside the church.

Little is known about the early history of San Pedro de Tejada, but it is thought that the monastery was founded in 850, at a time when land recovered from the Moors was being resettled. It lost its leading position in the area in 1011, when it was made subordinate to a new foundation in Oña, a few miles to the south-east. But in spite of this a new church was built, probably in the first third of the twelfth century, and that, unlike the church at Oña, has survived.

Monastic church of San Pedro de Tejada

Its most visible feature as you approach it from the village of Puente Arenas below is that it is narrow and so seems relatively tall. This is due to the fact that it has only a single nave, no side-aisles or transept and a single apse at the east end. In front of you there is the west front with its doorway. The doorway has the arrangement of receding archivolts that is common in the region, and above it is an uncommon feature: a small cusped window showing the influence of Islamic style.

Beyond it is the tower, with a little turret enclosing a spiral staircase on one side and an upper level that is unusually ornate. It has engaged columns at each corner, running up to a line of corbels under the cornice, and a similar column at the centre of each face. Between the columns are double arches, each with a column and a carved capital at the centre. The arches are open on all four faces of the tower, and in days gone by a fire used to be lit in this upper space once a year on St Michael's Day, which was visible all round the valley.

The outside of the nave has arched windows and columns topped with capitals in each of the two bays. The apse, on the other hand, is relatively plain. There are no windows, but five blind arches and a string course running over the top of them. There too, however, there are corbels under the cornice.

San Pedro has a wealth of carved stonework. The cornice that juts out over the

west doorway has a small figure in low
relief of Christ in Majesty, and on the
corbels on either side double representations of the four evangelists. On
the outer edges they appear as human
figures – though with angels' wings
– two on each side, all carrying their
books. But ranged alongside the
human figures are the 'four Beasts of
the Apocalypse' that also represent the
evangelists: the lion for St Mark, the
calf for St Luke, the eagle for St John,
and the winged man for St Matthew.

Below them are small carvings in
relief of the twelve Apostles, six on
each side of the arch and including, as
was often the case, St Paul. They are
talking to each other and gesturing in
an animated way.

San Pedro de Tejada: west doorway

Lower still, on the left side, is a small and original depiction of the Last Supper.
It consists of only three people sitting at a table. In the centre is Christ, who is
staring fixedly ahead, and on his left St John, who is holding a book in his hand
and resting his head on Christ's chest. On Christ's right is a haloed figure who is
being given some food by Christ and at the same time is grasping one of the two
fish that are on plates on the table. One interpretation is that this is Judas Iscariot,
whose wickedness is indicated by the furtive way in which he is taking the fish.

Opposite is a carving of a man on his back being mauled by a large lion.

One of the many riches of San Pedro de Tejada is the exceptional array of corbels. Their subjects range from the plant world – acanthus, vines – to animals, birds
and humans engaged in many different activities. As you walk round the outside of
the church you can see an eagle, a peacock, a deer, a wild boar, a domestic pig, a
goat, a wolf. There is a monkey, usually seen as representing greed.

As for humans, there are monks, pilgrims, musicians with several different
instruments, acrobats, a builder and, not surprisingly, some corbels that convey a
moral message: a devil complete with horns and a woman with her breasts being
devoured by serpents, the traditional representation of the punishment for lust.
Even Adam and Eve are there, each on a corbel, with the Tree of Knowledge, complete with serpent, on a separate corbel placed between them.

San Pedro de Tejada: detail of west doorway

The inside of the church is simple but, in the way of the little Romanesque churches of the region, has a harmony between its different parts. The short nave is covered with a barrel vault, and beyond it is a cupola resting on an octagonal base supported by squinches. There is then a further, very short stretch of barrel vaulting before the apse, which has a ring of blind arches, resting on capitals, at its base.

Here, as at Castañeda (see page 196), the Romanesque form of the apse can be appreciated without the introduction of a reredos that, however beautiful, prevented it from being fully seen.

There are capitals in several parts of the church, but the really unmissable ones are high up on three of the main arches: the transverse arch that divides the two bays of the nave and the two arches that support the cupola. One has eagles in a design of interwoven tendrils, another a scene in which a haloed person is being addressed by an angel carrying a cross – thought to be either Christ in the Garden of Gethsemane or St Peter being released from prison.

Two other capitals have finely carved figures, probably saints, who have cups and appear to be celebrating a ritual. It is not clear what the significance is, but the capitals, like so much else in San Pedro de Tejada, demonstrate the quality of both conception and workmanship in the church.

San Quirce

The little church of **San Quirce**, about twelve miles south-east of Burgos, is not easy to find. It is privately owned and so, though it is far out in empty country between the villages of Hontoria de la Cantera and Cubillo del Campo, there are no signs to direct you to it.

But it is worth making the effort to visit the church. Arrangements can be made with the help of the tourist office in Burgos, and when you come near local villagers will help with directions. After leaving the main road you drive across an expanse of almost flat countryside. You pass through some park gates and there, down in a slight dip, is a small church of great charm, attached to a country house and farm.

The bell-tower, or at least the upper part of it, is visibly later than the rest of the church. It has pointed windows and a balustrade at the top that were built onto the Romanesque base in the seventeenth century. But the sanctuary, consisting of the apse and a short choir, is early Romanesque, probably dating from the late eleventh or early twelfth century; and the nave and the transept crossing under the tower, although built in a second phase, were added only a short time later.

Monastic church of San Quirce

The form of the apse is interesting because it is very different from others in this part of Spain. It is thought that this could be the result of influence that derived ultimately from Byzantium. The apse is not covered by tiles, as was the normal practice, but by small stone slabs, and it is slightly pointed at the top, not rounded, giving it an exotic flavour.

As so often, little is known about the origins of San Quirce. It was once the church of a monastery, founded or refounded as the surrounding area was recovered by Christian forces from the Moors. There is a tradition that it was the site of a battle won by Fernán González, the count of Castile, in the early tenth century, and that he rebuilt the monastery. It is known that the church was consecrated in 1147 when the monastery, like several others in northern Spain, was converted to a college of canons. But it would have been built some time before that.

One of its best features is its carved stonework. This is to be seen on the capitals inside the church, and also on the decoration above the two outside doorways. One doorway is on the west front, leading directly into the nave. The other is on the north side, and must originally have been the entrance to the church for monks or canons coming from the cloister and the other monastic buildings.

The west doorway is the better preserved of the two. There are some capitals on either side of the door itself, but it is the line of corbels under a cornice just above, and the metopes between them, that are outstanding for the lively little figures carved on them. The corbels tell two stories: that of Adam and Eve and that of Cain and Abel. The metopes have a range of subjects: a cock; men fighting; a man ploughing; and, surprisingly, two carvings of a man defecating.

The north doorway is bigger than the other one and was once more ornate. It is now closed and badly preserved, but it is just possible to make out the figures of the twelve Apostles on the corbels. Underneath them are, on one side, a carving in relief of Christ in Majesty surrounded by the lion of St Mark, the calf of St Luke, the eagle of St John and the winged man of St Matthew, representing the four evangelists, and on the other the Annunciation and the Visitation.

Inside the church, the two bays of the nave have rib vaulting, also put there in the seventeenth century. But apart from that the interior has retained its Romanesque style. There is a good view through the tall round arches of the crossing to the round forms of the apse, and a fine array of capitals both in the crossing and in the sanctuary.

Below the apse there are two blind arches with tiny round windows set into them, and there was originally a third. But the small window was later replaced by a bigger, round-topped one, presumably to give more light.

The central feature is a hemispherical cupola that rests on four squinches high above the crossing, and was an important part of the second phase of the building of San Quirce. Here too the structure is a rare one, with more influence from the east, perhaps even from Persia. This is partly because of the form of the squinches, which each consist of a quarter of a sphere and are set immediately below the base of the cupola. Each squinch has an arrangement like a pendentive on either side of it, and they provide the transition to the circle of the cupola's base.

If there is eastern influence in the structure of the cupola, the capitals are western in style. Those in the sanctuary are a little earlier, and range from formal plant designs to scenes of great activity. There is another carving of Christ in Majesty, but also a man being released from chains, lions fighting, and a complex group in which a woman is resisting two lions, one on each side, while two snakes are gnawing her breasts – once again, a representation of the penalty for lust.

The capitals under the cupola are more specifically Biblical. There again are Adam and Eve, and Cain and Abel, but also Noah and the flood, Abraham's sacrifice of Isaac, and Samson grappling with a lion. They are lovingly carved, and offered some vigorous story-telling in this remote corner of the northern *meseta*.

Santa María de Wamba

The church of **Santa María de Wamba**, a few miles west of Valladolid, is a handsome building which stands in a pretty village square with pine-trees along one of its sides. It is also interesting in a number of ways.

In style, it is a mixture of Mozarabic and Romanesque. Its east end, including three chapels and one bay of the nave and side-aisles, has the horseshoe arches that are characteristic of Mozarabic architecture. So the presumption is that, like San Cebrián de Mazote (see page 231) and San Miguel de Escalada (page 309), it was the work of an abbot and his community of monks who had moved from the Moorish part of Spain in the early tenth century and brought their way of building with them.

The rest of the nave and the side-aisles, on the other hand, are Romanesque, and must have been added on later, towards the end of the twelfth century. There are two bays in which the nave is flanked by the pointed arches favoured by the Cistercians, and they have composite columns topped by some simple, but appealing carved capitals. The west doorway, too, is pure Romanesque, and an ornate example of that style.

There is also, however, a third element in Santa María, tiny carved capitals that may well date back to the period of Visigothic rule, before the arrival of the Arabs.

Monastic church of Santa María de Wamba

One of them, a lovingly carved version of the Corinthian theme of the acanthus, is on the outer upright of the arch framing the southern chapel. And other fragments from those days have been found.

So it seems clear that the history of Wamba goes back to that time. Wamba was the name of one of the last Visigothic kings – he ruled from 672 to 683 – and though that in itself is not conclusive, there are indications that the village may be the site of a domain then called Gerticos, in which his predecessor, Reccesuinth, was born and buried. Reccesuinth ruled from 653 to 672, and it is likely that he founded a monastery in what is now Wamba in about 670.

This link with the days of the Visigoths may in itself have been a reason for the foundation of a new monastery by Mozarabs in the tenth century. Another factor was that, like San Cebrián de Mazote, Wamba was in the area just north of the river Duero that had not long before been reconquered from the Moors by Alfonso III, king of Asturias. It was largely uninhabited, and Mozarabs were encouraged to settle there.

The exterior of the church of Santa María makes a satisfying ensemble. As in other Mozarabic (and Visigothic) churches the three eastern chapels each have a rectangular form on the outside, with sloping roofs and cornices. Above them is a lantern tower, added later, and the nave and side-aisles extend beyond that, also

Capital in Santa María de Wamba: weighing of souls

with sloping roofs and cornices. An open colonnade has been built onto the south side of the church.

The stone of the west front is worn, but it is worth a careful look. The doorway is framed on each side by three short columns on a raised base, and there is decorative carving in the archivolts, as well as traces of rosettes in the tympanum. There is a line of corbels under a cornice just above the doorway that includes some grotesque animal heads. A grimacing face peers at you from either side of the door itself.

Once inside, it is worth taking time to look at the Romanesque capitals on either side of the nave, which, like the side-aisles, is covered by a timber ceiling. They are very simple, but engaging. They include a scene of the weighing of souls in which St Michael and a devil each hold onto one arm of the scales, which have little heads in them. There are also Adam and Eve in front of the Tree of Knowledge, a cobbler biting into a piece of shoe leather, and crudely carved animals that must have been the sculptor's idea of an elephant.

There is one capital that is different in style from the others. Like the one at the entrance to the southern chapel, it is intricately carved and may date from the Visigothic period. It has a demonic head complete with horns and surrounded by entwined tendrils.

Interior of Santa María de Wamba

Santa María de Wamba; capital from Visigothic period

The eastern, Mozarabic end of the church has the charm and the exoticism that are given by horseshoe arches. Such arches not only frame the three chapels, but divide the nave from the side-aisles. The one framing the central chapel has been reduced from its original size, but has retained its horseshoe form. All three chapels are covered by barrel vaulting that runs east-west and is itself horseshoe-shaped.

Apart from the capital at the entrance to the southern chapel, there is little decoration. But there are traces of a fresco, probably from the Romanesque period, on the wall behind the main altar. It includes circular shapes with animals in their centre.

Another exotic feature is to be found in one of the rooms attached to the north side of the church on the edge of

Santa María de Wamba: capital from Visigothic period

what was once a cloister. It is a pillar that stands in the middle of a square space and, though badly worn, supports two groin vaults that cross the space diagonally. It is thought to represent a palm-tree and its branches, like the better-preserved one in San Baudelio de Berlanga (see page 228). As I pointed out, the palm was thought to be sacred by some early Christians, and Muslims too.

Santo Domingo de Silos

One of the outstanding cloisters of the whole Romanesque period is to be found in a picturesque village set in the low hills south-east of Burgos: **Santo Domingo de Silos**. Unusually, the cloister is on two levels, with a complete set of round arches and carving on both, and the lower level is exceptional for two features: the pairs of full-length panels carved in relief at each of its four corners and an array of imaginative, often fantastic, capitals along the sides.

Nothing is known of the artists, but it is generally accepted that the Silos carvings were the work of more than one. Six of the eight corner panels came from the hand of the so-called first master, and they are in a strongly individual style which combines an almost Byzantine formalism in the overall treatment of the various scenes with a depth of emotion in the faces of those taking part. It is thought that the first master worked in the closing years of the eleventh century, and was influenced by the ivory carving of the period.

The expressions on the face of the Virgin Mary as Christ is being taken down from the cross, of Joseph of Arimathea as he takes part in his entombment, and of the disciples from Emmaus when they encounter Christ after his resurrection, are unforgettable – and so are many of the others.

There is a similar style on a smaller scale, also quite formal, in the capitals of the north and east arms of the cloister and in four of those of the west arm. It is thought that they too were the work of the first master, and here too there are exotic influences, including those of the Islamic world. The capitals include animals caught in a thicket of tendrils, horned harpies confronting each other, fabulous creatures that are part bird and part animal, and a scene in which two youths, each mounted on a winged gazelle, attack each other with axes.

The subject-matter is largely the same in the other capitals of the west arm and all those of the south, which are thought to be the work of the second master. They too include harpies, animals caught in thickets and winged monsters, as well as two historiated capitals which illustrate the events surrounding the birth of Christ and those preceding his crucifixion. But the style is more rounded and three-dimensional and in some ways more realistic. These capitals, carved in the

Cloister of Santo Domingo de Silos

twelfth century, illustrate a later stage in the evolution of Romanesque sculpture.

This evolution is very marked in the two panels in the south-west corner of the cloister, also from the twelfth century, which could be the work of other sculptors. One depicts the Annunciation and the Coronation of the Virgin Mary, the other the Tree of Jesse. The first is a particularly moving scene, the second ornate but rather badly damaged. Both have a three-dimensional quality and an elaboration of detail which are quite different from the work of the first master, showing the transition towards Gothic.

Like other monasteries in the north of Spain, Santo Domingo de Silos has origins that lie far back in the country's turbulent history. It seems, on the basis of archaeological evidence, that a monastic institution was founded there during the Visigothic period, and that it continued to exist, like a number of others, after the Arabs had occupied the region in the eighth century.

According to a legend which probably has a grain of truth, the monastery was rediscovered and revived by Fernán González, count of Castile, when he reconquered the region in the middle of the tenth century. At that time it was dedicated to St Sebastian. Again like others in the region, it must have suffered from the raids into northern Spain carried out by al-Mansur, the Muslim leader from Córdoba, at the end of the tenth century, which left it in a much reduced state.

The monastery took on new life, however, with the arrival of Dominic, later St Dominic or Santo Domingo, in 1041. Dominic had been prior of the famous monastery of San Millán de la Cogolla (see page 241), but had been expelled from there because of his opposition to King García of Navarre, within whose kingdom the monastery then lay. He was welcomed by King Ferdinand I of Castile, who was not on the best of terms with his neighbour, who was also his brother, and installed as head of what was still the monastery of St Sebastian.

Dominic proved to be both a saintly man and a good administrator who took an active part in the public events of the time. He built up the reputation of the monastery, not least by the miracles that were credited to him, so that it became a pilgrimage centre. At the same time he set about enlarging the existing church and erecting other monastic buildings. He died in 1073, and three years later he was canonized. His remains were solemnly carried into his church in the presence of King Alfonso VI, and the monastery took on the name of Santo Domingo.

Dominic's church was further enlarged by his successor as abbot, Fortunio, in Romanesque style, but it was almost completely demolished in the eighteenth century, to be replaced by the present structure which, like other parts of the existing abbey, is neoclassical. Fortunately the Romanesque cloister, which may have been begun in Dominic's time, and was certainly planned by him and continued by

Cloister of Santo Domingo de Silos: detail of Entombment

Fortunio, has survived – due, it seems, to a lack in the eighteenth century of the funds needed for its demolition and replacement.

So has one small part of the Romanesque church, the south arm of the transept. In it can be seen, hung up high on the walls, the shackles and chains of people who were once prisoners of the Moors during the days of the *reconquista* and were released, so it was believed, through the intercession of St Dominic.

The focal point of a visit to the cloister has to be the pairs of carved panels at the corners. The two panels that are simplest in design, but no less compelling than the others, are those in the south-east corner which depict the Ascension and Pentecost. Both are stylized in form, with rows of Apostles who appear at first sight to be identical, but both, when you look more carefully, are full of exquisite detail. Even the bodies of the Apostles, beautifully moulded and some with elegantly crossed legs, some without, are each different.

In the Ascension, the movement is upwards. The Virgin Mary, the Apostles and, significantly, St Paul look up at the face of Christ as he rises into the sky, an angel on either side and the greater part of his body hidden by a cloud. In the Pentecost panel the movement is downwards as the hand of God reaches down from the sky towards Mary, the Apostles and, again, St Paul.

The presence of St Paul is interesting because he was not present at either event.

Cloister of Santo Domingo de Silos: Entombment and Visit of Three Marys

The artist plainly believed that in spite of this he should be included because of the crucial role he played in the early days of the Christian Church.

The panels at the north-east corner are more complex. One shows the Descent of Christ from the Cross, the other a sequence of events: his Entombment and his Resurrection. The Descent from the Cross is a poignant scene, as the faces of the participants display their emotion. Angels swing censers from the clouds and there are even two figures representing the sun and the moon. (See page 5.)

The panel also has an unexpected feature. The head of Adam, unfortunately badly damaged, is shown emerging from under the Cross as he pushes up the cover of his tomb, demonstrating that in the mind of the artist he too was affected by the Crucifixion. Adam makes a similar appearance in a painting of the Crucifixion in the Panteón de los Reyes in the church of San Isidoro in León (see page 298).

The panel depicting the Resurrection is surprising because the risen Christ is not himself shown. Instead the body of Christ is shown in the centre as he is being laid in his tomb, and his Resurrection is implied in the two other parts of the design. In the upper part the three Marys are told by an angel that the tomb is empty; and in the lower part the Roman soldiers are shown doing a wild dance in their helmets and armour out of astonishment at what they have seen.

The other two panels by the first master also show scenes that took place after the Resurrection. One, the meeting of Christ and the disciples from Emmaus, is different from the others in that the three participants, all with expressive features, are tall, dignified figures that occupy the whole panel.

The other, of Doubting Thomas, is perhaps the most dramatic of them all. There are three rows of Apostles, each slightly different from the others, who look on as Christ extends his right arm at a sharp angle to the rest of the scene and Thomas places his finger on the wound in his side.

Time is needed at Silos to look at these scenes, and also at the capitals, so rich in detail. The two artists treated subjects that were common in Roman-esque art – animals, birds and monsters

Cloister: Christ and the disciples of Emmaus

Capitals in cloister of Santo Domingo de Silos

in more or less contorted poses, and also purely decorative capitals using plant motifs – and they did so in distinctive ways.

Even the shapes of the capitals are different. In those carved by the first master the two columns on which they are placed are relatively far apart. The upper half of the body of each capital has a rectangular form, below which the carving contracts to form a circle at the top of each of the two columns.

In contrast, the columns used by the second master are closer together, so that the two capitals at the top of them form more of a unit than those of his predecessor. Also the body of the capitals does not have the rectangular upper section, and they begin to contract immediately below the abacus. And there is one curious feature: in the middle of the west arm of the cloister one of the historiated capitals rests on four columns which are not upright, but twisted round each other, an arrangement that is also found in the cloister of San Pedro de la Rua in Estella (see page 165).

The upper level of the cloister is not open to visitors, but the capitals can be seen from below. It has to be said that though their subject-matter is often the same, they are less appealing; they are simpler and often cruder than those at the lower level. The assumption is that they were carved at the end of the twelfth century or at the beginning of the thirteenth, when Romanesque art had passed its peak. But

Capitals in cloister of Santo Domingo de Silos

it can be seen that in order to preserve the unity of the cloister round arches were used instead of the pointed ones that were already being used elsewhere.

There are two other features that are worth noticing in the lower level. In the north-east corner there is an ornate doorway known as the Portada de las Virgenes which links the cloister with the south arm of the transept – although it is usually closed. It is largely Romanesque, with carved capitals, and has been dated to around 1120. But it has a Mozarabic-style horseshoe arch, which suggests that part of it could be older. The capitals are thought to be the work of yet another sculptor. They are vigorously worked, with scenes of men and animals struggling, and one in which a pair of crouching men share a head.

A few yards away in the north arm there is a full-length statue of St Dominic, recumbent over an empty tomb, that dates from the fourteenth century, and alongside it a small chapel which again commemorates his role in interceding for the relief of captives of the Moors. A carved relief of the late twelfth or early thirteenth century shows some of these captives, and their chains are hung up on the wall.

The abbey of Santo Domingo de Silos continues to have an active monastic life. It has an extensive complex of buildings, and in them an exceptional collection of reliquaries, manuscripts and other treasures that it has acquired over the centuries. But that is another story.

Segovia

Segovia is a lovely old city that is best known for the stupendous Roman aqueduct that strides across one of its lower districts; and it still has medieval walls that circle its centre, as well as a turreted fortress, the Alcázar, in a dramatic position at one end.

But it also has an exceptional number of Romanesque churches, and many of them are most handsome, with the distinctive porch-gallery that has already been described. It is thought to have originated in the small country towns in the area to the north-east, between Segovia and Soria.

The best-preserved of the churches is San Millán, which has porch-galleries on both the south and north sides, and an interior that has kept most of its original Romanesque style; the only unfortunate feature is the ornamental spire built onto its bell-tower some centuries later. But there are also fine porch-galleries on several others: San Martín, San Esteban, San Lorenzo and San Juan de los Caballeros.

One of the most intriguing of Segovia's churches is La Vera Cruz, a tiny polygonal structure built in imitation of the Church of the Holy Sepulchre in Jerusalem, probably by the Knights of the Holy Sepulchre, one of the military orders created in the course of the Crusades. Another small church that is well worth visiting is San Justo, which has some outstanding mural paintings.

Segovia has a splendid position on a spur of rock that rises above the junction of two small rivers, the Clamores and the Eresma; they flow below it on either side. It was an important town in Roman times – hence the aqueduct – but went into decline during the Visigothic and Moorish periods, and the central area was largely abandoned. It revived over a period of time after being taken over by the Castilians in the tenth century, as a result of the encouragement given to people from elsewhere to come and settle in the city.

Weaving was one of the city's main activities, and it seems that one of the reasons for building the porch-galleries was that the various corporations of weavers, merchants and others liked to hold meetings inside them.

Today it is an ideal city for walking around, with some fine views, several squares large and small – and the many Romanesque churches. There are said to be no less than twenty that are largely or partly in that style. This is attributed partly to the wave of building that accompanied the process of resettlement in the twelfth century, and partly to the affection that Segovians evidently felt for Romanesque, since they continued to build in it into the thirteenth and even the fourteenth century, rather than turning to Gothic.

San Millán is earlier than that. It dates from the first half of the twelfth century,

San Millán in Segovia

and its bell-tower is even older; it is constructed in brick and has horseshoe arches over its windows, which suggests *mudéjar*, or Muslim, work. The church stands in one of the outer districts, below the city walls, and the tower is the only surviving part of an eleventh-century building on the same site. It was put up by Mozarabs, and it was they who dedicated the church to the shepherd-boy saint who lived in the fifth and sixth centuries (see San Millán de la Cogolla, page 242).

The Romanesque church that took its place is a masterpiece, with the forms and proportions that give the style its appeal. On the outside, in addition to the bell-tower and the two porch-galleries, it has an east end made up of three apses – and a fourth one added a short time later. Above them are a short transept and a square tower over the crossing, and the whole east end is decorated with arched windows and lines of corbels under the various cornices.

Inside, there is a spacious nave flanked by two side-aisles, all three covered with flat timber ceilings, and it leads to a beautifully composed sanctuary. This has a short choir bay, an apse, and beneath the apse three tall windows framed by round arches. Below the windows is a ring of blind arches at ground level that spring from double columns topped by carved capitals.

There are also capitals on either side of the nave, and they have a wide range of subjects, from formal Corinthian-style acanthi to Biblical scenes.

San Millán: sanctuary and apse

One of the most remarkable features of San Millán is the Moorish-style cupola that rises over the transept crossing. It is octagonal and rests on four squinches. Pairs of transverse arches spring from the wall spaces between the squinches and support the cupola.

The basic plan and structure of San Millán are similar to those of the cathedral of Jaca in Aragon (see page 130). Both have composite pillars that alternate with single columns on either side of the nave, for instance, and both have Moorish-style cupolas, though their make-up is different. So the assumption is that the church was built between 1111 and 1126, when Alfonso I, king of Aragon, also ruled Castile, and that he brought in his own masons.

The two porch-galleries were added on later, the northern one in the thirteenth century, and they add a most attractive extra dimension to the church. They are similar in construction. Each has three sets of three arches resting on double columns and between them single arches that spring from composite pillars. Inside each, a decorative arched doorway leads into the church.

Many of the capitals on the northern gallery were not put there until the sixteenth century, although care was taken to ensure that they conformed. Those on the southern gallery are original. They are worn, but it is possible to make out Biblical scenes, animals, birds and entwined foliage. The corbels too are carefully worked and quite elaborate, with more patterns, monsters and the occasional human figure.

Several of Segovia's other churches are inside the city walls. **San Andrés**, which dominates a pretty square with trees, has an east end with three apses and above them a tall bell-tower that has open round arches on three levels, one above the other. Like the bell-tower of San Millán, it suffers from the spire built onto it in later years.

Not far away is an even more splendid bell-tower, one of the best of the Romanesque period, that of **San Esteban**. It is late Romanesque, dating from the early thirteenth century, and unspoilt. It has two levels of blind arches, the lower ones slightly pointed, and above them three levels of open arched windows, complete with archivolts and capitals. At the top is a simple conical roof, as other Romanesque churches would have had.

The interior of San Esteban was much modified in the eighteenth century, and in any case it cannot normally be visited. But the outside is magnificent, since it has not only the bell-tower, but a porch-gallery that runs along the south side of the church and continues along the west front. It too dates from the early thirteenth century. It has capitals with some Biblical scenes, formal plant designs and harpies. They, again, are much worn, however.

San Esteban in Segovia

One of the most impressive of Segovia's churches is **San Martín**, which is also in the centre of the city. It stands in a small square that is built on a slope and has some elegant townhouses and a massive tower along three of its sides; a busy pedestrian street is just below. Like several of the others, the church was much modified in its interior in later years, and it too had a spire built onto its bell-tower. But the exterior is very fine.

What you first see is the porch-gallery, which runs along the south side above the street, with a line of thirteen arches that all rest on double columns; and it also extends the whole length of the west front and along the north side of the church. Up above is the bell-tower, which is largely Romanesque and has two levels of paired windows in that style, with a column in the middle of each pair.

In the middle of the west front there is a large entrance portal, and this has a tall arch in its centre that is decorated with four elongated figures, two on either side. They are delicately carved, with serene expressions and flowing robes, and are one of the outstanding features of the church.

It is not known for certain who these figures are. But the one on the right must be Moses, since he is carrying the tablets of the law; above his head is a capital with two harpies apparently caught in foliage. The others are all carrying either a book or a parchment, and are often said to be Apostles. The one next to Moses has a capital that just has foliage on it; the other two capitals are more damaged, but appear to show people with chains on their legs.

Little is known of the history of San Martín, which was at one time the biggest and richest church in Segovia. But these figures are thought to date from the twelfth century, and the capitals in the various parts of the porch-gallery to have been some years later.

Many of these capitals are in bad condition, but they have a wide range of sub-jects, many of them historiated. They include formal plant designs, Biblical scenes – among them the Last Supper, the Massacre of the Innocents, the Kiss of Judas – and a number of symbolic themes, such as a battle between two warriors and a monster.

There are more capitals, and especially corbels, to be seen in **San Juan de los Caballeros**, another stylish church within the city walls of Segovia. This was once used for meetings of the assembly of local noblemen, 'caballero' meaning 'knight'. More recently it was taken over as his studio and residence by a local potter, Daniel Zuloaga, and his work is exhibited there.

The church has a traditional structure, with a broad nave that is covered by a timber ceiling, two side-aisles, and at the east end three apses. On the outside is a solid bell-tower that is partly Romanesque: it has some windows in that style that

San Martín in Segovia: saintly figures on west doorway

San Juan de los Caballeros in Segovia

are framed by round arches, and above them some more fanciful, later ones that are pointed at the top. There is also another of the city's porch-galleries, which runs along the south side of the church and continues along the west front.

Here are capitals with a thicket of tendrils, and more harpies, animals and humans caught in the midst of them. Here too are a Christ in Majesty, an Annunciation and other Biblical subjects. Above all, there is a sort of three-dimensional frieze that runs under the cornice for the whole length of the gallery, and even over the large entrance portal that is the main feature of the west front of the church.

This frieze is one of the most elaborate of its kind. It is made up of tiny trifoliate arches that have human heads in the middle and that rest on corbels, themselves carved. Above the arches is a strip of carving with formal plant patterns on it, and there are more carvings in the metopes between the corbels – mainly flower patterns, but with the occasional monstrous bird.

The church of **San Justo** which, like San Millán, is in one of the outer districts of Segovia, is mainly interesting for a different reason: its paintings. These were only discovered in 1962, when the layer of whitewash that had hidden them was removed in the process of cleaning, and they demonstrate the appeal of Romanesque painting at its best: its emotional power and the range of soft colours, red, black, green, brown and ochre.

The dominant feature, as so often, is the figure of Christ, powerful and yet gentle, who is seated in a mandorla in the centre of the apse. His right hand is raised in blessing, his left is holding a book, and he is looking down into the church. The scene is the Vision of the Apocalypse as described in the Book of Revelation beginning in the fourth chapter, and as depicted elsewhere in Romanesque work, not least in the carvings on the tympanum in Moissac in south-west France.

What is unusual in San Justo is that the Elders of the Apocalypse, some of whom are carrying a musical instrument, and others a cup of perfume, are themselves grouped within an outer mandorla and so are surrounding the figure of Christ. As always, they have great charm, and each of them is different from the others.

Around the outside of the mandorla are the 'four Beasts of the Apocalypse' that represent the evangelists: the lion for St Mark, the calf or bull for St Luke, the eagle for St John and the winged man for St Matthew.

Not all the paintings in San Justo are well preserved. Beneath this central scene are the Crucifixion on one side and the Descent from the Cross on the other, both clearly recognizable, but both in poor condition.

There is much to see elsewhere, however, and in better condition. On the inside of the arch leading into the sanctuary are Adam and Eve, two engaging figures that have the Tree of Knowledge and a huge serpent curled round the tree between

Painting in apse of San Justo, Segovia

them. Above them are two large birds with their necks intertwined, and higher up two more birds, perhaps eagles, that are head to head. Below is an elephant that is apparently carrying a load of grapes on its back.

Opposite are Cain and Abel. They are presented as two naked young men who both look harmless, though Cain has his index finger raised, possibly in reproach, and appears to be wielding the jawbone of an ass. Above them are two lions; below, a wolf and a dog.

And there are more paintings on the vault that covers the choir. The Lamb of God is presented in the centre in a circular shape that is supported by two angels, and lower down there are two scenes that can be easily identified: the Last Supper on the north side (with the inclusion among the Apostles of St Paul) and a dramatic rendering on the south side of the Kiss of Judas and the Arrest of Christ in the Garden of Gethsemane.

Two other paintings are less clear and have been explained in different ways. One, which is above the Last Supper, has a scene in which a priestly figure is stand-ing in front of an altar on which an angel is placing a chalice and three other per-sons are having an animated conversation in a group behind him.

The best-known interpretation is that this illustrates a miracle that took place at the time of Charlemagne when St Giles was celebrating Mass at a church in

San Justo in Segovia: tympanum over inside doorway – Discovery of the True Cross

Orléans. According to an account in the Codex Calixtinus, the twelfth-century collection of manuscripts relating to the pilgrimage to Santiago de Compostela, Charlemagne had confessed to incest in a document placed under the chalice. An angel appeared during the Mass, and the words were wiped out as a sign that Charlemagne had been forgiven.

On this interpretation the priestly figure is St Giles, who looks startled by the apparition of the angel, and the group behind him consists of Charlemagne, who is in the centre and is also looking astonished, and two companions.

The other difficult scene, which is placed above the one that depicts the events in the Garden of Gethsemane, has a group of several people, two of them with haloes. This has been interpreted as a description in two stages of the martyrdom of St Justus and St Pastor, to whom the church is dedicated.

On the left, according to this view, is Dacianus, the Roman praetor who is giving the order for their execution. On the right is the later scene in Paradise in which the two young martyrs are standing on either side of Christ and another martyr, perhaps St James the Apostle, is standing beside them carrying a palm branch.

The paintings in San Justo are superb, even when they are obscure, but the church also has other attractions. It dates from the late eleventh century, and is quite small, with a single nave, a timber ceiling and no side-aisles. But it has a decorative doorway in its largely plain west front, and behind it a particularly attractive bell-tower of the twelfth century. This has two levels of tall round arches, the lower ones blind, the upper ones open; and there is a good long-distance view to be had of it through the arches of the great Roman aqueduct.

Inside, there is a wooden statue of the crucified Christ, dating from the eleventh or twelfth century, that has articulated arms and is said to have been brought to Segovia by the inhabitants of a village in Gascony. There is also, over a small doorway on the north side of the nave, a fine twelfth-century tympanum that shows the Discovery of the True Cross by St Helena, mother of the Emperor Constantine.

St Helena stands in the centre, a statuesque figure wearing a crown, with two women companions to one side of her and beyond them a seated bishop. All three women are holding tiny pots of perfume. St Helena is gesturing towards a small covered stand that is decorated with a cross while a seated angel sprinkles incense over it. The little group is enclosed in an arch that is filled with a series of intricate patterns.

The polygonal church of **La Vera Cruz** is very different, with a special appeal of its own. It stands on a gently sloping hillside outside the walls of Segovia, beyond the Eresma river, and from it there is a good view of the city on its outcrop of rock, including the Alcázar.

As you walk up to it, its outline stands out clearly. La Vera Cruz is basically a twelve-sided structure with a tiled roof divided into matching segments. It has arched doorways in two of its sides and apses that extend from three others. The other sides are largely plain apart from some small windows and a line of corbels under the cornice. Over the centre is a tiny turret – a small section of tiled roof, also polygonal and divided into segments, that covers the cupola inside the church and is raised above the rest of the roof.

A bell-tower was added onto the original building a short time after it was completed, as was a fourth apse. But both are in the style of the church. The apse fits in well and the bell-tower is an important feature of the church's distinctive silhouette.

The interior of the church also has a distinctive form. There is a tall circular nave, covered with slightly pointed barrel vaulting, that runs round the whole building, with transverse arches that rest on engaged columns topped by simple capitals. A short stretch of barrel vaulting also leads off the nave to each of the three apses.

Interestingly, there is a shrine in the centre of the church, encircled by the nave, which must have had a special ceremonial function. It is on two levels, both

Interior of La Vera Cruz, Segovia

Crusader church of La Vera Cruz, Segovia

vaulted. The lower room, which is like a crypt, has two ribs that spring from short columns and cross in the middle. The upper, which is taller and lit by windows, has a Moorish-type cupola that is similar to the one in San Millán: it has two pairs of parallel transverse arches that form a square in the centre. It also has an exotic-looking stone altar whose sides are decorated with arches that intersect in Islamic style and on one side rest on twisted columns.

La Vera Cruz is not the only polygonal church to have survived from the Romanesque period. But it is unusual in being so well preserved. It was long thought to have been built by the Templars, but more recent opinion is that the Knights of the Holy Sepulchre were responsible for it.

What is certain is that it was completed in 1208, as an inscription makes clear, so that it was a relatively late example of Romanesque. It has been pointed out that it has similarities to some Lombardy churches, and in particular to San Tomaso in Limine, a church in Almenno San Bartolomeo, near Bergamo, so that it is possible that Lombard masons, who were often active in Spain, had a hand in its construction.

The church of **San Lorenzo** is also some way from the centre of Segovia, but it is well worth the journey, which takes you across some open country to one of the city's outlying districts. The church stands in a picturesque square that has old

San Lorenzo in Segovia, from east

San Lorenzo in Segovia, from south-east

houses on each side, and it dominates it with its three apses, its porch-gallery and its tall bell-tower.

The bell-tower stands out because, like the churches of Sahagún (see page 302), it is built in brick and this suggests that it too is *mudéjar*, or Muslim, work. It has four levels of simple, open arches, increasing from one at the lowest level to four at the top. They appear at first sight to be horseshoe arches because of protruding bricks, but are in fact round-topped.

The central apse is much larger than the other two and has three arched windows each with some well-shaped capitals; they show scenes from the life of St Lawrence and also the sacrifice of Isaac.

Horseshoe-shaped doorway into San Lorenzo

San Lorenzo in Segovia: porch-gallery

San Lorenzo: 'artesonado' woodwork over transept crossing

The porch-gallery is built onto the south side of the church, as was usual, and extends to the west front – where the door into the church is framed by a horse-shoe arch entirely made of brick. Like those elsewhere in Segovia the gallery is stylishly worked, with round arches resting on double columns, carved capitals and a line of corbels under the cornice.

As so often, the capitals are worn and it is sometimes hard to make out the subjects. But here, as elsewhere, there are thickets of intertwined tendrils with animals and people caught in them, and there are one or two historiated scenes.

The interior of San Lorenzo has been much altered over the centuries. It has a single nave, with no side-aisles. Most interesting, it has some ornate woodwork known as *artesonado*, that is also derived from the Islamic world, over the transept crossing. But it is worth travelling out to San Lorenzo for the exterior alone.

Sepúlveda

Sepúlveda is a picturesque little town in rolling countryside north-east of Segovia, and its church of **San Salvador** is a delight in many ways. It stands on a hillside above the town, with views far into the distance, and it is a well-proportioned and well-preserved example of a Romanesque church of the late eleventh century. Above all it has one of the porch-galleries that are found in that area.

The gallery has eight round arches, together with a number of capitals, on its south face. It has a larger arch at its eastern end, and the east front of the church as a whole is a beautifully balanced composition which can be well seen from the sloping ground below it.

From there you see the arch leading to the porch-gallery, and in the centre a tall apse that is decorated by engaged columns, corbels and, between the columns, three arched windows. On the north-east corner of the church is a bell-tower that is both stocky and stylish, with two levels of open windows at the top, paired and arched, that give it lightness.

San Salvador is in some ways a simple country church. It can be dated by an inscription to 1093 – presumably marking its completion and consecration. The body of the church has a single nave covered by a round barrel vault and a sanctuary consisting of a short choir bay and an apse. There are capitals which are quite unsophisticated, and mysterious: entwined lines and patterns, some formalized plants and the occasional mask.

But the church has its bell-tower and its porch-gallery; and above all it has preserved the various features and the sense of space of Romanesque style, both inside and outside, and that accounts for its appeal.

Sepúlveda, from south-west   *Sepúlveda: capital inside church*

The porch-gallery is a special attraction. When it was built, it extended round the west side of the church, like some of those in Segovia (see page 211). It still does, but the arches were filled in in the sixteenth century, so that there is now just a wall where the arches were.

The eight arches on the south face remain, however, grouped in pairs with a column and a capital in the centre of each pair. These capitals too are crude, but it is possible to make out several heads of monsters that reach out from the corners. They are part of the charm of a gallery that, open and spacious as it is, looks out over the town and the surrounding countryside.

Soria

The provincial capital of Soria, in north-eastern Castile, has several Romanesque churches, and they include two superb creations of the period: the western façade of Santo Domingo, in the centre of the town, and the cloister of San Juan de Duero, on the banks of the river Duero on the outskirts.

Both are relatively late works, from the late twelfth or even early thirteenth century, and both show foreign influence. But interestingly, they are very different from each other. Santo Domingo appears to have been the work of French stone-

Tympanum of San Juan de Rabanera in Soria: St Nicholas and followers

masons, while San Juan has an exotic character both inside the church and in the cloister that suggests the Levant.

Soria's other churches all have distinctive features and one in particular, **San Juan de Rabanera**, is well worth a visit. It is a well-proportioned little church with a cupola over the transept crossing and above all, a fine western doorway which was brought there from another church, San Nicolás. It has St Nicholas standing in the middle of the tympanum, surrounded by priests, and some lively capitals on the columns that flank it on either side.

It is the façade of **Santo Domingo**, however, which is outstanding. It dominates a little square, and is best seen in the late afternoon or evening, when its yellowish stonework, and the innumerable little figures carved into it, take on a golden glow in the sun; and the light catches the square Romanesque bell-tower behind.

Much of the façade is plain, with an almost classical severity. There are two rows of blind arches, one above the other, and over them a pediment which is undecorated except for a large rose window in the centre. But this formal design provides a setting for the decorative features, not least the wonderfully ornate central doorway, which is covered by carving – on the tympanum, in the four archivolts above it, and on the capitals on either side.

West front of Santo Domingo in Soria

The rose window is unusual in a Romanesque church, and is thought to be later than the lower parts of the façade, dating from the thirteenth century. It too is lovingly carved, however, and it forms a focal point at the centre of the pediment.

The central figure on the tympanum over the doorway is God the Father, a serene and masterful figure, who is sitting in a mandorla with the head of a lion emerging from each side of his seat. He is holding the young Jesus, his Son, who is stretching out his arms in an expansive gesture. On either side are angels representing the four evangelists, each with his symbolic attribute: a lion's head for St Mark, a calf's for St Luke, an eagle's for St John, and a book for St Matthew. Beyond them are two seated figures, the Virgin Mary and Joseph.

The four archivolts are packed with little figures and scenes, all carved with verve. In the first of them are the twenty-four Elders of the Apocalypse, who are engaging old men, as so often, and are each carrying a different musical instrument. In the second are violent scenes of the Massacre of the Innocents. A seated figure at the top is Abraham, who is receiving the heads of the slaughtered infants from two angels; while at one side Herod has the Devil whispering in his ear.

The third and fourth archivolts have scenes from the New Testament. The third illustrates events around the time of the birth of Christ. It begins with the Annunciation and ends with the Flight into Egypt. In between are the Nativity,

Santo Domingo in Soria: tympanum at centre of west front

the Announcement to the Shepherds, the Adoration of the Magi, and much else.

The fourth archivolt relates the Passion and the Resurrection of Christ. It shows Jesus in the Garden of Gethsemane, the Kiss of Judas, the Crucifixion. the Descent from the Cross and the Entombment. There are the Three Marys visiting the empty tomb, and the story ends with a scene which could be either Christ greeting Mary Magdalene or his meeting with St Peter; the stone is too worn for certainty.

Up above the doorway are two life-size seated figures. They too are worn, especially the one on the right, but there is little doubt that they are Alfonso VIII, king of Castile, who was

Tympanum on west front: Virgin Mary and angels representing the evangelists

Tympanum on west front: Joseph and angels representing the evangelists

responsible for the building of Santo Domingo, and Leonor (or Eleanor) of
Aquitaine, his queen.

There is more carving on the many capitals, and in particular on those on either
side of the doorway. The abaci above these are linked up to form a frieze – birds,
animals and humans in the midst of flowery tendrils – and the capitals have a
sequence of scenes from the Old Testament.

Those on the left begin with the Creation, and there is a dramatic little scene in
which God is shown standing against a background of rippling water, representing the separation of land and water. He has a disc in either hand, which are the
sun and moon, or planets, and there is an angel on each side, one of whom is holding out a sort of cloth with newly-formed stars on it.

The story continues with the creation of Adam, and after that his and Eve's mis-
adventures in the Garden of Eden. And it resumes on the capitals on the other side
of the doorway, which have Adam working the land, followed by the rivalry
between Cain and Abel. The sequence ends with Cain's murder of Abel.

Little is known about the circumstances in which Santo Domingo was built.
What is certain is that Alfonso VIII had a special link with Soria. He was only a
child when he succeeded his father as king of Castile, and he had powerful rivals,
not least Ferdinand I, king of León, who had designs on Castile. Alfonso was kid-

Archivolt on west front of Santo Domingo in Soria: the Elders of the Apocalypse and Massacre of the Innocents

napped and brought to Soria, but was hidden in a cape and smuggled out of captivity by local people, and he always remained grateful to the city.

The presence of French stonemasons is deduced from the fact that, unlike other churches in and around Soria, Santo Domingo is noticeably similar in style to churches in western France. Both the design of the western façade and the carving on it have a resemblance to those of Notre-Dame-la-Grande in Poitiers, for instance, though the façade of Santo Domingo is much plainer. So the assumption is that stonemasons were brought from the other side of the Pyrenees.

This must have been the doing of Queen Leonor. She was the daughter of Henry II, king of England, and Eleanor of Aquitaine, his queen, and like her mother she retained links with Aquitaine.

Apart from the façade, little is left of the church built by Alfonso and Leonor, which seems not to have been completed. There are just the three western bays of the nave, with their pointed barrel vaulting, composite pillars and formal capitals, decorated with plant patterns and a few animals and birds; also the two side-aisles, divided from the nave by more pointed arches.

The fourth bay is a survival from an earlier church, as is the bell-tower. The east end was rebuilt in Renaissance style in the sixteenth century.

But the façade is a memorial enough.

The church and cloister of **San Juan de Duero** seem to come from a different world. They are in a lovely setting, in a little park on the far bank of the Duero; and it is possible to get a view of both church and cloister, with the river and the city beyond, by climbing up the hillside behind.

The church itself is simple, with a single nave covered by a timber ceiling, a slightly narrower choir with a pointed barrel vault, and an apse. But it has two little domed structures, or aedicules, one on either side of the nave, that give it an eastern flavour. And above all it has its cloister, one of the most original of the Romanesque period.

The architect or architects decided against creating a homogeneous cloister, with the same style along each of its four sides. Instead, they gave it four different styles: each corner is flanked to left and right by arches of the same style, so that the style changes in the middle of each side of the cloister. And the styles are bold, to say the least. One, on either side of the south-east corner, has an arrangement of arches that is reminiscent of the Islamic world – or the cloister of Amalfi in southern Italy.

The arches not only overlap each other, but form loops over the square pillars, decorated with incised lines, on which they rest. In the corner itself is a doorway

Cloister of San Juan de Duero in Soria

with a horseshoe arch which immediately recalls Córdoba, and it enhances the impression of Islamic inspiration.

On the opposite corner of the cloister, by way of contrast, are two ranges of purely Romanesque arches, round and with well-carved capitals. These are the ones that you see first when you enter the cloister. Beyond them, on either side of the north-east corner, are pointed horseshoe arches which already have an Islamic tinge; and they have another decorative doorway, complete with horseshoe arch, in the corner between them.

The evolution is taken a step further on either side of the south-west corner, where there are pointed arches that overlap each other, and a third doorway with a horseshoe arch in the middle of the corner.

San Juan de Duero in Soria: horseshoe-shaped arch in cloister

So the south side is the most exotic of this altogether exotic cloister, since it has the two types of overlapping arches – and between them a sign that it was not completed, because in the middle there is a point at which two arches join at their base, but have no column or pillar to support it, so that the stone that links them is left hanging in mid air.

How a church and cloister of this sort came to be built in the depths of Castile is not known for sure. But there is a likely explanation in the tradition that one of the military orders that was created during the Crusades, the Knights Hospitaller of St John, had an establishment at Soria. They must have taken over the little country church of San Juan de Duero and embellished it – not forgetting what they had seen in Palestine.

The two aedicules in the church would have been part of this process, and they are quite elaborate, transforming the simple interior. One has a rounded top, the other a pointed one, and each of them has a tiny cupola inside. Both also have some well-preserved, and delightful, capitals on the multiple columns that support them.

The capitals on the right are devoted to the life of Christ, beginning with the

Annunciation and concluding with his Resurrection. In between, as at Santo Domingo, are the Visitation, the Nativity, the Adoration of the Shepherds, that of the Magi, and the Flight into Egypt. One of the most vivid is the scene of the Massacre of the Innocents which, again, is similar to the treatment at Santo Domingo. Herod is shown seated and listening to a tall and menacing Devil, who is whispering in his ear.

The capitals on the other aedicule have another dramatic scene in Herod's feast, which includes the beheading of John the Baptist and the presentation of his head by Salome to Herodias. Elsewhere there is a formidable collection of griffins and other winged monsters, including one hydra-like creature with several heads which is being attacked by a soldier in helmet and full armour.

It is thought that these capitals inside the church were the work of local crafts-men. The cloister, on the other hand, with its excellent stonework, may well have required skilled stonemasons from elsewhere, and the suggestion is that they may have come from Toledo or even Córdoba.

León

The region around León is today just part of Castilla y León, and it has been linked to Castile in one way or another for centuries. But from 914, when Castile barely existed, the city was the capital of one of the Christian kingdoms created in the north of Spain, as I have described, and the church of San Isidoro, which was built over the succeeding years by its kings and queens and is largely Romanesque, reflects the days of its ascendancy.

Members of the royal families were buried in the Panteón de los Reyes, or Royal Pantheon, which was attached to the church, and it has its splendid paintings in the vault.

The kingdom of León included much of the *meseta*, Spain's central plain, and there is a wide range of churches in it, both pre-Romanesque and Romanesque, reflecting its complex history. There is the delightful church of San Pedro de la Nave, north-west of Zamora, which dates back to the days of the Visigoths; and there are good examples of those built by the Mozarabs at San Miguel de Escalada, east of León, and Santiago de Peñalba, south of Ponferrada.

In Sahagún, south-east of León, there are two surviving Romanesque churches, San Tirso and San Lorenzo, which were both constructed in brick rather than stone; and there are others in that area. Brick was used by Moorish craftsmen, and so this is an indication that a number of them stayed on after the area was taken over by the Christians, and continued to work there.

In the convent of San Pedro de las Dueñas, south of Sahagún, stone was used when building of the church began, but the later stages were carried out in brick.

Much of León's importance derived from the fact that it not only had the pilgrim route to Santiago de Compostela, the Camino de Santiago, running across it from east to west, but that it also lay on an ancient north-south trade route which dated back to the days of the Moors. This passed through Astorga, Toro, Zamora and Salamanca.

Salamanca is an ancient university city, many of whose buildings date from the fifteenth and sixteenth centuries. But the old cathedral, which still stands alongside

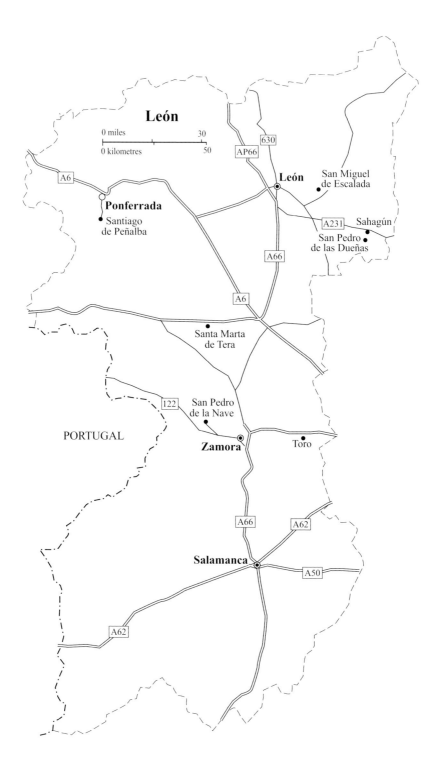

the newer one erected in the sixteenth century, is a good example of late Romanesque; and it, Zamora and Toro all have particularly fine lantern towers in that style, dating from a time when Romanesque was beginning to give way to Gothic.

León

The church of **San Isidoro** in the city of León is dedicated to the learned and saintly man who was bishop of Seville in the seventh century, before the Arab invasion (see page 13). Its outstanding feature is the paintings in the Panteón de los Reyes, or Royal Pantheon, in which members of the royal families were buried at one time. But it has good sculpture as well, as I wrote earlier.

There are two formal doorways on its south side, each with a carved tympanum and, on either side, life-size figures of saints. There are also carved capitals both in the Panteón and inside the body of the church, and they are full of life.

The paintings date probably from the late eleventh or early twelfth century. They cover the vaults of the Panteón, and they give a vivid presentation of a wide range of subjects, from the Annunciation and the Massacre of the Innocents to the Last Supper and Christ in Glory.

The depiction of the Annunciation to the Shepherds is particularly enchanting because of its scenes of country life in medieval times. There are the shepherds themselves, one sitting on a rock, another playing a sort of whistle, and a third blowing a horn as they listen to the message from the angel; and there are little groups of goats, sheep, cattle and pigs, as well as a large dog drinking milk from a pan held by one of the shepherds.

The Panteón was originally the narthex, or western adjunct, of a small church built in the time of King Ferdinand I and Queen Sancha, rulers of Castile and León, and consecrated in 1063. The church itself was pulled down later in the course of that century to make way for a larger building. But the Panteón survived, and it is interesting that it and the church of which it was part formed one of the earliest examples in Spain of the fully-formed Romanesque style, with its decorative features.

The later church was also Romanesque, and much of it can still be seen and admired. It was consecrated in 1149 after some years in the building. The first phase of the work was carried out on the instructions of Urraca, the daughter of Ferdinand and Sancha, who had charge of San Isidoro and other monastic institutions. The second phase was under Alfonso VII, who had taken the title of

Emperor, and his sister, another Sancha, who completed the work. Their architect's name is known – Pedro Deustamben – since his tomb is in the south side-aisle.

There have been some Gothic additions. One is the large extension at the east end which is a dominant feature of the outside of the church. It replaced the central apse in the sixteenth century and encloses the choir and sanctuary. Inside the church it has a monumental reredos containing twenty-four paintings, also from the sixteenth century. Another addition is a tribune that was constructed over the three westernmost bays of the nave in the fifteenth century; it overshadows and to a certain extent truncates it.

But the nave itself, which is tall and covered by barrel vaulting, the aisles and the transept are all those of the twelfth-century church, as are the two smaller apses off the transept. There are elegant round arches between the nave and the aisles and more over the windows above. And there is the unusual and striking feature from that time which was referred to earlier: the two high arches which link the arms of the transept to the nave are both cusped, a sign of the influence of Islamic design.

León has a long history which goes back to Roman times. It takes its name from the fact that it was the camp of the Seventh Legion, called Gemina. Stretches of the wall that surrounded the camp can still be seen below the bell-tower of San Isidoro, and excavations have uncovered other remains of the Roman period, including an underground watercourse.

Years later a monastery dedicated to St John the Baptist was built there, probably over a pagan religious site, and then a second one dedicated to St Pelagius, an early martyr whose bones were brought there from Córdoba. But everything was demolished in 988 in one of the raids into northern Spain by al-Mansur, the Muslim leader.

Rebuilding was carried out by King Alfonso V, but his church was made of poor materials, described as brick and mud, and was replaced by Ferdinand I's Romanesque structure. Ferdinand had maintained the close relations established by his father, Sancho el Mayor (see page 10), with the monastic world north of the Pyrenees, and one of the principal results was the adoption in Spain of the Romanesque style, not least in Ferdinand's own church in León.

There are Romanesque buildings in Spain which are earlier, among them the crypt of Palencia cathedral and some of the Catalan churches. But Ferdinand's church was particularly influential and is often described as the cradle of Spanish Romanesque.

Ferdinand was determined to emphasize the direct link that he had as king of Castile and León with the Visigothic rulers of Spain in the years before the Arab invasion. So, since he was a formidable military leader and through his successes on the battlefield was able to demand tribute from the Muslim ruler of Seville, he arranged for the bones of St Isidore, the renowned figure of the Visigothic period, to be brought to León from Seville.

They were formally deposited in the monastery church in December 1063, and the church was consecrated at the same time. It had previously been associated with Isidore, but from then on it had the sole name of San Isidoro, and it attracted large numbers of pilgrims.

It is said to have been at the request of Queen Sancha that the Panteón was constructed as the royal burial place. It is like a crypt, consisting of six low, vaulted bays all covered with paintings.

San Isidoro in León: Moorish-style cusped arch at opening of north arm of transept

The weight of the vaulting is borne by two single columns in the centre and by more substantial pillars that have engaged columns set into them on the outer edges.

All the columns have carved capitals, and two in particular, depicting the Raising of Lazarus and the Healing of the Leper, are interesting because they are said to be the earliest in Spain to show scenes from the Gospels. The others are equally accomplished. They range from decorative compositions made up of foliage and pine-cones and of birds and animals in formal poses to Old Testament scenes: among them, the Sacrifice of Isaac and Balaam on his ass.

The width of the Panteón is noticeably less than that of the nave of the church, to which it is attached. This is because it had the same width as the nave of the earlier, smaller church. The doorway that it used to have at the centre of its eastern side, leading into the church, can still be seen; it has the capitals with Gospel scenes on either side. But it had to be blocked when structural work was being done on the larger church and was replaced by the doorway to the south.

To the west of the Panteón there are three bays which appear at first sight to be part of it, though they have no paintings. In fact they are part of a portico which had its own capitals and which ran along the north side of the eleventh-century church and the Panteón and then round the north-west corner. The portico still makes up much of the south side of the cloister, the rest of which was built later in baroque style. In it can be seen the original door leading into the church.

The paintings in the Panteón were, it is generally accepted, later than the building itself. There are differences of opinion about their dating, but it is now widely believed that they had been completed before the middle of the twelfth century. In any case they are a splendid collection, with a sequence of largely Biblical scenes and, around them, little decorative designs, all painted in a distinctive range of colours: mainly browns, reds and blueish greys.

In addition to the religious scenes, one of the arches has a calendar for the farming year. There is a circular space for each month, and in each of the spaces is a peasant carrying out the appropriate task: pruning the vines in March, for instance, harvesting the grapes in October, and slaughtering the pigs in November.

The Biblical sequence begins with a charming Annunciation and continues on to the Crucifixion – in which Ferdinand I and Sancha, who were responsible for the building of the Panteón, are shown kneeling at the foot of the cross, each with a servant in attendance. Interestingly, the head of Adam is shown emerging from the rock on which the cross stands. This reflects the belief, also illustrated in the carved panel of the Descent from the Cross in the cloister of Santo Domingo de Silos (see page 263), that Adam was a beneficiary of the Crucifixion and Resurrection.

The Nativity scene had to be amputated to make way for the later door into the church, but it is still possible to see the heads of Mary and the infant Jesus, and engaging portraits of the ox and the ass. Some of the other subjects, among them the Flight into Egypt, are also badly preserved. But most of the paintings in the vaults are in good condition, not least the Announcement to the Shepherds and a dramatic and grisly scene of the Massacre of the Innocents in which Herod's soldiers are shown putting the infants to the sword.

Painting the Last Supper was difficult for the artist or artists because of the shape of the vault. The solution was to extend the table across the vault, with Christ and most of the Apostles sitting on one side, Judas across the table from Christ, and the corners of the vault filled by two sitting Apostles and two servants, one carrying a dish with a fish on it, the other holding a bowl and a large amphora.

Each of the participants is given his own individuality, which makes the painting a gallery of delightful portraits. And there are several decorative features, not least a fine cock perched on a leafy tendril.

The Arrest of Christ in the Garden of Gethsemane is another dramatic and complex scene. It has the Kiss of Judas, badly preserved, in the centre, together with Peter in the act of cutting off the ear of Malchus. There is a group of armed soldiers standing nearby, another of Jews brandishing sticks, and in one corner

Simon the Cyrenian carrying the cross. There are separate scenes of Pilate washing his hands, of Peter making his denials to the servant and of him weeping afterwards. Close to the scene of his denials is, significantly, another cock.

The Crucifixion is painted on a side-wall of the Panteón, between it and the nave of the church, so that it faces you as you look east, as does the Nativity on the opposite side of what was the central door. It is less well preserved than the paintings in the vaults, but the elongated figure of Christ on the Cross stands out clearly, with the sun and moon above. On one side are a soldier carrying a spear and Mary behind him; on the other, a soldier with a small bucket and John.

In the vault above the story goes beyond the events of the Gospels to the vision of St John as described in the Book of Revelation. God sits enthroned in the centre, with John prostrate on one side and an angel who is presenting God with a book on the other. Above God's head is an altar with seven candlesticks, and below his feet an angel is presenting John with a book. Around the central scene are small paintings of the seven churches listed in Revelation: Ephesus, Smyrna, Pergamum, Thyatira, Sardis, Philadelphia and Laodicea.

The climax of the cycle is the painting in the central vault immediately above what was the door into the church. It shows Christ in Glory, a serene and compelling figure sitting in a mandorla surrounded by stars, his right arm raised and his left holding an open book. Around him are the winged figures of the four evangelists, surrounded by an irregular fringe of what could be clouds: Mark with the head of a lion, Luke that of a calf, John that of an eagle, and Matthew that of a man.

The figures are strongly drawn, as are those elsewhere in the Panteón, and demonstrate the vitality of the work carried out for the rulers of León.

The same can be said for the sculpture on the two doorways on the south side of San Isidoro and also that on a third doorway which leads off the north arm of the transept. The principal one, known as the Doorway of the Lamb, leads into the south aisle and now has a baroque superstructure that was built above it in the eighteenth century. But the Romanesque doorway itself, thought to date from the first phase of the building of the church, is largely intact.

It has its name because its tympanum is dominated by a carving of the Lamb of God standing in a circle supported by two angels. Below is a dramatic presentation of the Sacrifice of Isaac. Abraham is standing in the centre, his knife raised, and Isaac has his head bent back as he waits for the blow. Abraham is looking over his shoulder as he is about to strike and sees a huge hand, the Hand of God, and a ram being pushed forward by an angel.

There are decorative trees on both sides, and a number of other figures whose

San Isidoro in León: Sacrifice of Isaac on tympanum of Doorway of the Lamb

identity is not altogether certain. But one view is that the woman standing in front of an open door on the right is Sarah, Abraham's wife, and that the man on horseback with a bow and arrow at the opposite end is Ishmael, Abraham's older son. The person apparently taking off his shoes is thought to be Isaac preparing himself for his ordeal, and the two other figures, one of them on horseback, servants of Abraham.

It has been suggested that the inclusion of Ishmael was significant, since he was regarded as the ancestor of some of the Arab tribes, and that he has deliberately been given a peripheral, and so subordinate, position.

There is less controversy about the carvings around the edge of the arched doorway, which are thought to come from the earlier church built by Ferdinand I and Sancha. On the left is St Isidore, a tall figure holding a bishop's crozier, with a smaller soldier carrying a sword, perhaps an executioner, at his side; on the right St Pelagius, obviously younger. In the row above are David and his musicians, delightfully portrayed, and above them the twelve Signs of the Zodiac

The other tympanum, on the doorway into the south arm of the transept, was carved later and presumably installed in the second phase of the building of the church. It is considered to be an early work by one of the few sculptors of

San Isidoro in León: David and musicians on Doorway of the Lamb

the period whose names are known: Master Esteban, who went on to work in the cathedral in Santiago de Compostela (see page 374) and elsewhere.

It is another movingly presented group of scenes. In the centre two of the disciples are taking the body of Christ down from the cross, while Mary clings to one of his arms and two angels swing censers above. On the right the Three Marys look on as an angel lifts the lid of the empty tomb. On the left two angels support Christ as he ascends to Heaven.

This doorway too is flanked by tall figures of saints: on the left St Paul carrying a book, on the right St Peter with his keys.

The third doorway is less easy to find and it is plainer, with no carving on its tympanum. But it has four vigorous capitals, thought to be the work of the same sculptor as the tympanum of the Doorway of the Lamb. One shows two animals in a thicket, another an extraordinary struggle between humans, a monster and two snakes.

It is in the inside of San Isidoro, however, that the great majority of the capitals are to be seen, and they are a most impressive collection. They are considered to be the work of at least three different artists: the sculptor of the Doorway of the Lamb, Master Esteban and Pedro Deustamben.

There is a rich variety in both the subject-matter and the treatment. The subjects range from a formal Christ in Majesty to scenes of men fighting, with each other or with snakes or lions, animals in formal confrontations, birds in thickets, acrobats, musicians and much else. They are a feast for the eyes, and it is worth taking the time to go round and study them.

Two other parts of San Isidoro should be noted. One is the tall bell-tower, built over part of the Roman wall and largely Romanesque. The other is the exceptional collection of ivories, metalwork, jewellery and silver in the church's treasury, much of it on display in the Royal Tribune immediately above the Panteón de los Reyes.

San Isidoro in León: detail of Doorway of the Lamb, with St Pelagius

The collection includes gifts from members of the royal family, among them the gold and agate chalice donated by Urraca, daughter of Ferdinand I and Sancha, in the eleventh century, and it is a further demonstration of the special place of León in the story of Spain.

Sahagún

Sahagún, a town that lies on the flat plains south-east of León, was the setting in the twelfth century for the most powerful abbey in Spain. It was also an important stopping point on the pilgrim route to Santiago de Compostela. Little remains of the church that formed part of that abbey, but there are still two other churches there from that period, San Tirso and San Lorenzo. Both are largely Romanesque, and they both have impressive east ends in that style.

The two churches are especially interesting for having been built almost entirely in brick. I have pointed out that Sahagún was the centre of an area where Moorish or Mozarabic masons introduced the use of brick for the construction of churches, in place of the stone which was normal further north. **San Tirso**, which dates from the early twelfth century, is the earliest known of a number of these brick-

built, or *mudéjar*, churches, known as
'*Sahaguninas*'.

It has a tall, rectangular tower that
rises above the three apses of the east
end and, with its three rows of round-
topped arches, one above the other, is
a sort of façade in its own right. Unusually, it is built over the single bay of
the choir rather than the transept, with
a pyramidal base. The arches are open
on all four sides, and they give it lightness and form.

The lowest row has the widest
arches, and they, like the narrower ones
in the row above, rest partly on stone
columns, each with a base and a capital, whose whiteish colour contrasts
with the surrounding brick. The top

San Tirso in Sahagún

row, under a projecting cornice, are simple round-topped openings in the brick-
work, which is set slightly in from the rest of the tower.

The three apses below are encircled by a range of blind arches, also round-
topped. Some stand alone; others are set in a rectangular frame that derives from
Moorish architecture. It is interesting that the lowest levels of the central apse,
both outside and inside the church, are in stone, showing that that is where construction of the church began, as so often, before the builders made the switch
from stone to brick.

At this point it should be pointed out that the tall, rectangular tower that
dominates the east end of San Tirso had to be rebuilt after collapsing in 1949; and
the smaller apse to the north of the main central one was also reconstructed in the
twentieth century. But in both places the work was faithful to the original design,
and the overall effect is still most pleasing.

San Lorenzo was a later construction, from the thirteenth century, and it has
different proportions and a less appealing design than San Tirso. But it too is
a powerful presence, with a tower that soars above the surrounding buildings and
a complex arrangement of arches, mainly open in the tower and blind on the three
apses. Interestingly, most of the arches on the apses are horseshoe-shaped, while
there are tall, narrow arches in the tower, one row of them pointed, that give it a
sense of upward movement.

The use of brick was common in the Moorish part of Spain, and in buildings in *mudéjar* style constructed in places that had recently been under Moorish rule, as we have seen. Apart from stylistic considerations, it was economical to use it in Sahagún, since there is little stone to be found in the area; and there were qualified masons on the spot, so that others, more used to working in stone, did not have to be brought in.

San Lorenzo in Sahagún

The history of Sahagún goes back to Roman times. A small river, the Cea, runs by it and according to tradition a chapel was put up beside it to mark the spot on which two brothers, Facundus and Primitivus, both Roman legionaries, had been martyred in the third century.

Many years later the area was overrun by the Arabs, and the chapel demolished, but the cult of the two martyrs was revived after the area was recovered by the Christians in the tenth century. An abbey was founded, and a town grew up around it. The name of Sancto Facundo became first Santfagund and eventually Sahagún.

The abbey was promoted by the kings of León, and reached the peak of its power and influence under Alfonso VI, who was king of León and, later, Castile from 1065 to 1109. He brought it into the orbit of the great French abbey of Cluny, with which he had close relations, and he chose it as the place in which he himself would be buried. Monks from Cluny arrived in 1080 to carry out reforms, and Sahagún came to rival Cluny itself, with more than fifty abbeys and priories dependent on it.

Both San Tirso and San Lorenzo date from the period of Sahagún's greatness. Both were extensively rebuilt in later years, and San Lorenzo is less striking inside than out. But in addition to its splendid east end San Tirso has in its interior a simple but stylish transept with the three apses leading off it, all of them almost entirely in brick.

Horseshoe arches support a timber ceiling over the transept, and others frame the entrances to the sanctuary and to the chapels in the two smaller apses.

The sanctuary has a short barrel-vaulted choir – that supports the weight of the tower above it – before the apse.

Salamanca

Salamanca is the site of Spain's oldest university, and it is a city that is a joy to walk around because it has a wealth of delightful architecture, often built in a golden stone. Much of it dates from the fifteenth and sixteenth centuries, as I have written, but the city also has one of the best buildings of the late Romanesque period, the old cathedral, and there are a few smaller churches in that style.

Interestingly, one of them is dedicated to Thomas à Becket, the archbishop of Canterbury who was assassinated in 1170 and canonized by Pope Alexander in 1173. It was founded in 1175 by two brothers from Britain and is known as **Santo Tomás Cantuariense**. It has been rebuilt inside, but the outside is pure Romanesque, with three apses, transept and nave, and a decorative door on the north side.

The **old cathedral** is overshadowed by the much larger new cathedral that was erected alongside it in the sixteenth century. But most of it remains in place, and as well as an impressive interior it has a superb lantern tower over the transept

Santo Tomás Cantuariense in Salamanca

Old cathedral of Salamanca: Torre del Gallo

crossing, known as the Torre del Gallo, or Cock Tower, because of its tall silhouette, with a weathercock at the top.

It is an intricate and carefully modelled structure that has turrets at the four corners, narrow gables on each side and, worked into them, two levels of round arches of different designs. Above them it rises to a peak, covered by tiles that create a scaly effect.

The tower is one of three similar ones, all within a short distance of each other, as already noted, and it is the outstanding example. The first to be built was the tower over the cathedral in Zamora (see page 326), which was the inspiration for Salamanca's. The third was the one over the collegiate church of Toro (see page 323), which followed that of Salamanca.

Like many other Spanish cities, Salamanca was a substantial town in Roman times, was largely abandoned during the years of Muslim rule, and began to be resettled with encouragement from the kings of Castile and León at the end of the eleventh century. It still has a Roman bridge over the river Tormes, from which there is a good view of the city.

Work began on building the old cathedral in the middle of the twelfth century. It was spread over a number of years so that, while the older parts are purely Romanesque, as work went on the style evolved to one that was closer to Gothic.

The basic plan of the cathedral is Romanesque, and so are the lower levels of the nave, side-aisles and transept, up to the springing of the arches of the vault. The apses at the east end were one of the first parts to be built, and the two that remain, in the centre and south, have the rounded form of the earlier style. They have arched windows on the outside, decorated with some particularly fine capitals: winged monsters, the head of a bearded man with horns, and another face apparently spewing out some noxious matter.

But the short choir bay over the sanctuary has a pointed barrel vault, and there is Gothic-style ribbed vaulting over the nave, the side-aisles and the transept. Above all, there is a magnificent circular cupola, resting on pendentives, that crowns the transept crossing and is one of the outstanding features of the cathedral.

It is, of course, the inside of the Torre del Gallo. The cupola rests on eight slender arches that criss-cross at the centre, forming a star effect, while below them, at the springing of the arches, are two complete circles of sixteen small arched windows, a few blind, but most of them open.

The result is that the nave soars upwards from its Romanesque beginnings and is enhanced by the cupola over the crossing. It culminates in the pointed arch of the choir and the fifteenth-century reredos that fills the central apse beyond it. This consists of fifty-three paintings of the life of Christ and the Virgin Mary, and

Old cathedral of Salamanca: capital on outside

is thought to be the work of Nicolás Florentino, as is the larger fresco of the Last Judgment immediately above it. In the centre of the reredos is a bronze-plated statue of the Virgin and Child from the twelfth century.

There are also excellent capitals along the nave and in the transept, as well as on the arch that frames the sanctuary, and they are a typically Romanesque feature. They are a lively collection: more winged monsters, scenes of men battling with them, large human heads, Samson fighting a lion, Daniel in the lions' den, and some purely decorative designs based on formalized plants.

Also Romanesque is an arched doorway complete with capitals that leads from the chapel in the south apse to the main sanctuary. And there is another doorway that leads from the cloister into the south arm of the transept and shows the Romanesque style that the cloister once had. It too has two engaging capitals showing men, animals and birds entangled in thickets.

The Romanesque cloister was badly damaged in 1755 by the earthquake that also destroyed much of Lisbon. It was rebuilt in neo-classical style, and there is much to be seen in the chapterhouse and in the various chapels that lead off it, though very little is Romanesque.

San Miguel de Escalada

San Miguel de Escalada, which stands alone on a bare hillside fifteen miles or so east of León, is both a lovely building in itself and a memorable example of a church built by Mozarabs. It dates from 913, when it was consecrated, and was the work of monks who had left Córdoba, the Muslim capital, and set up a new monastery under the leadership of their abbot, Alfonso, in what became the expanding kingdom of León. (See page 23.)

The first of its distinctive features, immediately visible as you approach the church, is a long, elegant portico of twelve horseshoe arches that runs along its south side. The interior of the church also has great charm, with an array of more horseshoe arches whose effect is enhanced by the soft light. Some run along either side of the nave, supported by marble columns; three of them form a chancel screen that divides the nave from the transept; and yet others frame the entrances into the transept from the two side-aisles and the three apses beyond them at the east end.

It can be seen that the church, built some two hundred years after the Arabs had first invaded and then occupied most of Spain, is in the basilica style that dates back to late Roman times, and has many similarities to those, like San Juan de

Monastic church of San Miguel de Escalada: portico

Baños de Cerrato (see page 217), that were built while the Visigoths still ruled. There are also a number of decorative features, and a refinement in the stonework, which show Islamic influence. But San Miguel demonstrates the extent to which many Mozarabs resisted the attractions of that culture, then at its peak in southern Spain, and retained their own traditions.

The site was given to Abbot Alfonso and his monks by King Alfonso III. Like many others, it had previously been occupied by a religious institution in Visigothic times, as has been proved by excavations, and before that by buildings of the late Roman period. It seems that the community got briskly down to work and, according to an inscription seen in the eighteenth century but since lost, built the new church in twelve months.

This was a time of much cultural activity in the kingdom of León, and the monastery flourished, with an influential scriptorium, in which monks copied out and illustrated ancient texts. They decided to add the south portico a few years after completing the church itself, in about 925; and the chunky tower and chapel that stand at the south-eastern corner of the church, and already have Romanesque characteristics, towards the end of the eleventh century.

The portico must have been one side of a cloister. Only the seven westernmost

Monastic church of San Miguel de Escalada: interior

arches and the marble columns that support them, topped by capitals in a formalized Corinthian style, formed part of the original structure. The five others were added when the tower was being built. But it is clear that great care was taken to ensure that the later ones had the same size and form.

All the marble columns, both in the portico and inside the church, appear to have been taken from dismantled buildings of the Roman period, as happened generally. In the portico the two sets of capitals are clearly different from each other: those of the five later arches are larger, and one face is plain, showing that they had been placed against a wall. But they are stylistically similar, and are thought to be the work of the same group of stonemasons, who formed a Mozarabic school active all over León. These capitals may have come from a neighbouring monastery, in Eslonza.

A feature that shows Islamic influence is the small window in the wall at the western end of the portico. It is made up of a pair of horseshoe arches with a typically Islamic rectangular frame, known as an *alfiz*, above them. Also Islamic in origin is the narrow masonry frieze, consisting of pointed stones set between two rows of bricks, which runs all round the outside of the church below the eaves. So are various modillions around the east end and under the eaves of the nave roof.

There is some decorative carving on the semicircular tympanum over the door-way from the portico into the tower. This is Mozarabic work, and is almost certainly composed of two stone screens that used to stand inside the church, but were given a new use.

The entrance into the church is through a simple horseshoe arch. The interior is small but well proportioned, with a high timber roof over the nave, lower ones over the side-aisles and small windows high up on either side of the nave which provide the gentle light. There is a transept that does not project beyond the aisles, and three apses which are circular and vaulted inside, but not visible outside because they are enclosed within a plain, rectangular shape.

The most prominent feature inside the church is the triple-arched chancel screen, a delicate structure which also has leafy capitals derived from Corinthian style at the head of its marble columns and a frieze along the top consisting of lions, eagles and other birds, all encircled by tendrils.

The screen marks off the transept, which must have been reserved for those officiating at church services, and there is a similar arrangement in the two aisles. Smaller stone screens stand there, upright and exquisitely carved, to mark the transition from one part of the church to the other, and it is thought that there would have been others under the arches of the main chancel screen – probably those that have been re-used over the doorway from the portico into the tower.

The carving on these stone screens is one of the high points of San Miguel de Escalada. It is quite simply superb. The masons have drawn on the work of their Visigothic predecessors and brought in various Islamic motifs. The result is an exuberant display of birds, leafage, bunches of grapes, palm-trees, abstract designs and much else, all set inside closely-packed patterns, some square, some circular.

There is more fine carving in the capitals of the nave, and in various friezes similar to the one on the chancel screen. One frieze runs above the arch leading into the central apse, and another round the inside of the apse.

San Miguel de Escalada: carved screen

The nave capitals are thought to be from different periods, several of them earlier works that came from buildings elsewhere. They too derive from Corinthian style, much formalized and elaborated, and no two are the same. So here again there are birds picking at grapes, shells and convoluted patterns, emerging from what once were the leaves of acanthus.

Together with the building itself, they show the riches that Spain could draw on on the eve of the arrival of Romanesque.

San Pedro de la Nave

North-west of Zamora, on the outskirts of the village of El Campillo, is **San Pedro de la Nave**, an exquisite little church that survives from the last years of the Visigothic period in Spain. It dates from the late seventh century, just before the Arab occupation, and was moved to its present position, stone by stone, in 1930/31 to save it from being engulfed when a dam was built across the river Esla a few miles away.

In the process it was restored, but care was taken to preserve its original structure and, above all, its superb carving.

San Pedro de la Nave, Visigothic period

There are capitals in the church with decorative and arresting depictions of two Old Testament stories, Daniel in the lions' den and Abraham's sacrifice of Isaac; tiny portraits of St Peter, St Paul, St Philip and St Thomas; birds pecking delicately at bunches of grapes; and an array of other designs that run above the capitals and around the inside of the church in friezes. (See page 15.)

It is thought that San Pedro was once part of a monastery and, presumably, a prosperous one. Some of the motifs – circles representing the sun, for instance, and rosettes – have their origins in ancient Hispanic art, while the scenes on its capitals reflect the influence of Byzantium, and were possibly copied from illustrations in manuscripts of the day.

The church that you see today when you emerge from El Campillo is a well-proportioned structure whose different parts stand out clearly: a nave and two side-aisles, tall porches on the north and south sides, a short turret in the centre, and a rectangular east end. The arches leading into the two porches are slightly horse-shoe-shaped and still have traces of carved designs. On the sides of the porches are pretty little windows that each have a double horseshoe arch and a column topped by a carved capital in the centre.

Inside, the walls of San Pedro are mainly constructed of sizeable blocks of well-cut stone, but some of the higher levels and some of the vaulting have an amalgam of smaller pieces of masonry held together by mortar. The western part of the nave has a timber ceiling.

Though it is small the church has a good balance between its various parts, with a nave and two side-aisles and an open space in the centre beneath the turret. This has a horseshoe arch on each of its four sides. Beyond it there is a further stretch of the nave that has barrel vaulting overhead, and on either side a small chamber that opens onto it through three small windows and a door; their original use is unknown.

At the east end a smaller horseshoe arch, resting on two columns, provides an attractive focal point by framing the entrance to the sanctuary, which also has barrel vaulting.

It is the carving and its quality, however, that immediately capture your attention. The Daniel scene is on the left, on the top of one of the columns that stand at the four corners of the central space. Daniel is standing in some water with his arms raised while on either side an elegant lion is approaching him, not very aggressively. On the two sides of the capital are St Thomas holding a book and St Philip raising a crown over his head.

Opposite is Abraham. Isaac is bent over an altar in front of him, and Abraham is grasping him by the hair while wielding a knife over his head. The Hand of God

St Philip on capital in San Pedro de la Nave, Visigothic period

is emerging from a cloud to one side and indicating the ram caught in a thicket. This capital too has a pair of saints: St Peter carrying a cross and a book marked 'LIBER' and St Paul holding a scroll.

The other two capitals each have a pair of birds surrounded by foliage and pecking at grapes. At the sides are unidentified human faces.

Almost as fine as these little scenes on the capitals are the decorative friezes that run across the top of them and continue onto the wall at the side. They have birds, human faces, bunches of grapes and other formal designs, all set in circular tendrils. There must also have been good carving on the bases of the columns, but although it is possible to make out some human faces at the corners, they are badly damaged.

There appear to have been two master masons, or two workshops, who were responsible for the carvings in San Pedro. One of them produced the capitals and the friezes in the central space, and it is he or they who are thought to have been influenced by manuscript illustrations and perhaps Byzantium.

The other mason or masons did similar work on the two capitals in the arch that frames the entrance to the sanctuary, as well as on the long frieze that runs along either side of the eastern stretch of the nave and all round the three walls of the sanctuary itself. Here are the solar circles and the rosettes which are thought to derive from ancient Hispanic motifs, and stars and other shapes set in circles, but also some stylized leaves and bunches of grapes.

These carvings are less sophisticated than those of the central space, since they consist largely of formal designs. But they too are distinctive, and beautifully carved, and they contribute to the exceptional appeal of San Pedro.

San Pedro de las Dueñas

The convent church of **San Pedro de las Dueñas** towers over the village of that name just a few miles south of Sahagún (see page 302). I have already mentioned that it is interesting for having been begun in stone, as can be seen at the lower levels, and completed in brick.

The feature that stands out, however, is the carved capitals in the nave and the two side-aisles. They range from formal plant designs, including some large spherical shapes, to action scenes in which lions with elaborate manes are shown back to back, face to face, and devouring both other animals and children.

One capital has seven human figures in long robes standing side by side with doves spreading their wings overhead. They are thought to be nuns. Another

Capital in San Pedro de las Dueñas

Capital in San Pedro de las Dueñas

shows tiny human figures sitting astride the lions as they go about their grisly business. Yet another has dragons with the head of a lion, the body of a bird and the tail of a siren.

San Pedro is unusual in that it had a double function from its earliest days: as a church both for the nuns and for the local parish. The convent, which still exists, was founded in 973 and put under the authority of the great abbey in Sahagún – though the nuns in due course broke away and established their independence.

Building of the church began in 1109, and the basic plan dates from that time: three apses at the east end and a nave and two side-aisles, each of two bays. So the supporting walls of the apses and the arched windows in them are in stone. The same is true of the arches between the nave and the south side-aisle and, above all, of the various capitals, which are similar in style to those of the same period in San Isidoro in León (see page 295).

The transition to brick took place at the end of the twelfth century, in line with the techniques being used in Sahagún. The hemispherical vaults of the apses are in brick, as is the barrel vaulting over the short choir bays. So is the tall pointed arch which frames the entrance to the central apse.

One very obvious innovation was to wall off the north side-aisle from the nave and decorate the partition with a design consisting of blind arches, also in brick. This had the effect of separating the main body of the church, which was used by the nuns, from the northern aisle and a porch that was built onto it to increase the space, which were used by the parishioners.

The two side-aisles have barrel vaulting, but the nave has rib vaulting.

On the outside, the three apses make a splendid east end, with the upper parts in brick, but they are hard to see because they are surrounded by a garden used only by the nuns. The tower, however, is very fine – not least because of a colony of storks that have built their nest at the top. It has three stages, also all in brick, and an array of arched windows.

Santa Marta de Tera

The church of **Santa Marta de Tera**, which is in a village some way north-west of Zamora, dates from the end of the eleventh century, when it was part of a monastery much favoured by the kings of León. It is not large, but it is thought to have been modelled on the church of San Isidoro in León (see page 295), which was being rebuilt at that time, and may even have had the same architect.

It is worth visiting above all for its many carvings, on both the inside and the outside of the church. They are in a pinkish stone that contrasts with the rest of

Santa Marta de Tera: St James on south doorway

the stonework, and many of them are similar in style to those in San Isidoro. There is a handful of historiated subjects, and a wide range of other designs, from Corinthian-style acanthus and intricate arrangements of foliage to animals, birds and monsters.

The church has a simple floor plan: a single nave, a transept that extends beyond it on each side, and a square sanctuary. The nave is covered by an arrangement put in place at the end of the twelfth century, after the rest of the church: two pointed arches that support groin vaulting over the three bays. The crossing tower rests on four round arches, and it and the two arms of the transept have a timber ceiling.

The sanctuary has a stone barrel vault. Its square shape and in particular the flat east end derive from the style of churches of the Visigothic period.

That outer wall, however, has decoration that is original and purely Romanesque. It has three arches, one in the centre that frames a tall and narrow window, the other two blind, and they all have carved capitals. So have the taller columns that stand against the wall on either side; and the line of the roof has both a chequerboard frieze and a string of carved corbels.

The large capital on the right-hand side has the Adoration of the Magi, which is rather worn but still moving. The smaller capitals on either side of the three windows have a pair of lions confronting each other, a design in which lion heads are spewing out tendrils while in the abacus birds are caught in a thicket, and other fanciful creations.

There are a number of other windows around the sides of the church, and they too have their charm. They are linked up by chequerboard friezes similar to those at the east end, and have such subjects as a pair of harpies, a winged monster pecking at the neck of a four-legged beast, and various floral and plant motifs.

The doorway on the south side is also noteworthy. It has two archivolts, each of which rests on a pair of columns, and all four are topped by capitals. Not least, it has a pair of life-size statues of Apostles, one on either side of the outer arch. One is clearly St James because he is holding a staff and has a pilgrim's bag with a shell on it; the other is thought to be St John, since he has a book or roll of parchment in his hands.

Both statues came from elsewhere in the church, and have lost their feet. But they are powerful figures with similarities to some of the statuary in San Isidoro.

There is more carving to be seen inside Santa Marta: four large capitals inside the sanctuary, two more on the columns supporting the arch between the nave and the transept, and several smaller ones on either side of the windows. Here too many have Corinthian-type acanthus or other plant designs, but there is a particularly engaging one on the left-hand side of the arch that frames the apse.

It shows a small naked figure inside a mandorla that is being held by two angels, and represents the soul of a righteous person being taken up to Heaven. Interestingly, it is similar to a capital in San Isidoro.

Santiago de Peñalba

The little Mozarabic church of **Santiago de Peñalba** is not the only one in Spain to have a remote and beautiful setting. But the approach to it is an unforgettable one: a good half-hour's drive south from Ponferrada, west of León, up the narrow valley of the river Oza, with mountains on either side.

The road ends at Peñalba, a well-kept village with slate roofs on all its houses, magnificent views and at its centre the well-defined outlines of the early tenth-century church of Santiago. It too has its various roofs covered with slate. A freestanding belfry was added to the east of it at a later time, but the church retains the form and proportions given to it more than a thousand years ago.

Monks are known to have established themselves in this mountainous region as long ago as the seventh century, when the Visigoths ruled Spain. The tradition

Mozarabic church of Santiago de Peñalba

continued after the Arab occupation of the eighth century, and Santiago is thought to have been part of a monastery founded between 909 and 920 by Genadio, a hermit who had been appointed bishop of Astorga – although some experts date it two decades later.

Like other Mozarabic churches, it is largely plain on the outside, its rough stonework carefully aligned. A tower rises above the east end, with extensions on all four of its sides, and the slopes of their roofs form a satisfying ensemble. There are the characteristic corbels, similar to those found in Islamic architecture, under the eaves, though they are quite worn.

Above all Santiago has a superb doorway on its south side, of a form known as an *ajimez*. It is made up of two horseshoe arches resting on columns topped by Corinthian-style acanthus capitals. A narrow frieze consisting of three lines of stonework forms a rectangular shape around the top of the doorway and also runs round the outer edge of the arches.

It is interesting to note that there is the outline of a taller arch in the stonework above the doorway, suggesting that there was once an earlier, less decorative structure there that was replaced.

There are more horseshoe arches inside the church. Santiago is unusual, if not unique in early churches, in hav-

Doorway of Santiago de Peñalba

ing an apse at both its east and west ends, which creates two focal points; and both of them have such arches leading to them. The eastern apse even has a horseshoe-shaped floor plan, while the floor plan of the western one is a slightly elongated round arch.

In both, the hemisphere of the apse itself has groin vaulting that divides it into segments.

The body of the church is made up of two main sections, both with a square floor plan, which together form a sort of nave. A tall horseshoe arch resting on columns and capitals is set between them, with a smaller arch built into the wall above it.

The western section is covered by barrel vaulting. The eastern one has the tower high above, as if it was a transept crossing, and that too has vaulting that is divided into segments by groins. Small arched doorways on either side lead to chapels.

Like all other medieval churches, Santiago would originally have had painted decoration all over its walls. Traces of such painting, dating from the tenth century, have been uncovered in recent years in several parts of the church, not least on the barrel vault of the nave, where plant designs, set in a pattern of circles, can be seen.

Toro

Toro, like Zamora (see page 326), was once a fortified town overlooking the river Duero, and it still has numerous churches and other monuments from different periods in its long history. And like Zamora it has, as I stated earlier, one of the ornate lantern towers that date from the late Romanesque period, when the transition to Gothic was under way.

The tower is the most prominent feature of Toro's collegiate church of **Santa María la Mayor** and you see it ahead of you as you walk along the street leading from the main square, the Plaza Mayor. The church also has two doorways with

Collegiate church of Toro, from south-east

some delightful carving, one on its north side that is Romanesque and the other in Gothic style at its western end.

It stands in an open space at the high point of the town, from where there are views out over the Duero and the flat countryside beyond. From there you see the church's east end, which has the lantern tower as its culminating point and which, unlike that of the cathedral in Zamora, has largely retained its Romanesque form.

There are three apses and, beyond them, the almost solid wall of the transept. The peaked end of the choir bay is filled by a rose window that was added later. The central apse has a ring of attractive round arches complete with columns, and there is a sequence of tiny arches that mark the cornices of the apses and the transept; but much of the east end is plain.

The lack of decoration is more than made up for in the lantern tower. Unlike the other two similar towers, on Zamora cathedral and on the old cathedral in Salamanca (see page 305), Toro's is roofed with tiles rather than stone slabs, so that it does not have the scaly surface of the two others. Also, though it has four corner turrets, it does not have gables in the spaces between them.

But it has two levels of tall arched windows, with two sets of three between each pair of corner turrets, and there are decorative designs both on them and on the turrets, which also have tall, narrow window openings. So the overall effect is a rich and distinctive one.

The building of Santa María began in about 1160, a few years later than the cathedrals of Zamora and Salamanca, whose influence it would have felt. Salamanca was its immediate predecessor, and like the old cathedral there Toro has two levels of windows in its lantern tower – compared with only one in Zamora – though its dimensions are quite different.

It too has a Romanesque plan, and the interior of the church retains a Romanesque feel in spite of later additions. The nave has a pointed barrel vault, as have the two arms of the transept, while there is rib vaulting over the two side-aisles. Gothic-style rose windows have been added at each end of the transept, as well as the one over the choir bay. But the three apses remain in place.

There are few carved capitals. But there are a handful of historiated ones high up on the pillars of the transept crossing. One shows Daniel in the lions' den, another a knight saying goodbye to his wife as he leaves his castle.

As in Zamora and Salamanca, the cupola over the transept crossing, borne on four pointed arches, dominates the interior of the church. The two circles of windows beneath it, sixteen in each, rest on pendentives and the windows are framed by columns and round arches. Eight arches spring from columns set between the windows and support the dome, forming a star pattern in the centre.

Collegiate church of Toro: Elders of the Apocalypse on north doorway

Then there are Santa María's doorways. The northern one is round-arched and much decorated, with a charm that is characteristically Romanesque. The arch over the door is cusped, with tiny figures in the rounded spaces and decorative patterns above them. The first of the archivolts has a succession of angels standing under little round arches and all turned towards the central figure of Christ.

The outer archivolt has the twenty-four Elders of the Apocalypse, and at the centre Christ seated with the Virgin Mary and St John on either side. Each of the Elders is wearing a crown and carrying a different musical instrument, apart from the two who, just like two of the Elders on the Pórtico de la Gloria in the cathedral of Santiago de Compostela (see page 372), have a single larger instrument, an 'organistrum', across their knees.

The Gothic doorway once formed the western entrance to Santa María, but is now enclosed in a chapel built onto the west front. It is of course pointed, and it too is richly decorated. There is a statue of the Virgin and Child on the central pillar and above that in the tympanum the Coronation of the Virgin. On either side are statues of David and Solomon, four prophets and two archangels.

In the archivolts there are scenes of the Last Judgment, Heaven and Hell, as well as a profusion of angels, saints, martyrs and, once again, the twenty-four Elders of the Apocalypse with their musical instruments.

Zamora

Zamora, a city that stands on a rock high above the river Duero and still has traces of its medieval walls, possesses a great number of churches that are wholly or partly Romanesque. The principal one is the **cathedral** which, though it is in a mixture of styles, has several Romanesque features: a handsome and distinctive lantern tower over the transept crossing, a much plainer bell-tower at its western end and an elegant façade at the southern end of the transept.

The lantern tower is the one that stands out, with an exotic appearance that indicates influence from the Byzantine world to the east, probably via Sicily. It consists of a domed cupola that rests on a ring of arched windows and has four corner turrets, with tiny gables between them. The dome, the turrets and the gables are all covered by stonework that creates a scaly effect, similar to that found in some churches in western France.

It seems that the dome and the windows were erected first, and that the corner turrets and the gables were added later because they were felt to be needed to maintain stability. The result is complex and original.

The tower is late Romanesque, dating from a time when Spanish builders were

Zamora cathedral: lantern tower

receiving many influences from elsewhere and putting their own construction on them. It was the first of three similar ones, all to be found within a relatively small area. As recorded elsewhere, it was followed by the Torre del Gallo, or Cock Tower, on the old cathedral in Salamanca (see page 305), and later by the tower on the collegiate church in Toro (see page 323).

Zamora, like many other Spanish cities, has a history that goes back to Roman times. It too suffered from the raids by al-Mansur, the Moorish leader from Córdoba, in the late tenth century, and like many others it began to be rebuilt at the end of the eleventh century, with people from elsewhere being encouraged to settle there.

Work began on the cathedral in 1151, and must have been well advanced by 1174, when a service of consecration took place. By then architectural style was moving into the transitional phase between Romanesque and Gothic. So though the basic plan was Romanesque, with a nave and two side-aisles, a transept and three apses at the east end, there are pointed arches in the nave, the side-aisles and the transept crossing. The Romanesque apses were later demolished and rebuilt in Gothic style.

The outstanding feature of the interior, as of the outside, is the cupola over the crossing. There you see the sixteen windows that surround the base of the dome, four of them blind because of the turrets on the outside. Springing from columns that are placed between the windows are eight arches that support the dome, forming a star pattern where they criss-cross in the centre.

There is little sculptural decoration inside the cathedral, perhaps a result of the austere influence of the Cistercians. The bell-tower at the western end is also largely plain. It has three levels of arched windows at the top, providing a decorative feature, but otherwise is a robust, four-square structure that makes a striking contrast with the curved exoticism of the lantern tower.

The south front too, known as the Bishop's Façade, is relatively plain. But this is another well-proportioned construction, with three levels of arches and some strong vertical lines; and it has carved decoration both over the central doorway and in the blind arches on either side. (See page 9.)

It is possible to see the influence of church fronts in western France in this façade. But it has a distinctive form of its own, and its central doorway has an arrangement that is typical of Zamora. Circular holes have been drilled in the stonework of the main arch and the three archivolts, creating the impression of tiny stone cylinders stacked together.

On either side there is a circular flower design and below it a carved tympanum. The left-hand tympanum has a scene in which St Paul and St John, both with

South doorway of La Magdalena in Zamora

flowing robes, are talking. St Paul is pointing at a large book that he is carrying, while St John, who appears to be setting off, is holding his gospel.

The other tympanum shows the Virgin Mary enthroned under a decorative awning and holding the infant Jesus on her knee, with an angel on each side. The arch above her is filled by a small thicket of plants, including some rounded ones that look like artichokes above her head.

The Bishop's Façade was originally one of three. The other two, on the northern and western fronts of the cathedral, have both been demolished and replaced by additions in later styles. On the north side there is now a tall, neo-classical arch, and that is the central feature when you look at the cathedral across the square in front of it. It is a fine view, in spite of the mixture of styles, which also includes the fifteenth-century east end, the lantern tower, the bell-tower, and the entrance to the seventeenth-century cloister.

The other churches in Zamora that are wholly or partly Romanesque are dotted around the city both inside and outside the line of the old walls. Provided they are open, which is very often not the case, it is possible to do a rewarding tour, since it is a pleasure to walk around Zamora, particularly the older parts. The churches are built in a golden stone, and have a variety of forms. A charming feature, once again, is the many storks that have built their nests on the tops of towers and can often be seen perched on them.

A church that should be visited is **La Magdalena**, which also dates from the late twelfth and early thirteenth century. Its basic structure is unexceptional, with a tall nave and no side-aisles, but its height is unusual and it is a beautifully pro-portioned structure both inside and out.

On the outside there is a single apse at the east end. It is tall, in keeping with the rest of the building, is decorated with engaged columns and arched windows, and has a round window in the wall above it. But above all there is a doorway on the south side of the church that has some splendid carving.

The central arch of the doorway is cusped in Moorish style and has flower and plant patterns. Radiating out from it are four archivolts which are also filled with patterns, but have one human face, the bust of a bishop and, at the top, the face of a grimacing monster. Round the outer edge are forty-five tiny human faces. Down below there are carved capitals on the supporting columns, with a fine array of harpies and other similar creatures on them.

Inside, the focal point is the sanctuary, and the view from the back of the nave is a magnificent one. First there is a high pointed arch that rests on very tall en-gaged columns. Beyond that is a short choir bay that is covered by a barrel vault, also pointed, and has the round window in the east wall. Then a round arch that

La Magdalena in Zamora, from south-east

La Magdalena in Zamora: detail of south doorway

rests on pilasters incised with vertical lines frames the semicircular form of the apse.

La Magdalena is unusual in having two aedicules, small roofed structures, one on each side of the nave. They have columns and capitals that are reminiscent of those in San Juan de Duero in Soria (see page 290). It is not known what their purpose was.

It also has a particularly fine tomb from the Romanesque period. The outer frame is made up of a line of three columns and above them two little scenes in which monstrous creatures have their necks entwined. In the centre is the death-bed with an angel on either side, and above it the soul of the deceased being carried up to Heaven by two more angels.

Another appealing church is **Santiago el Viejo**, also known as Santiago de los Caballeros, which is just below the city walls to the west. It is small and simple, and the stonework on the outside is rough. But it has a number of capitals that, though they are often crude, are most engaging.

The church also has its place in Spanish history – or rather, legend. The hero El Cid is known to have grown up in Zamora and is said to have been dubbed a knight in the church. This is thought to have been unlikely, but the story persists.

Santiago el Viejo is dated to the beginning of the twelfth century, and consists

Santiago el Viejo in Zamora

of no more than a single nave covered by a timber ceiling, a short choir bay and an apse. The nave may once have had a barrel vault, since there are two engaged columns that are free-standing and may have supported the vault.

These columns have elaborate capitals, and there are more on three pairs of columns which support an arch and two archivolts and provide an elegant entrance to the apse.

The first two capitals have scenes on them that are full of life, but hard to interpret. The one on the south side has a heaving mass of some eleven people, one on top of the other, and is interpreted as depicting sinners in Hell. The one opposite has two scenes: in one a man is astride an animal with large teeth, presumably a lion, while a second man is tied to it by a rope; in the other are two other lions, one of them with a rope round its neck.

The six capitals at the entrance to the apse are simpler but equally inscrutable: on the south side acanthus leaves, a man and a woman surrounded by a snake and another man and woman with a pair of lions; on the north more lions, two large birds together with a man, and yet more lions.

Not far away and also outside the line of the city walls is one of the oldest churches in Zamora, **San Claudio de Olivares**, part of which dates from the late eleventh century. It too has a simple floor plan, consisting of a nave, a short choir bay and an apse, but it is larger than Santiago el Viejo and it has more excellent capitals, though their style is different.

On the outside its apse is entirely plain apart from three narrow slits for windows and a cornice that is decorated with an array of corbels – foliage, human and animal figures and much else. By way of contrast it has a doorway on the south side that is lavishly decorated, though unfortunately much of the carving is worn.

There are four archivolts. The innermost is plain apart from a representation of the Lamb of God in the centre. Of the other three the central one has plant designs, and the others have another range of animals, birds and humans. It is thought that the third one in from the outside illustrates the labours of the months, with a lion at each end.

Inside, San Claudio also has a timber ceiling over its nave, put there after a round barrel vault had collapsed. As in Santiago el Viejo it is the area of the sanctuary that is the most decorated. It is framed by a tall round arch that rests on a pair of engaged columns. Beyond it are two bays with a barrel vault above them and blind arches on each side, and beyond them is the apse, which has three windows in the circular space below it.

Most striking are the various capitals: large ones on the columns supporting the main arch, and smaller ones on those of the blind arches. One of the large ones has

San Claudio de Olivares in Zamora: capital inside church

San Claudio de Olivares in Zamora: another view of the same capital

two griffins drinking from a cup, the other Samson struggling with a lion while an eagle looks on.

Those on the blind arches have more plants, animals and mythical creatures. A particularly dramatic one presents a battle between two centaurs, one male, the other female, on the front, and on either side a dragon and a siren, both in contorted positions.

All the capitals have carefully worked abaci, most of them with plant patterns. One of them has a small human figure, a bear and some birds caught in circular tendrils.

Many of Zamora's churches that were originally Romanesque had their naves widened in later years by means of tall, overarching structures. That is the case with **San Cipriano**, but its Romanesque east end, which dates from the eleventh century, is intact, and the effect is unusual when you see it from the western end of the church. There are three arches in a line. A tall pointed arch that was put in place in the twelfth century frames the sanctuary in the centre; two round ones the side-chapels.

All three arches have capitals on the engaged columns that support them: on the central arch are Adam and Eve on the left and the Magi on the right. There are

San Cipriano in Zamora: interior view

San Juan in Zamora: south doorway

more capitals in the sanctuary, which has blind arches on each side: a siren holding a fish, for instance, on the left.

San Cipriano is built in a beautiful spot, on high ground with a handful of trees to the east of it and a view far out over the surroundings to the south. On the outside the sanctuary and the two side-chapels all have a rectangular shape, and each of them has a small, narrow window set in an arch.

The arches of the side-chapels are elaborate. They each have two archivolts, and the inner one rests on two columns that have carved capitals and abaci (though the capitals of the southern one have been lost). Not least, each of the tympana has a scene that, while worn, has a tiny group of people, some with haloes and one carrying a cross. Who they all are is not clear, but it is thought that the scene on the right, or north, is the sacrifice of Isaac.

Another church that was much transformed in later years is **San Juan**. The doorway on its south side has survived, however, and it is an attractive feature on one side of Zamora's main square, the Plaza Mayor.

San Juan was built relatively late, at the beginning of the thirteenth century. But its style was initially Romanesque, and the doorway is a particularly ornate example. It has three archivolts that are all covered with floral patterns set in squares, and is framed by two tall columns, one on each side, that run up to a cornice above. A rose window is set into the wall beneath the cornice.

On either side of the door are two clusters of columns, each with simple capitals above them, that support the outer archivolts.

Asturias

The creation of the kingdom of Asturias was an extraordinary achievement. Its rulers not only held off the Arabs, as was described earlier, but proceeded over the years to recover territory from them. They also built churches, and those that survive are a most interesting group, both for themselves and for showing the evolution of a pre-Romanesque style.

Construction in this style began in the eighth century and continued into the tenth. It reflects the confidence of a small kingdom that had established itself in difficult conditions and was going from strength to strength.

The earliest of the surviving churches is Santianes (St John) in Pravia, which dates from the reign of Silo, who ruled from 774 to 783 and had moved the capital there from Cangas de Onís. It has been much restored, but it has or had features that were developed some years later in the church of Santullano in Oviedo and formed the basic plan for Asturian churches after that.

These features derived from the Roman basilica, as described earlier. They were a nave and two side-aisles divided from each other by plain round arches, a transept, and at the east end a sanctuary and two side-chapels, all rectangular. Like other Asturian churches, Santianes also has a raised tribune at the west end, which would have been used by the king and his entourage.

The next phase of building was under Alfonso II, known as 'the Chaste', who ruled from 791 to 842. He was a great builder who moved the capital once again, from Pravia to Oviedo, and erected a number of churches there, including Santullano, as well as the chapel known as the Cámara Santa, or Sacred Chamber.

The high point, architecturally speaking, was the reign of Ramiro I, from 842 to 850. It saw the erection of Santa María de Naranco and San Miguel de Lillo, two ambitious buildings in which barrel vaulting was used for the first time to cover the width of a nave or, in the case of Santa María, the wide hall. It also saw another innovation, the extensive use of decorative carving.

Ramiro was succeeded by Ordoño I, who reigned from 850 to 866, and another ambitious building, the chapel of Santa Cristina de Lena, dates from that time. This

is not big, but has features that recall the churches of Ramiro I's reign: barrel vaulting and decorative carving.

It is interesting that although the Asturian kings saw themselves as the successors of the Visigoths, these early churches do not use something that was a structural feature in churches of the Visigothic period: the horseshoe arch. In Asturias
the principal arches are round, and while there are small windows that have horseshoe arches in Santianes in Pravia, it appears that they were later additions.

During the reign of Alfonso III, however, who ruled from 866 to 910 and came
to be known as 'the Great', a new influence was making itself felt. This was the
Mozarabs, who arrived in considerable numbers at that time and brought their
style, which included the use of the horseshoe arch, with them.

So two churches that were built in Alfonso III's reign, San Salvador de Valdediós
and Santo Adriano de Tuñon, both reflect the presence of Mozarabs. In Valdediós
windows with horseshoe arches are an integral part of the church's design. In
Tuñon, too, there is a small window at the east end with two horseshoe arches, and
there are traces of painting in the barrel vault over the sanctuary which are thought
to be in Mozarabic style.

The last of the surviving churches in the pre-Romanesque style of Asturias is
Priesca. It is much simpler than those built in the heyday of the style, but the basic
features are there, together with some delightful capitals.

Oviedo: Cámara Santa and Santullano

Oviedo was promoted to be the capital of the kingdom of Asturias by Alfonso II,
'the Chaste', who ruled from 791 to 842, as already recorded. He set out to make

Oviedo a worthy successor to Toledo, which had been the Visigothic capital of the whole of Spain before the Arab invasion, and a few of the monuments that he erected are still in existence, at least in part.

Attached to the cathedral is the Cámara Santa, or Sacred Chamber, a chapel on two levels, the lower one a crypt, that was originally part of a palace complex. Nearby is the east façade of the church of San Tirso. Above all, there is the handsome and well-preserved church of Santullano, or San Julián de los Prados, which stands a little way out from the centre, beyond the original city walls.

Santullano has the features that came to be characteristic of Asturian churches of the ninth century, as I wrote earlier: a nave and two side-aisles, a non-projecting transept and three rectangular chapels at the east end, aligned on the outside. Particularly noteworthy, however, are the outstanding paintings to be seen on its walls.

The Cámara Santa is interesting, partly for being an early example of the architecture of the kingdom of Asturias, and partly for the Romanesque statues carved for its upper level when that was rebuilt in the twelfth century.

Alfonso's buildings took the place of the ruins left behind after Arab raids in 794 and 795. Oviedo had previously had a monastery and at least two other churches built by Fruela I, Alfonso's father, who ruled from 757 to 768, but these were all destroyed when the Arabs marched in.

The **Cámara Santa** was badly damaged in more recent years, in 1934, when in the course of political disturbances dynamite was placed in its crypt and exploded, bringing much of the building down. But it has since been thoroughly restored.

The crypt is covered by a low barrel vault and has a latticed window at its east end, framed by a round arch resting on slim columns. It was dedicated by Alfonso to St Leocadia, an early martyr in Toledo, and was subsequently used for the tombs of St Eulogius and St Leocricia, two ninth-century martyrs, when their coffins were brought from Córdoba.

Above it is the chapel of St Michael, which was much modified in Romanesque style in the twelfth century, but has retained its original eastern section, that also has a barrel vault and a latticed window. The chapel was used from the beginning to store precious objects brought by Christian immigrants from the Muslim south, and this section still has an exceptional collection of crosses inset with jewels and other pieces of engraved metalwork – though a grille prevents them from being looked at closely.

The main body of this upper level now has a high barrel vault supported by transverse arches that was erected in the twelfth century, replacing the original timber ceiling, which was lower. It also has underneath it an outstanding collection of

Cámara Santa in Oviedo

full-length Romanesque statues that take the place of columns, as well as some accomplished capitals and a frieze of plant designs running above their heads.

On the west wall are three carved heads in early Gothic style that are all that is left of a Crucifixion. The head of Christ is particularly moving; those of the Virgin Mary and St John are reconstructions, because the originals were virtually destroyed by the explosion in 1934.

The full-length statues are of the eleven Apostles and St Paul who, as was common, replaces Judas. They are grouped in pairs, with St Peter and St Paul in a central position on the south wall with a small monster attacking a cock at their feet. The statues all have a charm and vigour that makes them stand out as examples of late Romanesque.

The capitals above them are a little later in style, with a naturalism typical of early Gothic, and are presumably the work of another sculptor. They include the Three Marys at the empty tomb, which is above the statues of St Peter and St Paul. Elsewhere are the Annunciation, Christ in Majesty, and scenes of warriors fighting monsters and lions.

San Tirso is not far away, on one side of the cathedral square, and while the greater part of it was rebuilt in the seventeenth century, it is still possible to see the original east end of Alfonso II's church in a side-street. It has three arches that rest on columns topped by Corinthian-type acanthus capitals. Interestingly, it has a Moorish-style *alfiz*, or rectangular frame, above them.

Santullano is further away, and a walk to it is rewarding. It stands in a little park, and its structure can be clearly seen on the outside: the slightly projecting porch, the nave and the two side-aisles, the tall transept and, at the flat east end, three lattice windows that mark the sanctuary and the two side-chapels.

There are a number of such windows elsewhere in the church, in the nave and the transept, but only the one in the north side-chapel is at least partly original. Above the sanctuary window is a larger one that has three arches resting on columns; behind it is an upper room whose function is not known.

Inside the church the nave has three round arches on each side, all resting on square pillars topped by plain, undecorated capitals. Most striking is the large arch that leads to the transept, which is itself both tall and wide. Beyond it are three more round arches, the central one bigger than the others, that lead to the sanctuary and the two side-chapels. The nave, side-aisles and transept all have timber ceilings. The sanctuary and the side-chapels are barrel-vaulted.

It is interesting that though church builders in the Visigothic period regularly used horseshoe arches, as I have described, there are none in Santullano. There are, however, columns and capitals in the sanctuary, as well as two carved marble

Santullano in Oviedo: east end

pilasters that flank the entrance, that must have been taken from buildings of the Visigothic period and re-used.

The pilasters have a pattern of squares and hexagons. The capitals are variations on the theme of the Corinthian-style acanthus, and decorate the various arches: a central one that frames the window in the east wall, the two blind ones that flank it, and the three blind arches that line each of the two side-walls.

All round the church are the paintings. These were only discovered in 1913, but since then have been revealed to the world and, if the colours are not strong – red, blue, ochre, black – they are a vivid example of early medieval painting. There are stylistic links to late Roman painting, at Pompeii for example, and later work else-where around the Mediterranean, and they give an idea of how a church of the ninth century would have been decorated.

There are no figures, human or animal. There are various geometric patterns, in the vaulting of the sanctuary and side-chapels for example. There are also floral patterns, and some depictions of flowers in vases.

Above all, there is an array of buildings, great and small, from palaces to simpler dwellings: a total of thirty-eight, according to one count, many of them emerging from behind drawn-back curtains.

There is also, in a prominent position above the arch leading from the transept to the sanctuary, an ornate cross. It stands inside a painted arch, with symbols representing alpha and omega hanging from it, and both it and the arch are decorated with patterned shapes.

Oviedo: Santa María de Naranco and San Miguel de Lillo

Santa María de Naranco, which stands high on a hillside above Oviedo, is a building that is both distinguished and original, and unlike any other that has survived from the early Middle Ages in Spain. It was built in the middle of the ninth century by Ramiro I as part of a palace complex, and must have been used as a royal audience chamber or even courthouse, only later being converted for use as a church. (See page 19.)

Not far away, and with the same magnificent views of distant mountains, is San Miguel de Lillo, which was built at about the same time, also by Ramiro I. Sadly, the greater part of the church, including much of the nave and side-aisles, as well as the transept and the chapels at the east end, collapsed some time later. But the part that has survived gives a good idea of how it would have been – like Santa María, a tall, ambitious creation with some fine carving.

The secular function of Santa María is clear from its layout, and the decoration on its walls shows that it was designed to impress. It is on two levels, with a crypt down below. The main floor, which would have been reached by external staircases on two sides, is a tall, impressive hall that is covered by round barrel vaulting and has a two-bay loggia, or belvedere, opening out from it at each end.

The crypt has a low barrel vault that is like the one beneath the Cámara Santa in Oviedo (see page 339), except that it has transverse arches. The hall above is an early example of vaulting over the main body of a building, such as the nave of a church – by contrast with, for example, the church of Santullano (see page 341), also in Oviedo, that was built only a few years earlier and has a timber ceiling.

The inner walls of the hall are lined by round arches that are mostly blind (some frame windows or doors) and of slightly different heights, and they are covered with carving. There is spiral fluting on the engaged columns, which are mostly grouped together in clusters of four, and lines are incised into the arches, creating a decorative effect. There are carved designs not only on the capitals, but in the spandrels between the arches and on the surface of the wall immediately above them.

The carvings have different compositions, reflecting a wide range of influences, from Persia, Byzantium and elsewhere: on the capitals, tiny heraldic animals in frames like a twisted rope; in the spandrels, circular designs in which single animals or monsters are surrounded by plant patterns; and above them, a rectangular design which has two human figures with raised arms at the top and two horsemen confronting each other below.

The two loggias are decorated in a similar way, with spirals on both single and engaged columns and Corinthian-style acanthus capitals above them. The eastern loggia now has a copy of the ninth-century altar that once stood in San Miguel, commemorating its consecration in 848 when it too was

Santa María de Naranco, outside Oviedo: carved decoration in church

dedicated to the Virgin Mary. It was placed in Santa María when that was converted for use as a church and similarly dedicated.

When you see Santa María from the outside as you approach on foot, it is these
two loggias that are immediately striking. They are identical in style, each a mirror
image of the other. Each has three round arches on its main face, the central one
higher than the two others and all slightly elongated; and above them a smaller
trio that also rests on columns with spiral fluting and acanthus capitals, and that
reveals the existence of a small upper chamber.

With their spiral fluting and their acanthus capitals the two columns that support the main arches have a special elegance; and there are engaged columns in the
same style elsewhere in the loggias. Above the two main columns are carved
designs like those inside the hall – animals in a circular frame – while higher up
are designs that are characteristic of ninth-century Asturias: crosses with alpha and
omega dangling from their arms.

Pairs of arches open out on each side of the loggias, and along both the north
and the south side of the building there is another distinctive feature: buttresses
that run all the way up the side of the building, providing support for the barrel
vaulting inside and, like the arches inside, decorated with incised lines. On the
south side the staircase that was once there, and that led to a terrace, has gone, but
the double one on the north side is still in place, and leads up into the main hall.

San Miguel is only a short walk away. It still has its west front, and this is a
sight in itself: a tall and well-proportioned composition that is made up of several
different features, each covered by a roof pitched at a different angle. There is a
central block that encloses the entrance porch and the tribune above it, a higher
section that marks the beginning of the nave, and extensions on either side for the
two side-aisles.

There are buttresses that are similar to those in Santa María and several lattice
windows with their carved stonework, although only the one that is set into the
wall on the south side is original. It is protected by a transparent screen, so that it
is hard to see, but it has three arches resting on columns with spiral fluting and
acanthus capitals in its lower part, and a pattern of intricately entwined circles in
the upper.

Inside the church it is again the height that is impressive. The single surviving
bay of the nave has a tall barrel vault – which is supported, significantly, by
columns rather than pilasters – while on either side of it an arch leads to another
barrel vault that runs at right angles to it, like a transept. On either side of the
entrance porch staircases lead up to the tribune, which was presumably designed
for the use of the king and his entourage.

San Miguel de Lillo, outside Oviedo: west front

As at Santa María there is much carving to be seen, and there are even a few fragmentary paintings, including geometric patterns and two human figures: a lute player and a person sitting on a throne.

Of the carvings, two panels that stand on either side of the west door are specially noteworthy. They are considered to be copied from an ivory diptych that commemorates the consulate of a certain Areobindus in 506 and that is now in the Hermitage in St Petersburg. Areobindus is shown presiding over games at the top and bottom of each panel, while in the middle there is a lively scene in which an acrobat stands on his hands with a threatening lion on one side and its trainer on the other.

Much of the other carving is of various forms of floral design – on capitals, for example, and on tall strips that run up the walls in parallel with the columns of the nave. The tribune has two arched doorways on either side, and they too are decorated in that style.

There is one other feature that is unusual. The plinths of the columns are themselves carved, with tiny human figures inside rows of round arches.

San Salvador de Priesca

San Salvador de Priesca, which stands in the centre of a small village east of Gijón, with good views of the valley below, has a structure that is similar to that of other pre-Romanesque churches in Asturias. Its exterior is fairly plain, but when you go inside its east end is more ornate, with some decorative capitals in the arches that frame the sanctuary and the two side-chapels, and others in the sanctuary itself.

They are variations on the theme of a formalized leaf. Some of the capitals have large leaves that each fill a side or an angle, with a simple pattern running round the abacus; others have a pattern of several smaller leaves. The church in Valdediós (see page 348), which is only a few miles away and, like Priesca, was one of the last to be built in the Asturian style, has some similar capitals with the large leaf design.

Priesca was built several years later than Valdediós, being consecrated in 921. By then Ordoño II had become king – he ruled from 914 to 923 – and he had taken the decision to move the capital of the kingdom from Oviedo to León in 914. As a result Asturias became something of a backwater, and new projects were launched further south, not least in León itself (see page 295).

Like other pre-Romanesque churches in Asturias, Priesca has a rectangular plan. It has a nave and two side-aisles that are divided by plain round arches resting on pillars and simple capitals. In the east end it has a sanctuary and two side-chapels,

San Salvador de Priesca: capital inside church

all rectangular and aligned on the outside; and at the west end a porch flanked by two small rooms.

But it is noticeable that unlike Valdediós and some churches built earlier during the reign of Ramiro I Priesca has timber roofing, which was an older style, over its nave and side-aisles, rather than the more ambitious barrel vaulting (the present roof is a modern replacement because the original was destroyed in a fire in 1936).

When you enter, the sanctuary makes a good focal point. It has three blind arches on the flat east wall, all resting on columns and capitals with the leaf designs; and three smaller blind arches on each of the side-walls, also resting on columns and leaf capitals. There is a rectangular window with carved latticework in the central arch.

Another point of interest is that it is possible to see traces of painting on the east wall and the vault of the sanctuary, as well as on the vaults of the side-chapels. They include geometrical designs that are similar to some of those in Santullano (see page 341), in Oviedo.

On the outside, the west front of the church has a doorway with a round arch, but little decoration. The east end has three carved lattice windows and, high up in the centre, a window that shows Mozarabic influence. It has two horseshoe arches and a single carved column complete with a capital in the centre.

San Salvador de Valdediós

San Salvador de Valdediós, which stands in a pretty valley north-east of Oviedo, is a handsome church, like several others built by the rulers of the kingdom of Asturias. It was one of the later creations, being consecrated in 893, and it is interesting for the fact that, while its structure is broadly similar to that of other Asturian churches of the ninth century, it also has a number of decorative Mozarabic features, particularly in its windows, as I wrote earlier.

At the east end, for instance, the sanctuary has a window formed by three horseshoe arches, and there is another window with two such arches in the wall above it; both have a rectangular frame, or *alfiz*, over the top. There is a similar pair of arches on the west front, also with an *alfiz*.

The church makes an immediate impact when you first see it across the open ground that surrounds it. You see the outline of the tall nave and two side-aisles, the two small extensions on the north and south sides, and on the south side a porch that was built on a little later than the main body of the church.

The west front has an arched doorway with columns on either side and carved capitals with acanthus designs

Arched window in San Salvador de Valdediós

that also show Mozarabic influence. Above is the window with the horseshoe arches, and above that a small, typical Asturian cross has been carved, with alpha and omega dangling from its arms.

Running along the crest of the roof is a row of tiny shapes that show Islamic influence, brought by the Mozarabs. On the south side the porch shows another sign of their workmanship: an exquisitely carved lattice window.

San Salvador was the work of Alfonso III, 'the Great', as pointed out earlier. He ruled from 866 to 910 and was an impressive military commander who expanded the borders of the kingdom. He welcomed the Christians that chose to come north, fleeing troubled conditions in the Muslim-ruled part of Spain, and they

San Salvador de Valdediós, from west

brought their style with them. In spite of his successes, Alfonso was deposed by his sons, and retired to end his days on his estate in Valdediós.

It is recorded that the consecration ceremony in 893 was attended by no fewer than seven bishops from different parts of Spain and what is now Portugal. They would have seen a church that was virtually rectangular in floor plan, with a nave and two side-aisles, all three barrel-vaulted and divided from each other by round arches resting on pillars topped by plain capitals.

At the east end was the sanctuary, which was also barrel-vaulted and protruded slightly on the outside, making a small break in the rectangular form; and on either side were smaller, barrel-vaulted chapels. Balancing this arrangement at the west end were a tribune constructed above the entry porch and small rooms at floor level on either side of it. The assumption is that, as in other Asturian churches, the tribune was for the use of the king and his entourage.

Today the nave, which has no carved decoration, seems rather narrow and bare. But it is tall, and its height enabled the architect to insert windows in the wall above the roofs of the side-aisles. There are four on each side, and they too are each filled by a pair of horseshoe arches and a central column, with an *alfiz* over the top.

The sanctuary has a marble column on either side of the entrance arch, and each of them has a capital carved in a style that was characteristic of the later Asturian churches: there is a large formalized leaf on each face and on the angles, and a pattern running along the abacus.

There are also traces of painting in several parts of the church. The sanctuary has three crosses representing Golgotha in the semicircle of wall above the window and various patterns in the vault. The vault of the nave also has a pattern of squares and circles.

Santa Cristina de Lena

The chapel of **Santa Cristina de Lena**, which stands alone on a hilltop some miles south of Oviedo, with more tall hills dominating the surrounding countryside, is a delightful survivor from the days of the kingdom of Asturias. It is thought to date from the reign of Ordoño I (850-66), as already noted, and may have been part of a royal estate.

It has a distinctive floor plan on several levels, with a short nave of three bays, a raised tribune at the west end, and an elaborate arrangement of its east end. There is a screen of three round arches and above them carved lattice windows that pro-

Santa Cristina de Lena, from north-west

vide a sort of façade for the choir, which is also raised. Beyond that are three more arches, the central one leading into the sanctuary and those on either side framing plain niches.

Both the screen and the choir are much decorated with carving – as are other parts of the chapel – and that adds to the charm of this original structure. The columns supporting the arches of the screen have capitals that are made up of Corinthian-type acanthus but, unusually, have a shell in the middle. Above them are the lattice windows, two in the spandrels and three more over the tops of the arches.

A pair of columns stands on either side of the entrance to the sanctuary, and they not only have spiral fluting all the way up, but are topped by carved capitals that have tiny animals in inverted triangular shapes and human figures in the upright triangles between them. There are pairs of shorter columns, also with fluting, supporting the arch that leads into the sanctuary.

Carved decoration in Santa Cristina de Lena

As I wrote earlier, there is much in Santa Cristina that recalls the style of Santa María de Naranco (see page 342), that was built by Ramiro I, the father of Ordoño, not least the carved decoration. So the assumption is that though it may not have been exactly contemporary, or have had the same architect, it was built not long afterwards.

One obvious similarity is the barrel vaulting, supported by transverse arches, that covers the nave. Such vaulting was an innovation in Santa María, not having been used to cover such a wide span before. In Santa Cristina the vaulting had collapsed by the nineteenth century, when the chapel was extensively restored, but it was replaced in confidence that it was authentic.

The tribune at the west end may well have been intended for Ordoño and his entourage, like those in other Asturian churches. From it there is a fine view of the whole chapel, and in particular of the east end with its three-dimensional effects. The walls on either side of the nave have blind round arches which have, or had, carvings in the spandrels between them. Not all of them have survived, but where

Santa Cristina de Lena: interior

they have, the carving is similar to that in Santa María: an animal in a circle, for example, and above it a rectangular shape enclosing a man on horseback.

An interesting feature is the two pieces of carved stone that form a smaller screen in the middle of the central arch of the main choir screen. They have panels containing circles, stars and plant designs, and are thought to date from the days of the Visigoths.

Down below the tribune is an entrance porch that forms the western end of the chapel's main axis, the eastern end being formed by the sanctuary. On either side of the nave is a small room, each of them barrel-vaulted.

On the outside Santa Cristina has a simple, well-proportioned shape that stands out on its hilltop, with forms that reflect the structures of the interior. It has roughly carved stonework and buttresses that once again are similar to those of Santa María. At the east end is a small extension that covers the sanctuary and has a square window filled by four small columns. At the west end a similar extension covers the entry porch and part of the tribune. Between them is the long shape of the nave.

Extensions on the north and south sides complete the chapel's outline. The one on the north side has a window made up of three small round arches supported by columns.

Galicia

Galicia is a remote part of Spain. But in the Middle Ages its very remoteness made it attractive to pilgrims because of the challenge it presented, and so after it was announced that the bones of St James had been discovered there, people from all over western Europe took to the various pilgrim routes to Santiago de Compostela.

Santiago's cathedral is one of the great churches of the Romanesque period – for the building itself and for its carvings – and its style was influential when other, smaller churches were being erected all over the region. There are a great number of them, often far out in the country in picturesque settings.

But Galicia was never as inaccessible as Asturias, Cantabria or the Basque Country, which were separated from the rest of Spain by the mountains. The Romans were there, and so were the Visigoths, after they had defeated the Suevi, who arrived there before them, and there is still a small church from the Visigothic period to be seen at Santa Comba de Bande.

After the Arabs had occupied most of Spain, and been driven out of Galicia soon afterwards, Mozarabs began to arrive there from the south, and there is a delightful little chapel in their style to be seen in Celanova.

The Romanesque churches often appear rustic when compared with the cathedral in Santiago. But there are some fine east ends to be seen, with one or more apses – in Aciveiro, Vilar de Donas, and Hospital de Incio, for example – and some good west fronts that have a range of carvings in Cambre, Serantes and, once again, Vilar de Donas.

There are other attractions. Mondoñedo has some carvings inside the church that are well worth seeing. Aciveiro is one of a group that have a 'false triforium' high up above the nave. Cambre has an ambulatory that was modelled on the one in Santiago.

Last but not least, there is a second Romanesque church in Santiago de Compostela itself: Santa María de Sar. It suffers from tilting columns in its nave which create a strange effect, but it too has a good east end, and also one surviving wing of what must have been a superb cloister. They fully justify a short walk through the city to its outskirts.

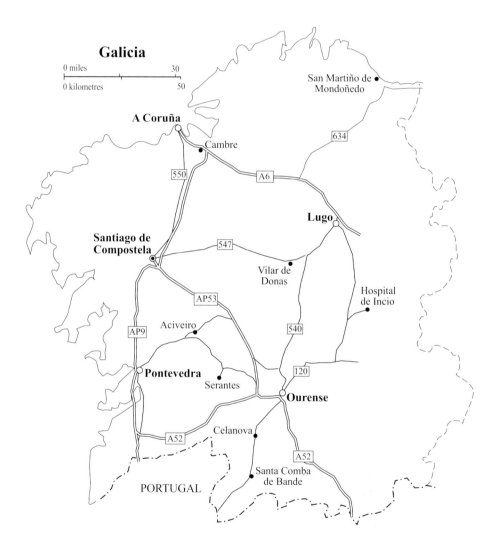

Galicia

0 miles   30
0 kilometres   50

San Martiño de
Mondoñedo

A Coruña

Cambre

634

550

A6

Lugo

Santiago de
Compostela

547

Vilar de
Donas

AP53

Hospital
de Incio

Aciveiro

AP9

540

Pontevedra

120

Serantes

Ourense

A52

Celanova

A52

Santa Comba
de Bande

PORTUGAL

Church of Hospital de Incio

Aciveiro

Santa María de Aciveiro, or Acibeiro, which is deep in the countryside south-east of Santiago de Compostela, is a large and handsome church that dates from the last decades of the twelfth century and like many others was once part of a monastery. On the outside it has a stylish east end; in its interior is the unusual and attractive arrangement known as a false triforium.

Like a normal triforium this consists of pairs of small arches above the main arches on either side of the nave. It is different because there is no floor behind the small arches, and therefore no gallery. Nor are there windows, since the church's roof has a single, unbroken slope above it on each side.

According to an inscription the monastery was founded in 1135 by a group of twelve monks, and it was so successful, thanks to its pattern of life and royal or other donations, that in a few years' time it had become a community of one hundred and six. At some point in the late twelfth or early thirteenth century it was taken over by the Cistercians, though there is no agreement among specialists about when that was.

Aciveiro: chapel off north arm of transept

Aciveiro: false triforium

The monastery went into decline some centuries later, and apart from the church its buildings were until not long ago little more than ruins. But they were taken over and restored for a hotel, and today the church is attached to that.

Its west front is largely plain, but it is worth walking into the nearby field for a good view of the east end. This is not quite traditional. The central apse is very much larger than the two side ones, which are built onto it on each side and are not the same size as each other. The central apse is polygonal, with five sides divided by engaged columns, and the two others are rounded, each with three segments.

There are five windows in the main apse, one for each of the sides. The three in the middle are blocked, but they all have arches and decorative patterns carved on them; and there is more carving high up under the cornice, mainly of rosettes.

Inside, the nave is tall and wide, with a wooden structure overhead. It seems that it was originally intended to construct a barrel vault – or that it was built and later dismantled. But the two sides are imposing, each with a line of tall round arches and the smaller arches of the false triforium above them.

There were structural reasons for having the false triforium, since it meant that the main arches below did not need to be so tall. At the same time it was decorative.

At the far end the main apse no longer has its Romanesque form, since the vaulting is in a later style and a tall and elaborate reredos has been installed behind the altar. But it is still possible to see part of the two rows of arches that run round under the apse.

The two side apses are of different heights, as could be seen outside, and both also have a ring of arches, most of them blind, but with a window in the central one, probably added later. The northern apse has carved capitals and patterns in the arch that frames it.

Many of the capitals in Santa María have versions of the Corinthian-style acanthus. But some are historiated with, for instance, lions confronting each other, and others have various plant patterns.

Cambre

The church of **Santa María de Cambre**, which stands in the centre of the small town of that name a short way south-east of A Coruña (Corunna), is a good example of late Romanesque in Galicia. Built in the late twelfth and early thirteenth century, it had to be extensively repaired in later centuries, but it has retained considerable elegance both inside and out.

On the outside it has a well-balanced west front, with a central doorway set between two tall pilasters, a rose window above it and arched windows on each side; and an east end made up of five apses. In the interior a nave and two side-aisles lead to a transept and beyond that to the sanctuary, the ambulatory and the apses, which radiate out from it.

Little is known about the origins of Santa María, except that a monastery was founded on its site in the second half of the ninth century, and that in 942 this was attached to the monastery of Antealtares in Santiago de Compostela with the rank of a priory. The present church presumably replaced an earlier one. According to an inscription that has been found on a piece of the stonework, at least part of it was completed in 1194.

The assumption is that this date refers to the western part of the church, the nave and side-aisles, and that the eastern end, consisting of the sanctuary, the ambulatory and the apses, was erected later, in the early thirteenth century.

The whole church went through troubled times in later years, not least partial demolition in 1589 at the hands of troops commanded by Francis Drake, the English sea captain, who was besieging A Coruña at the time. Much of the roofing had to be replaced after that. There was further damage when Napoleon's army invaded Spain at the beginning of the nineteenth century.

Today Cambre is a more peaceful place, and there is a little park to the east of

Cambre: west front

the church from which there is a good view of the apses. Their roofs and those of the transept and the nave behind them all had to be replaced in the sixteenth century, but they all combine well together, with three windows in each of the three central apses and two in each of the other two.

There is also much to see on the west front. The doorway has two archivolts, each of which rests on columns that have carved capitals – struggling monsters on one, acanthus leaves on another. The inner archivolt is largely plain, but there is patterned decoration between it and the outer one, and that has a man with a book on his knees in the centre, surrounded by a succession of tiny animals on either side. They are all quite worn.

Above the door itself is a small tympanum that has the Lamb of God in the centre, standing in a circle that is supported by two angels. On either side an engaged column is set into one of the pilasters. Further out are the two windows, each framed by columns, capitals and a cusped arch, though the cusping is different in each.

Inside the church the nave is, like the outside, well-proportioned. Engaged columns attached to composite pillars support a sequence of round arches on each side that lead to the transept and the sanctuary, which has a choir bay covered by barrel vaulting and an apse at the far end.

Cambre: capital inside church

Here the changes that had to be made in the sixteenth century are more obvious. Both the nave and the side-aisles are covered by a high timber ceiling that rests on stretches of wall built over the various arches.

In the sanctuary the decoration of the vault is not Romanesque, nor is that of the arch that frames the apse. But the original form has been preserved, and it is very fine: there is a round arch on either side of the choir bay, and beyond it under the apse a semicircle of large columns that are set close together and have very simple capitals provides a backdrop. They support the apse, which is divided into segments by groin vaulting.

Many of the capitals in the nave are formalized versions of the Corinthian acanthus. But there are also a few lively scenes of animals fighting each other and human beings being attacked by them.

The ambulatory is a distinctive feature of Santa María, and one that is clearly influenced, like much else in the church, by the cathedral in Santiago de Compostela. It circles round the sanctuary, from which it is divided by the two arches of the choir bay and the semicircle of columns under the apse.

It has round barrel vaulting, but its relatively late date is shown by the fact that the chapels radiating out from it in the various apses are framed by pointed arches.

Celanova

Tucked away on a piece of open land behind the largely baroque monastery of San Rosendo in Celanova, a town south of Ourense, is a tiny and enchanting Mozarabic **chapel**, the smallest in Spain. Completed in 942, it has the characteristic features of the style, from horseshoe arches to decorative corbels similar to those found in Islamic buildings, that are under the eaves on the outside.

The chapel is part of the monastery, which was founded in the tenth century by San Rosendo – or Rosendo Guterres Eiriz, bishop of San Martiño de Mondoñedo (see page 362) – and later extensively rebuilt. The chapel was dedicated to St Michael, and it is thought that it would have been used for putting up priests who were visiting the monastery from elsewhere.

Intriguingly, it was built in memory of Rosendo's sister, Froila. An inscription over the little entrance door asks for prayers for her, whom it describes rather ungallantly as 'a sinner and unworthy servant of God'.

The chapel is in some ways a miniature version of Santiago de Peñalba (see page 321), although it only has one apse, at the east end. It is made up of three spaces,

Mozarabic chapel of Celanova

that are clearly visible on the outside and divided from each other on the inside by
two horseshoe arches: a square space at its west end that is covered by a barrel
vault; a slightly larger one, also square, that has a little tower rising above it; and a
small, almost circular apse in the east.

The smaller of the two arches forms the entrance to the apse, and is the outstanding feature that you see when you enter, together with the window that is
visible in the wall behind, also horseshoe-shaped. It is enhanced by an *alfiz*, a rectangular frame, made of stone, that encloses the arch. As at Peñalba, the apse itself
is divided by groin vaulting into segments.

The tower has small, embrasured windows set into it, and vaulting provided by
two groins that run diagonally across it. Unusually, the groins are extended downwards, and rest on four stone supports, one at each corner, that have a form like the
corbels under the eaves on the outside.

Mondoñedo

The church of **San Martiño** (or **San Martín**) **de Mondoñedo**, which is in
rolling country north of Lugo and a short way inland from the Galician coast, was
once the seat of a bishop. So it is a relatively large building that towers over a small
village, and it has a good collection of simple but appealing carvings on its capitals and elsewhere in the church.

One exceptional carving, which is on a stone slab placed in the centre of the
main apse behind the altar, is a complex and mysterious scene in which a seated
Christ is surrounded by angels and figures that could be priests or monks. The
capitals have a range of subjects, from abstract patterns to the beheading of John
the Baptist.

The site of San Martiño has a long history that goes back to the fifth century,
when Britons fleeing the Anglo-Saxons in Britain settled, not just in Brittany, but
also on the north coast of Galicia. There was an area known as Britonia, and a
monastery was established there on, it is thought, the site now occupied by San
Martiño.

The monks and the other inhabitants had to leave and take refuge in Asturias
from Arab attacks in the ninth century. But they returned later in the century, and
in 866 Alfonso III, king of Asturias, decided to make Mendunieto, as it was
known, the seat of a bishop. This it remained until 1112 when, possibly for fear of
Viking attacks, the bishop's seat was transferred to Valibria, which was some twelve
miles away to the south-west and has been known as Mondoñedo ever since.

The church of San Martiño was built during that period, in three main phases. So it is partly pre-Romanesque and partly early Romanesque. The first phase, it is thought, was in the tenth century, and parts of the north and south walls survive from then. The second was in the eleventh century and was the most significant because much of the interior, including the carvings, dates from that time, as well as the two side apses. The third phase, during which the central apse and the west front were added, is dated to the early twelfth century.

Since then the east end has had to be supported by substantial buttresses, put there in the nineteenth century, and so has the north wall. But the church is still imposing when you approach it from below, the two side apses decorated with Lombard bands, the central one with corbels, and the transept, crossing tower and nave stretching out beyond them.

Former cathedral of Mondoñedo, from north-east

The west front has an arched doorway, with several archivolts and two columns on either side, each topped by simple capitals – the two outer ones going back, it is thought, to the days of the Visigoths or perhaps of the Suevi, who occupied Galicia before them. The tympanum has the chi-rho symbol carved on its lower part and above it the Lamb of God.

The interior of the church is well-proportioned and spacious. The nave has a timber ceiling, as have the two side-aisles, which are divided from it by round arches resting on plain pillars. Beyond it is a non-projecting transept, which has the three apses leading off it. The crossing tower is rectangular with rounded corners and supported by squinches.

It is the carvings that attract attention. The stone slab behind the altar is in two parts, and it is thought that there was once a third one, which would make for greater symmetry. But Christ is there, his hand raised in blessing and seated in a mandorla that is almost round and is being held in place by two angels. To one side is the Lamb of God in a smaller but similar mandorla, and below it an eagle.

Down below are two almost identical scenes in which an angel is holding out

Former cathedral of Mondoñedo: capital inside church

a hand to a standing figure who has his head bowed in reverence; one of them is wearing a chasuble, the other a cope. Between them is a small person who is also wearing a cope. The faces of all the participants are simple and expressionless, almost crude, but the scene has great solemnity and one suggestion is that it relates to the consecration of a bishop.

The capitals are in the east end of the church, in and around the transept. They are thought to date from the same period as the carving behind the altar and like that, show an engaging naivety. In the scene depicting the beheading of John the Baptist three people are sitting with fixed expressions at a table, and one of the plates has John's head on it. A figure to one side could be Salome.

There is a similar scene on another capital, which appears to represent the story of the rich man and the poor man. Here too are three people sitting comfortably at a table while servants attend to them on either side. Lazarus is shown on the right, rather curiously lifted up from the ground, while a dog placed under the table licks his leg.

There are many other intriguing capitals in San Martiño, many of them with a distinctive pattern of formalized palm leaves on the abacus; and interpretation is not always easy. On one there is an eagle with outstretched wings and to one side a human figure, presumably a woman, with toad-like creatures attached to her breasts – a scene that usually shows the punishment for lust. On another are two pairs of large animals shown back to back; each pair shares a head with which they are devouring small humans.

A less gruesome feature is a corbel that is attached to the wall and decorated with three tiny musicians, squatting peacefully as they play their instruments.

Santa Comba de Bande

A Roman road once ran along the right bank of the river Limia in the south of Galicia, linking Braga, which is now in Portugal, with Astorga in Spain. Today a dam has turned the Limia into a lake, but the foundation walls of an extensive Roman military camp, home to a cohort, can still be seen on its bank, and in the village above is a little church built when the Visigoths, successors to the Romans, ruled Spain.

Santa Comba de Bande is a simple and engaging church in a beautiful position, with the lake below and rolling hills all round. It dates from the late seventh century, before the Arabs occupied most of Spain, and it is thought that it originally belonged to a small monastic community.

Santa Comba de Bande, church of Visigothic period

Santa Comba de Bande: arm of transept

It is carefully structured, with large blocks of roughly cut granite on the outside and a combination of granite blocks and long, narrow bricks inside. Inside the church a horseshoe arch resting on marble columns provides the entrance to the sanctuary, and it is a good focal point when you see it from the western end of the narrow nave, beyond a short choir that is framed by a taller arch.

The floor plan is a straightforward one: basically that of a Greek cross, with a short tower in the centre, an eastern arm made up of the choir bay and the sanctuary, a western arm of the same length, and extensions at the two sides that form a transept.

Each of the arms is covered by barrel vaulting, which is round and made up of the narrow bricks. More bricks make up groin vaulting for the central tower, which is supported by four arches that are horseshoe-shaped, but only slightly. The tower has small windows on three sides, set into deep embrasures and framed by more horseshoe arches.

Excavations have shown that there were once other covered spaces both between the arms of the cross and at the western end of the church, where there are now a porch and a belfry added in the sixteenth century.

Santa Comba has little decoration, perhaps reflecting the asceticism of its first monks. But a narrow marble frieze, carved with plant designs, runs round the walls of the sanctuary and over the arch of its single window, which has a carved latticework pattern. The walls of the sanctuary also have some sixteenth-century frescoes.

The two pairs of fine marble columns that flank the entrance to the sanctuary must have come from some Roman building, and so must the capitals, which all have Corinthian-style acanthus, but are in different styles. It is thought that they were installed in the ninth century, when the church was restored after more than two centuries of neglect.

There are more relics of the Roman period in the church. The main altar is made up of two such relics, a flat marble slab and an upright piece of stone on which it rests. There is also Roman stonework in each arm of the transept, one of them a milestone.

Santiago de Compostela: Cathedral

The cathedral of **Santiago de Compostela** is the goal towards which pilgrims have been making their way, most often on foot, for centuries. At first sight it appears to be a baroque building because of the very elaborate west front, erected in the eighteenth century and known as the Obradoiro, that towers over the central square and has given it its name.

But behind that façade is a Romanesque masterpiece that was built, as I wrote earlier, between the late eleventh and the early thirteenth century. It was a great achievement, both for its structure and for its wealth of carvings, especially on two doorways, the Pórtico de la Gloria and the Portada de las Platerías.

The Pórtico de la Gloria is enclosed by the narthex, and you see it ahead of you when you walk through the Obradoiro to enter the cathedral. The Portada de las Platerías, or Silversmiths' Doorway, so named because of the silversmiths who once did business in the little square outside, is at the entrance to the south arm of the transept.

Between them is the main body of the cathedral, which has a tall and majestic nave that is covered by barrel vaulting and transverse arches; and running across it a transept that has the same height and vaulting.

High and slightly elongated arches line both sides of the nave, dividing it from the side-aisles, which have groin vaulting. This arrangement continues around the two arms of the transept, which also have side-aisles. Higher up is a triforium that consists of pairs of smaller arches set within a larger relieving arch, behind which is a gallery that is covered by a half-barrel vault.

Cathedral of Santiago de Compostela: carved figure on left tympanum of Portada de las Platerías

Cathedral of Santiago de Compostela: central figure of Portada de las Platerías

Nave of cathedral of Santiago de Compostela

There have been many additions to the cathedral over the centuries, often of chapels. The cupola over the transept crossing replaced the original Romanesque structure at the end of the fourteenth and beginning of the fifteenth century; and it is Gothic. The area of the sanctuary retains its original form, with a semicircle of arches behind it, but though it has an early thirteenth-century statue of St James, there is now a tall and ornate baroque structure that fills the space around the altar – and is very visible when you look the length of the nave from the west end.

The Romanesque ambulatory is still there, however, and though not all the chapels that radiate out from it are still in that style, the central one, which is one of the earliest parts of the cathedral and is simple and stylish, has not been altered. It has a single bay that is covered by barrel vaulting and has arched windows on either side – although the one on the north side is now blocked – and beyond it an apse.

There are capitals in the nave, and they are mainly, but not exclusively, simplified versions of the Corinthian acanthus. But there is a wide range of historiated capitals in that central chapel and elsewhere in the ambulatory. They include birds and animals in formal poses, sirens in the form of a mermaid with two tails and the story of the martyrdom of St Foy, to whom one of the chapels is dedicated.

The present cathedral is the third church to have been built on this site. The first was put up by Alfonso II 'the Chaste', king of Asturias, in the ninth century, soon after the discovery of the tomb of St James had been announced. It was quite small, however, and it was replaced by a larger one later in the same century by Alfonso III 'the Great'. This second church was badly damaged by al-Mansur, the Moorish leader, in 997, in one of his raids into the Christian kingdoms.

Work on a replacement began in 1075, when Alfonso VI was king of León and Castile, and continued in phases until the cathedral as a whole was formally consecrated in 1211. The east end was the first part to be erected, when a certain Bernardo, or Bernard, the Elder directed the work. Inscriptions indicate that the Portada de las Platerías was finished in 1103, and the Pórtico de la Gloria not until 1188.

The Pórtico de la Gloria, which replaced an earlier doorway, is one of the outstanding achievements of that time. It is in a late Romanesque, almost Gothic, style, and was largely the work of Mateo, about whose life almost nothing is known, but who was both architect and sculptor.

Mateo and his team started work on the doorway in 1168. But they did more than that, because during his lifetime Mateo was responsible for reshaping the whole western end of the cathedral. The ground on which the cathedral is constructed slopes down at that point, and as a start he extended and embellished the crypt that already lay beneath the west front, providing the level surface that it needed.

This crypt has its own entrance at the foot of the staircases leading up into the cathedral. It is often known as the 'old cathedral' and it is in fact like a church in its own right, with several bays, clusters of columns that support rib vaulting, and a small rectangular sanctuary flanked on each side by two apses.

It has some very good carving, on the column capitals and up the side of some of the pillars: flower patterns, birds, animals and much else. Up above, at two of the points at which the ribs cross, are small figures representing the sun and the moon.

Mateo also rebuilt the western end of the nave, adding new capitals to the columns and remaking the tribune that had been erected there above the nave. The tribune had two pairs of arches complete with capitals that continued the design of the triforium in the front of it. Mateo kept them in place but added the large cusped window above them and the two smaller openings with their four-leafed shape on either side of it, as well as the vaulting.

Above all, he created the Pórtico de la Gloria. This consists of three arches which make a dramatic presentation of two themes: mainly the Vision of the Apocalypse as described in the Book of Revelation, but also the Last Judgment. In addition it has an exceptional array of lifelike and engaging statues that are ranged in two groups: the Prophets of the Old Testament and the Apostles of the New.

The Prophets are on the left, occupying both sides of the smaller arch and one side of the central one; the Apostles are similarly placed on the right. Not all of either group can be identified, but the four Prophets under the central arch are, from right to left, Moses, Isaiah, Daniel and Jeremiah. The Apostles opposite them are, from left to right, St Peter, St Paul (here presented as an Apostle, as he often was), St James and St John.

Prominently placed in a central position, on the pier that supports the tympanum of the main arch, is the seated figure of St James, complete with a halo that has precious stones set into it. Below him is an engaged column with portraits of several of Christ's ancestors, taken from the Tree of Jesse, carved on it – and a place where the stone has been worn smooth by the hands that have been placed on it by pilgrims over the centuries.

Not to be missed is a small kneeling figure on the back of the pier and facing into the nave: Mateo himself.

The main arch is dominated by a powerful representation of Christ. He is seated and is displaying his wounds – on his hands, his ribs and his feet. There is a small angel on either side of his head, while the four larger figures that surround him are the evangelists, each with the symbol that identifies him. St Mark is holding a lion,

St Luke a calf, and St John an eagle, while St Matthew has faintly carved wings.

Beyond them are four angels on each side who are holding various instruments associated with the Crucifixion. On the far left one of them is kneeling and holding a pillar that represents the Flagellation. Next are two who have a cross and another with a crown of thorns. On the other side are an angel with four nails, another with a jug, a third with a whip, and the last with a sponge.

Above them is a crowd of tiny worshippers massed on either side of Christ, many of them holding their hands together in prayer.

Much larger are the twenty-four Elders of the Apocalypse, who occupy a whole archivolt and surround the central scene. Each is individually carved, with his own personality; some of them are talking to each other, others looking straight ahead. They do not all have both a musical instrument and a cup of perfume, as was often the way in other Romanesque works, but all of them have either an instrument or a flask, and some have both; and there are several different instruments on display, all carefully carved.

One is an organistrum, which is being played by two of the Elders sitting together – just as two of the Elders on the north doorway of the church of Santa María la Mayor in Toro (see page 325) are doing.

It is thought that each of the side-arches of the Pórtico de la Gloria may well have had a tympanum originally. Neither has one now, but both have carved figures in their archivolts, as well as the statues of Prophets or Apostles on either side.

The figures on the left are thought to represent the world of the Old Testament. Some are partly hidden by one of the outer archivolts which is made to appear to be pinning them in. Others are sitting more comfortably in the innermost archivolt with foliage around them. The central figure is thought to be God, who is holding up the Book of Life and has Adam and Eve on either side. In the spandrel between this arch and the central one angels are apparently leading two naked figures, representing human souls, to Paradise.

It is on the archivolts of the other side-arch that the Last Judgment is evoked. On the right are sinners being tortured by devils. On the left angels are holding tiny figures that represent souls going to Paradise; and there is a scene on the spandrel that is similar to the one on the opposite side.

As was the case with Santiago's earlier churches, one of the main functions of the cathedral was to house the bones that were believed to be those of St James, and to make them accessible to pilgrims and others.

The idea was that they could use the side-aisles to walk the length of the nave, go round the transept and enter the ambulatory and its various chapels without interrupting whatever services were under way in the nave and the sanctuary. They would also be able to use the gallery that runs along the nave and the transept above the side-aisles.

It is interesting that Santiago de Compostela is one of five churches that were built in this style at about the same time. The others were all in France: St Sernin in Toulouse, Ste Foy in Conques and two others, in Tours and Limoges, that were pulled down some years ago. So the assumption is that a French architect or architects were responsible for the overall plan of the cathedral.

A crypt was constructed under the main altar in which to put St James' bones and to provide a space where they could be venerated. It has been altered over the years, but a large and elaborate casket is still there, with steps leading down to it from the aisles on either side.

Another feature designed with pilgrims in mind is the *botafumeiro*, a censer that is suspended on ropes from a point high up in the transept crossing and can be swung on special occasions from one end of the transept to the other, spreading incense over the whole of that part of the cathedral. It is not known exactly when a device of this sort was introduced, but it is thought that it may go back to the twelfth century.

A good place from which to look the length of the nave is the tribune at the west end. It is linked to the two galleries that run above the nave, and as well as the pair of double arches already described it has rib vaulting overhead that rests on small human figures at the four corners.

From there you see the arches that line either side of the nave, supported by engaged columns that form part of tall composite pillars. Other engaged columns run all the way up the side of the nave to provide support for the transverse arches of the vault; and they contribute to the impression of loftiness.

The transept is as lofty as the nave, and has chapels that lead off it on its eastern side, though the original Romanesque ones have been replaced. There are still Romanesque capitals to be seen, however, including some bloodthirsty scenes in the north arm of tortures being inflicted on sinners in Hell; and the south arm has a tympanum in which St James is shown riding a horse into battle and swinging a sword as he goes: a good illustration of his reputation as *matamoros*, killer of Moors.

This is a reference to the battle of Clavijo in 844 when Ramiro I, king of Asturias, is said to have seen St James appear as a knight in shining armour and to have been helped by him to defeat the Moors.

There were originally doorways in Romanesque style at each end of the transept. The one at the north end, the Portada del Paraiso, also known as the Portada de la Azabachería, was reshaped in the eighteenth century, but the Portada de las

Platerías, which is on the south side, has survived, and it forms the principal feature of an impressive façade.

Up above are two broad arches, each of which has a small window at its centre and above it several archivolts, all of them carved and the innermost cusped in Islamic style. Below them is the doorway itself, which also has two arches and is covered with sculpture: on the supporting columns, the buttresses on either side, the two tympana and the expanse of wall above the arches.

Not all the sculpture was originally intended for this doorway. Some of it is believed to have come from the Portada del Paraíso and some from the doorway at the western end of the cathedral that was erected at about the same time as the other two and was replaced by the Pórtico de la Gloria. So there is now no sense of an overall design, even on the two tympana, which both have a mix of subjects that are unrelated to each other.

But many of the individual pieces have great power, not least those attributed to Esteban, a sculptor who is known to have worked in Pamplona as well as in Santiago de Compostela, and is thought to have played a leading role in the design of both the doorways leading into the transept. His work is believed to include two fine pieces on the buttress to the left of the doorway – David seated with a

Cathedral of Santiago de Compostela: south façade

Cathedral of Santiago de Compostela: David on Portada de las Platerías

stringed instrument in his hands and God creating Adam – as well as a woman holding a skull on the left-hand tympanum.

The main subject on that left-hand tympanum is the Temptation of Christ, with some monkey-like devils doing the tempting while Christ confronts a snake twisted round the trunk of a tree and two angels offer him food and incense. Just who the woman with the skull might be is not known. Above are two lions confronting each other and a man apparently riding on a lion.

There is also uncertainty about some of the figures on the right-hand tympanum. The two principal scenes are clear: on the upper level the Adoration of the Magi, on the lower the Arrest of Christ and the Flagellation. What is not certain is the subject of the two little scenes on the far left of the lower level. But it can be argued that they represent the healing of the blind man and the placing of the crown of thorns on Christ's head.

There is much more to be seen on and around this doorway. Each of the arches has archivolts that rest on three pairs of columns. The column at the centre is shared, and that column and the two outer ones have tiny figures carved in relief on them: on the two outer columns Apostles and angels, and on the central one people carrying books who are taken to be prophets, above them angels who are also carrying books and at the top pairs of doves drinking from chalices.

Cathedral of Santiago de Compostela: right tympanum of Portada de las Platerías with Flagellation of Christ in centre

Cathedral of Santiago de Compostela: Creation of Adam on Portada de las Platerías

Saintly figures on doorway at east end of cathedral of Santiago de Compostela

There are larger figures on the uprights on either side of the doors: Moses and St Andrew on the left, Aaron or Melchisedec and a woman holding a lion cub on the right. Then on the buttresses there are, on the left, the two scenes carved by Esteban, David and the creation of Adam, under a depiction of Christ giving a blessing; and on the right God with Eve, Christ in Majesty and the sacrifice of Isaac.

The space above the arches is dominated by two striking figures, Christ and, on his right, St James. Down below are four angels blowing horns, two above each of the arches, and on either side a number of smaller figures, many of whom may well not have been in this position originally and are generally thought to be Apostles. (See page 11.)

There are also several unrelated subjects: on the far left, the expulsion of Adam and Eve from the Garden of Eden; over the left-hand arch a centaur holding a bow; over the other one a mermaid with a long fishy tail. These last two are thought to represent signs of the Zodiac, Sagittarius and Pisces.

One compelling work is the bust of a man with his hands held out who is in the centre immediately below the figure of Christ. Who this may be is not clear. An inscription suggests that it is Abraham rising from his tomb. So it is deduced that the figure below him is Moses, and that together with that of Christ they represent the Transfiguration. But it is also proposed that such a powerful presence could only be that of God the Father, and that the sculpture was originally on the doorway on the west front.

There is another work in Santiago that is by Mateo, but it can no longer be seen in its entirety or in its original place. This is a choir that was built in stone and used to occupy the four bays of the nave before the transept. It was full of carvings – of prophets, Apostles, saints and others – which were set into an elaborate structure that included the stalls.

This choir was demolished in the late sixteenth and early seventeenth century. Part of it has been reconstructed, however, and can be seen in the cathedral museum; and twenty-four seated figures from the choir were set into the doorway that surrounds the seventeenth-century Puerta Santa, or Sacred Door. This opens onto the square at the east end of the cathedral and is only unlocked in Jubilee years. Above the figures from the choir are statues of St James and his two followers, all dressed as pilgrims, that were carved in the late seventeenth century.

Finally, it is well worth visiting the **Palace of Gelmírez**, which is built onto the north-west corner of the cathedral alongside the Obradoiro. It has been much added to over the centuries, but the building dates back to the days of Diego Gelmírez, who was appointed bishop in 1100 or 1101 and archbishop in 1120.

Gelmírez was a wealthy and powerful man who was active not only in the religious field – spurring on the work on the cathedral, for instance, and promoting the pilgrimage to Santiago – but in civil matters, politics and even military affairs. He is said to have been a skilled commander of troops, and to have created a navy to protect the coasts of Galicia against Vikings from the north and Moors from the south.

In Santiago he was so authoritarian that there was an uprising against him in 1116-17 by the bourgeoisie in the course of which a great deal of damage was done to the cathedral, including the Portada de las Platerías, and to the residence he had then. On one occasion he had to slip out of the city by night to avoid being captured.

Today there is still an impressive room on the ground floor of the palace, known as the armoury, which is thought to be from Gelmírez's time. It is quite long, with a line of tall and slender pillars down the middle, each made up of four engaged columns and topped by Corinthian-style foliage.

Immediately above is a longer and even more ambitious room, clearly designed to be a ceremonial hall, that was built by one of Gelmírez's successors, Juan Arias, in the middle of the thirteenth century. It is covered by a single wide span that is supported by a succession of transverse arches and has rib vaulting in the bays between them. Both the arches and the ribs rest on stone supports at eye level, each of which has a little scene carved on it.

The scenes reflect the influence and style of Mateo, and are all related to a formal meal accompanied by music. So it is speculated that the room may have been a banqueting hall, and that it commemorates a royal wedding feast, perhaps of Alfonso IX or Alfonso X. One scene is of a royal couple holding hands at a table. Others are of a priest giving his blessing, servants bringing food and a family at table.

Santiago de Compostela: Santa María de Sar

The collegiate church of **Santa María de Sar** stands on the outskirts of Santiago de Compostela, near the banks of the river Sar. It looks unusual when you approach it because of the huge flying buttresses that prop it up on both the north and the south sides; and when you go inside the tilting of the pillars that line the nave shows why the flying buttresses, placed there in the eighteenth century, were necessary.

But Santa María de Sar retains the features and the appeal of a church of the twelfth century, and one with similarities of style to the cathedral a short distance away. It has a nave and two side-aisles that are divided from each other by tall round arches that rest on composite pillars, not unlike those in the cathedral. There is no transept, but there are three apses in the east end, all of which are exemplary both inside and out.

On the south side it still has one wing of a cloister, as I have mentioned. It was built soon after the church itself, and has some intricately carved arches, complete with columns and capitals – even though they have the flying buttresses erected over them.

The building of the church was set in motion by Munio Alonso, who had been bishop of Mondoñedo (see page 362) from 1112 to 1134 and on retiring from that position decided to establish a college of Augustinian canons. A key factor was the close relationship that he had always had with Diego Gelmírez (see page 379), the powerful archbishop of Santiago, and on Alonso's death in 1136 Gelmírez took over responsibility for the college and its church until his own death four years later.

Relations were always close between the canons of Santa María and the cathedral chapter, and it seems likely that workmen from the cathedral were brought in from time to time, particularly for the cloister. The church was completed between 1168 and 1172, and the cloister some years later.

Santa María de Sar in Santiago de Compostela: east end of church

It is now thought that the tilting of the pillars resulted from a combination of two factors. One was structural: Santa María was given a single sloping roof on each side, and beneath that the pillars of the two side-aisles were built up too high, with buttresses that were not robust enough, so that they were not able to support the sideways thrust of the central vault. The other factor was environmental: the church was built on marshy ground.

The result was that the vault of the nave collapsed in the sixteenth century, and was rebuilt in the style that it has today. The tilting of the pillars was not reversed, but the nave was given slightly pointed barrel vaulting that rested on transverse arches. This eased the problem, but was found to be inadequate in the eighteenth century, when the flying buttresses were constructed.

These flying buttresses are impressive in their own way, at least on the north side. It is possible to see the original Romanesque windows between them, each set within a relieving arch in a style similar to that of the cathedral, as well as an arched door. There is a similar door on the west front, though the upper part of the façade was remade in later years.

It is the east end that is the most satisfying part of the exterior. It is very largely

Santa María de Sar in Santiago de Compostela: detail of cloister

in its original form, with three well-proportioned apses and a wealth of decorative carving on the various capitals and corbels. The central window of the main apse has been modified, as have several of the capitals and corbels of the smaller apse on the south side, but the other four windows of the main apse, two open and two blocked, are unchanged, and it is worth taking time to look at the carvings, most of them quite small.

Some of the capitals have a single human or animal head. Elsewhere there are several miniature scenes: men reading books, for example, a contortionist, a man struggling with an animal, and the weighing of souls, with St Michael and a devil confronting each other over some scales.

There is a rose window in the wall above the central apse; and in two places, above the apse and on the angle of the roof, the carved figure of the Lamb of God.

Inside the church the eye is led to the three apses, which are as stylish there as they are on the outside. They all have rings of arches along their walls, several of them topped by some good capitals. The two side apses each have a single ring of seven arches, most of them blind, but two with small windows in them.

The central apse has two rings of nine arches, one above the other. The lower arches are blind and rest on plain pilasters. The upper ones all rest on columns and capitals, and three of them have windows in them.

The cloister now has three sides that date from the eighteenth century, when they replaced the Romanesque ones. The surviving side is richly decorated, as mentioned earlier, and shows the influence of the school of Mateo, the creator of the Pórtico de la Gloria in the cathedral. The capitals, the abaci and both the inner and outer faces of the arches are covered with carvings, almost all of them consisting of a range of plant designs.

It is of course unfortunate that they are overshadowed by the flying buttresses. But this one side of the cloister is exceptional.

Vilar de Donas

The little church of **San Salvador** in Vilar de Donas, which is far out in the country east of Santiago de Compostela and surrounded by a handful of houses, now serves the local parish. But in the thirteenth century and for some time after that it was the heart of a monastery belonging to the Knights of the Order of Santiago, and it still has the tombs of some of them.

Its east end is imposing but relatively plain, consisting of a high central apse and two smaller ones, with a tall transept behind them. By way of contrast, it has a very

East end of monastic church of Vilar de Donas

ornate doorway at its west end, with carving on the archivolts and the capitals of the supporting columns.

The early history of the site is not known, but it is assumed that since 'donas' means 'ladies' in the Galician language there was originally a convent there. At any rate it was donated to the Order of Santiago by the family that owned it, the Arias de Monterroso, in 1184. The present church was built during the first half of the thirteenth century, probably replacing one that was there before.

The east end is the part that you usually see first when you arrive at Vilar de Donas. The three apses have tall and narrow windows, three on the central one and one on each of the others; and most of them have tiny round arches resting on columns that have capitals on them. Given its simplicity it is thought that this part of the church may be earlier than the rest.

The west front is flanked by a short arcade of pointed arches, presumably the surviving part of a porch. The carvings on the doorway are a little worn, but the patterns of the archivolts are still clear; and it is possible to make out a pair of harpies and a person reading a book among the capitals. Intriguingly, there is a Celtic design on the right-hand of the two pilasters set into the wall on either side.

Inside, San Salvador has a single nave that is short and covered by a timber ceiling. It is unusual, for a Galician country church, in having a sizeable transept with barrel vaulting over each arm and rib vaulting over the crossing.

There is a good view to be had from the west end of the nave of the two tall round arches of the crossing, which rest on engaged columns and simple capitals, and the central apse beyond it, which is also tall, with its three narrow windows topped by round arches. The apse has some well-preserved paintings from the fourteenth century, among them an Annunciation, Christ in Majesty and prophets.

The two side apses have similar proportions. In the right-hand one are three little statues, also post-Romanesque, of the Virgin and Child, St Michael and St Bartholomew.

Vilar de Donas: Celtic design on west front of church

Index